CQ GUIDE TO

CURRENT AMERICAN
GOVERNMENT

CQ GUIDE TO

CURRENT AMERICAN GOVERNMENT

Spring 2002

CQ PRESS

A Division of Congressional Quarterly Inc.

Washington, D.C.

Congressional Quarterly Inc.

Congressional Quarterly Inc., an editorial research service and publishing company, serves clients in the fields of news, education, business and government. It combines the specific coverage of Congress, government and politics contained in the *CQ Weekly* with the more general subject range of an affiliated service, the *CQ Researcher*.

Under the CQ Press imprint, Congressional Quarterly also publishes college political science textbooks and public affairs paperbacks on developing issues and events, information directories and reference books on the federal government, national elections and politics. Titles include the *Guide to the Presidency*, the *Guide to Congress*, the *Guide to the U.S. Supreme Court*, the *Guide to U.S. Elections* and *Politics in America*. CQ's A-Z collection is a reference series that provides essential information about American government and the electoral process. The *CQ Almanac*, a compendium of legislation for one session of Congress, is published each year. *Congress and the Nation*, a record of government for a presidential term, is published every four years.

CQ publishes the *Daily Monitor*, a report on the current and future activities of congressional committees. An online information system, CQ.com on Congress, provides immediate access to CQ's databases of legislative action, votes, schedules, profiles and analyses. Visit www.cq.com for more information.

CQ Press
A Division of Congressional Quarterly Inc.
1255 22nd St. N.W., Suite 400
Washington, DC 20037
(202) 822-1475; (800) 638-1710

www.cqpress.com

Cover photo: Scott J. Ferrell

Printed and bound in the United States of America
05 04 03 02 01   5 4 3 2 1

♾ The paper used in this publication meets the minimum requirements of the American National Standard for Information Sciences—Permanence of Paper for Printed Library Materials, ANSI Z39.48-1992.

ISBN 1-56802-608-0
ISSN 0196-612-X

Contents

Contents

Introduction

Congressional Quarterly's *Guide to Current American Government* is a collection of articles selected from the *CQ Weekly*, a trusted source for in-depth, nonpartisan reporting and analyses of congressional action, presidential activities, policy debates and other news and developments in Washington. The articles, selected to complement introductory American government texts with up-to-date examinations of current issues and controversies, are divided into three sections: Government Institutions, Political Participation and Politics and Public Policy.

Government Institutions. This section explores the inner workings of the major institutions of American government. The presidency, Congress, the judiciary and the bureaucracy are examined in light of recent events at home and abroad. In this edition of the *Guide*, the articles focus on changes in government caused by the Sept. 11 terrorist actions in New York City, Pennsylvania and suburban Washington, D.C. Shifts in the balance of power among the major government institutions and new priorities in foreign policy and domestic security are some of the results of the war on terrorism.

Political Participation. The articles in this section examine current issues in electoral and party politics, including race and representation, redistricting and significant congressional personnel changes that may affect party representation on Capitol Hill.

Politics and Public Policy. This portion of the *Guide* focuses on major social policy issues, such as homeland security, changes in the aviation industry, the economic stimulus package, the battle over stem cell research, energy conservation, managed care and new education proposals from the White House.

The *Guide to Current American Government* reprints articles largely unchanged from their original appearance in the *CQ Weekly*. The date of original publication is provided with each article to give readers a time frame for the events described. Page number references to related and background articles in the *CQ Weekly* and the *CQ Almanac* are provided to facilitate additional research. Both publications are available in many school and public libraries.

Government Institutions

The articles in this section provide insight into the inner workings of the major institutions of American government, focusing in turn on the presidency, Congress, the judiciary and the bureaucracy. Most of this section is devoted to the impact of the Sept. 11 terrorist attacks on American government. It examines major actions by the federal government to address the challenges stemming from the attacks.

As a result of the crisis, President George W. Bush faced a new political agenda and re-ordered priorities in his administration. The basis for presidential action in a time of national emergency is the focus of the first article. President Bush's efforts to build alliances with foreign governments and strike a balance between personal freedom and increased security are detailed in the following two articles.

A significant burden also was placed on Congress in the wake of the attacks, as the articles under the Congress heading attest. For the first time in many years, Congress set aside party agendas, offering support to the president and facilitating swift retaliation. Congress was called on to address new proposals from the president, aid the floundering airline industry and the shaken economy and consider the best course of action for combating new threats of bio-terrorism. Perhaps the biggest challenges for Congress during this time were maintaining the balance of power and protecting civil liberties as new legislation was proposed. The articles on Congress explore these challenges and their historical contexts.

The stories on the judiciary address a variety of topics. The first article measures the pace of judicial confirmations against that of nominations in previous administrations. The next two articles discuss the judiciary's role in determining the constitutionality of the administration's new proposals—specifically in response to Attorney General John Ashcroft's efforts to broaden his powers—and explain the debates about the courts' influence on lawmaking.

In the final section, the focus shifts to the bureaucracy. The articles under this heading explore new defense and anti-terrorism efforts. Old debates about missile defense and military readiness were set aside as the Defense Department considered new ways to wage war and worked to defend the United States against non-traditional acts of war. The creation of a new cabinet-level agency, the Office of Homeland Security, marked a change in the focus of the administration and in the shape of the bureaucracy. Congress and the president worked together to refine new anti-terrorism legislation, including a number of unusual provisions. The last article describes the debate in the Senate about a defense bill that placed high priority on counter-terrorism efforts.

For Bush, a Transforming Event

Low-key leader takes on the challenge of inspiring, consoling and mobilizing a nation

President Bush reflected the shock of his nation in the immediate aftermath of the terrorist attacks of Sept. 11. His remarks, some made during stops on a circuitous trip back to Washington from an event in Florida, were brief and subdued.

In the ensuing days, though, Bush found a stronger voice as he sought to reassure the people he leads.

"This is now the focus of my administration," Bush said Sept. 13. "Now that war has been declared on us, we will lead the world to victory."

It was often said that Bush's predecessor, President Bill Clinton, governed as though searching for his place in history. Bush will not have to search: History has found him.

The unprecedented terrorist assault was a pivotal moment for the United States, one bound to change Bush's image and his relationship with the people — and with Congress.

Lawmakers rallied behind him without having to be asked. Congress passed resolutions condemning the attacks and endorsing military strikes, and appropriated $40 billion for recovery efforts and to prepare for armed conflict. Bush moved to win support from the international community for a war on terrorism.

Opinion polls showed overwhelming public support. During a service at Washington Cathedral on Sept. 14, a day he had declared to be one of prayer and remembrance, Bush quoted President Franklin D. Roosevelt from an earlier time of national trial: Americans, he said, had been strengthened by "the warm courage of national unity."

And Bush revealed an understanding that only he, as president, can communicate to the public the magnitude of the sacrifices — and the patience — that will be required in carrying out a war against the shadow world of international terrorists.

"The commitment of our fathers is now the calling of our time," Bush said at the cathedral. "We ask almighty God to watch over our nation and grant us patience and resolve in all that is to come."

Men in Los Angeles watch Bush speak on Sept. 11 during a stopover in Louisiana. It was the second of several statements by the president to a nation shaken by that day's terrorism.

Bush exhibited a range of emotions shared by his nation's citizens: anger, grief, compassion. He comforted victims, thanked rescue workers at the Pentagon in Arlington, Va., and at the World Trade Center site in New York, and was moved to near tears in the Oval Office as he spoke of a "terrible moment" for the nation.

He talked tough, saying at the cathedral service, "This conflict was begun on the timing and terms of others; it will end in a way and at an hour of our choosing." But he also counseled patience for a root-and-branch effort to eradicate terrorism that will go beyond imposing justice on those responsible for the attacks.

A Tentative Start

Bush made two brief statements about the attacks, one from Florida and one from Louisiana, as he followed a winding route to Washington on the advice of security personnel. His first formal response came from the White House, 12 hours after the attacks.

"Terrorist attacks can shake the foundations of our biggest buildings, but they cannot touch the foundation of America," he said. Bush promised to root out those responsible for the attacks and vowed to make "no distinction between the terrorists who committed these acts and those who harbor them."

"He didn't look particularly good on Tuesday," said George C. Edwards III, director of the Texas A&M Center for Presidential Studies. "His address that night was not great. It was adequate, but it was no more than adequate."

In ensuing days, Bush was considerably more visible, convening his Cabinet, meeting with congressional leaders, and visiting the scenes of destruction and recovery at the Pentagon and the World Trade Center.

2

Addressing reporters Sept. 13, Bush became visibly emotional as he recounted his thoughts of the effect the tragedy has had on families and children. "I'm a loving guy. And I am also someone, however, who's got a job to do, and I intend to do it," Bush said. "And this is a terrible moment."

Politics on Hold

When the week of Sept. 10 began, Congress was in the midst of a fall endgame for the first session of the 107th Congress marked by sharp partisan debate over Bush's domestic policy priorities.

Democrats were arguing loudly that the tax cut Bush pushed through Congress in May would force him to break a "lockbox" pledge not to spend any of the Social Security surplus. Republicans countered that the ongoing economic slump might require further tax cuts.

"I came to work yesterday focused on two things that are for me enormous policy issues — the farm bill and keeping the budget out of Social Security funds," said Rep. Earl Pomeroy, D-N.D., the morning after the terrorist attacks. "Both of those sound trivial to talk about in light of what's going on now."

Bush will have a hiatus from partisanship. "We are working together here in the Congress in a completely nonpartisan way," said House Minority Leader Richard A. Gephardt, D-Mo. "There is no division between parties, between the Congress and the president."

Anyone walking the halls of the U.S. Capitol in the aftermath of the disasters could sense a palpable change in the atmosphere. "I was rooting hard for the president," said Sen. John D. Rockefeller IV, D-W.Va., of Bush's address to the nation on the night of the attacks.

With six years as Texas governor his only previous political experience, Bush became president after a disputed election win and amid lingering doubts that he was up to the job. Even his allies admit he is not a "great communicator" in the mold of predecessors Roosevelt, Ronald Reagan or Clinton.

Millions of Americans whose skepticism colored their views of Bush deferred their doubts in the days after the terrorist assault. In an ABC News/Washington Post poll released Sept. 13, 86 percent of respondents approved of how Bush was doing his job.

Yet he faces a task that would prove daunting for any president, much less one who has been in office barely eight months and who lacks the foreign policy experience of his father, George Bush, who was CIA director, ambassador to China and vice president before becoming president.

"Would any president, even Poppa Bush, be up to this challenge because of the nature of it?" said Charles O. Jones, professor emeritus at the University of Wisconsin. "It's so unprecedented, and analogies don't work very well."

> "*This is now the focus of my administration. Now that war has been declared on us, we will lead the world to victory.*"
>
> — President Bush,
> in a televised statement Sept. 13

"This is a new president who is untested, who needs to grow very quickly into this job," said Sen. Robert G. Torricelli, D-N.J. "This is not a routine problem. We're going to deal with something on a scale that the nation has not faced before."

How presidents responded to crises create indelible images, ones that often determine how their presidencies are viewed by history.

Roosevelt bucked up public morale during the Great Depression by saying "the only thing we have to fear is fear itself," and led the nation to the sacrifice of world war with his "date which will live in infamy" address to Congress following Japan's attack on Pearl Harbor.

John F. Kennedy's successful handling of the Cuban missile crisis brought the nation back from the brink of nuclear war in 1962.

Reagan in 1986 calmed a nation whose confidence in itself was chafed by the explosion of the space shuttle Challenger.

The manner in which Clinton handled the 1995 Oklahoma City bombing — the nation's biggest previous terrorist atrocity — helped resuscitate his presidency just months after his party lost both chambers of Congress and weeks after he had to defend his relevance.

Bush's task promises to be far more difficult than any undertaken by Clinton, or even any faced by Bush's father, who as commander in chief during 1990-91 directed the war in the Persian Gulf to free Kuwait from occupation by Iraq.

Until Sept. 11, Bush seemed satisfied with being a low-profile leader of a general public that often appeared passionless about politicians and the policies they pursue.

One pundit said that Bush was the "A4 president," meaning his daily actions often ended up on an inside newspaper page rather than the front page. When asked about the moniker, Bush said it did not "bug me in the least."

In crucial times for the nation, though, politicians matter. And the president matters far more than members of Congress, who acknowledge theirs is a supporting role.

Americans are suddenly engaged in what their leaders are saying, and are anxious for them to find solutions.

Bush's ability to inspire, console and mobilize the public — and his skill at conducting the war he has declared on terrorism — now becomes the gauge for measuring his success as president.

Bush's challenge is magnified because the victory will be difficult to win — and perhaps harder to maintain — against diffuse, insular and ruthless enemies driven by fanatical hatred of the United States and dedicated to finding any way to attack Americans.

Bush must prepare a military response to the terrorists who planned the attack, and a strategy of arms, diplomacy and economic pressure to shatter the multinational network that supports terrorism. They must devise an effective long-term plan to try to fix intelligence and security weaknesses that left the nation's capital and financial nerve centers so vulnerable.

Important issues of governance will not be permanently dismissed by the current sense of national emergency. "We're all supporting the president in this crisis, but it's hard to say how lasting the change in the relationship will be," said Sen. Joseph I. Lieberman, D-Conn.

Still, the lawmakers who have pledged their support for Bush in this effort say they know it will not be quick or easy. "It's not over," said Sen. Ted Stevens, R-Alaska, who flew transport planes in World War II. "It's not going to be over for a long time." ◆

Executive Powers in Crises Are Shaped By Precedent, Personality, Public Opinion

There is no rule book to tell President Bush or the Congress exactly what emergency powers are available to the president in a time of crisis.

Bush's latitude to respond to the terrorist attacks of Sept. 11 depends as much on his own assertiveness and ability to shape public opinion as it does on any power explicitly granted him by the law of the land.

The Constitution itself does not give the White House any explicit emergency powers. Instead, presidents typically have drawn on a mix of implied constitutional powers, statutory authority and Supreme Court decisions in reacting to domestic and international crises.

Even that does not fully capture the complex foundation for presidential action in a time of emergency: The will of the nation, Congress' attitude and precedents set by earlier presidents also play major roles.

"This is an area where a lot of law has been made by history and circumstances, rather than by adjudication or strict legal analysis," said Carnegie Mellon law professor Peter M. Shane.

So far, the Bush administration has stressed the president's constitutional responsibilities as the basis for his powers, while acknowledging his broad responsibility to consult with the legislative branch.

"The administration is gratified by Congress' show of unity," White House spokesman Ari Fleischer said Sept. 12. "But, also, as previous presidents have maintained — and as President Bush does — under the Constitution, the president of course has the authority as commander in chief to protect our nation."

"One of the greatest strengths of our country is that we are a Constitution-based democracy," Fleischer added. "Our Constitution and our nation have survived acts of terror and attacks on our nation before. And the president knows that the strength of our nation comes from that Constitution, which gives an important role to Congress, and he will continue to consult closely with Congress and its leaders."

Executive Power Struggle

While Congress has traditionally kept a close watch on any presidential effort to broaden executive powers, lawmakers also are reluctant to do anything to undermine the president during a national crisis.

Emergency powers available to the president range from detaining individuals, restricting travel and suspending habeas corpus to fixing wages and prices and withholding sensitive information from Congress and the public.

Congressional efforts to circumscribe the president's emergency powers peaked in the turbulent 1970s — resulting most notably in the 1973 War Powers Resolution (PL 93-148) and the 1976 National Emergencies Act (PL 94-412). Both were passed in an era of intense struggle between the legislative and executive branches.

But the practical effect of those laws, particularly the War Powers Resolution, in constraining the president has been limited.

The War Powers Resolution, enacted over President Richard M. Nixon's veto, states that the president can commit U.S. armed forces to hostilities or imminent hostilities only if there is a declaration of war, specific statutory authority, or a national emergency created by an attack on the United States, its territories or its armed forces. (*1973 Almanac, p. 905*)

It requires the president to consult with Congress "in every possible instance" before committing U.S. troops, report such a commitment to Congress within 48 hours, and terminate it within 60 to 90 days unless Congress authorizes an extension.

Presidents, however, have refused to acknowledge the constitutionality of the War Powers Resolution, seeking congressional support — but not prior authority — for decisions to use U.S. troops abroad. And Congress has been reluctant to act while U.S. forces are in harm's way.

A Sept. 11 report by the Congressional Research Service found that presidents have submitted 90 reports consistent with the resolution. Although they have met with congressional leaders, the "consultation" has been after, not before, the decision to deploy has been made.

President Gerald R. Ford set the precedent when he sent the Marines to free the ship *Mayaguez*, a U.S. merchant marine vessel that was captured by Cambodian forces in May 1975. Ford did not seek prior congressional approval, relying instead on inherent constitutional powers. He did report to Congress within 48 hours but consulted with selected lawmakers only after the attack order had been issued.

The 1976 National Emergencies Act set up procedures for declaring emergencies and established automatic deadlines for the expiration of such declarations. At the time, several states of emergency dating to the 1930s technically were still in effect.

The law requires that if the president declares a state of emergency he must cite which law or part of the Constitution gives him the power to do so. The administration must keep records of rules, regulations, expenditures and other activities carried out under the declaration.

The law also set up a timetable for expiration of the emergency declaration, requiring Congress to consider ending it every six months until it is terminated. The president can also unilaterally terminate the state of emergency. (*1976 Almanac, p. 521*)

Bush invoked the National Emergencies Act on Sept. 14, using it largely to suspend most personnel regulations governing the armed forces.

Presidents Push the Limits

The most famous case of a president asserting vast powers is that of Abraham Lincoln, who blockaded Southern ports, expanded the size of the Army and suspended habeas corpus, all in the name of preserving the Union.

While Lincoln relied almost exclusively on the argument that such powers were inherent in his constitutional duty to "preserve, protect and defend the Constitution," most presidents have tried to show that their emergency actions had some basis, however slight, in statutory authority.

Both Presidents Woodrow Wilson during World War I and Franklin D. Roosevelt during World War II relied heavily on broad statutory authority given them by Congress to fight the wars. That does not mean they did not stretch the power — Roosevelt got Congress to repeal legislation regulating farm prices in 1942 by saying he would do so on his own if Congress did not act — but it does indicate they were cognizant of the need for a link to the will of Congress for the exercise of that power.

During the Korean war, President Harry S Truman learned the danger of ignoring that need. In 1951, Truman ordered the seizure of strike-threatened steel mills, citing constitutional authority as president and commander in chief. "The president," Truman said, "has very great inherent powers to meet national emergencies."

Though Congress was not willing to challenge his assertion in the middle of the war, the Supreme Court in the 1952 case *Youngstown Sheet and Tube Co. v. Sawyer*, declared the seizure unconstitutional. The court found that, because Congress in passing the 1947 Taft-Hartley Labor Act had not given the president the authority to take over industries shut down by strikes, the president could not assume that power.

Justice Robert Jackson's concurring opinion in the case has become a guide for presidents trying to determine the reaches of their emergency powers. Jackson pointed to the crucial role of consensus in a govern-

Early in the Civil War, Lincoln stretched the limits of presidential power to preserve the Union.

ment whose powers are deliberately divided among separate branches.

The president's authority, Jackson wrote, is at its strongest when he is acting with the expressed or implied consent of Congress. "A seizure executed by the president pursuant to an act of Congress would be supported by the strongest of presumptions and the widest latitude of judicial interpretations," he wrote.

The justice found that there is a "zone of twilight in which he and Congress may have concurrent authority or in which its distribution is uncertain. Therefore, congressional inertia, indifference or quiescence may sometimes, at least as a practical matter, enable, if not invite, measures on independent presidential responsibility."

But, he cautioned, when the president exercises emergency powers that appear to go against the will of Congress, "his power is at its lowest ebb, for then he can rely only upon his own constitutional powers minus any constitutional powers of Congress over the matter."

A Longstanding Issue

The recognition that the president must sometimes assert extraordinary executive powers goes back to the

roots of our democracy.

John Locke, the British political philosopher whose work was influential to those crafting the Constitution, wrote that the executive should have some discretion to act in emergencies since "the lawmaking power is not always in being and is usually . . . too slow for the dispatch requisite. . . . Therefore, there is a latitude left to the executive power to do many things of choice, which the laws do not prescribe."

The debate over just how much latitude the president should have also has been debated since the beginning of the republic. While Alexander Hamilton, John Jay and James Madison acknowledged in the Federalist Papers that preserving the nation might be cause for superseding constitutional restrictions, they also warned that the actions of the president would have to withstand the later scrutiny of the Congress.

In a report on the status of emergency presidential powers, a special congressional committee in 1973 concluded that "to what extent the Founding Fathers adhered to [Locke's] view of the executive role in emergencies is a much disputed issue. Whatever their conceptions of this role, its development in practice has been based largely on the manner in which individual presidents have viewed their office and its functions."

Experts also agree that the role of commander in chief gives the president the right to unilaterally respond to aggression against the United States such as the Sept. 11 attacks. "The president has inherent authority to repel attacks on the United States," said Shane.

"Presidents have absolutely always been given enormous discretion for defensive actions — and this is a defensive action," agreed Shirley Anne Warshaw, a political science professor at Gettysburg College, pointing out that the president's responsibilities as commander in chief "put the entire military establishment at his beck and call."

Fixing U.S. Intelligence: A Cultural Revolution

Failure to foresee the attacks spurs a re-examination of national objectives

Graham, chairman of the Senate Intelligence Committee, said the nation's intelligence capabilities once were the standard for the world, but in light of the Sept. 11 terrorist attacks on the World Trade Center and the Pentagon, "we have fallen behind."

There is no room for error now. In recent years, America's disparate intelligence agencies operated through the prism of scandal. Senior intelligence officers and Congress' intelligence committees reacted to the latest turncoat drama — from father and son spies John and Michael Walker in 1985 to Aldrich H. Ames in 1994 — by charging toward an overhaul of the nation's espionage apparatus but achieving only modest reforms.

In the aftermath of Walker, the House endorsed random polygraphs for defense and contractor employees with access to classified information. Two years after Ames, Congress gave the CIA director a few more managers and a bit more say in Defense Department spending for intelligence. (*1985 Almanac, p. 160*)

But what has happened now is no mere spy scandal. The most audacious, bloody and unanticipated terrorist assault ever on U.S. soil is fueling an imperative for change.

The Sept. 11 attacks not only shook the American psyche and sense of security; they may well have destroyed the Cold War mentality that American spy agencies tried but failed to shed after the collapse of the Soviet Union.

The clarity of a superpower rival disappeared more than a decade ago, yet U.S. intelligence never adjusted to the murkier danger of a stealthy network of suicidal terrorists. Now the attacks have set into overdrive the push not just for modest organizational tinkering but for the adoption of a new world view to counter these transnational adversaries and religious fundamentalists who are determined to destroy the United States.

"Our intelligence capabilities were the standard of the world," Bob Graham, D-Fla., chairman of the Senate Intelligence Committee, said the day of the attacks. "We have fallen behind."

Terrorism brought into sharp focus the nation's intelligence deficiencies: few contacts with foreign nationals who could infiltrate terrorist groups, a failure to communicate between the many government agencies and a lack of linguists to decipher intercepted clues.

In coming weeks, congressional committees and special panels will examine the shortfalls and review the specific so-

Intelligence Sources Compared

U.S. intelligence gathering relies on a broad array of techniques, including imagery, in which satellite photos are analyzed; signals intelligence, which is the interception of communications; and open sources such as newspaper and magazine articles. Each form of collection has its strengths and weaknesses.

INTELLIGENCE	ADVANTAGES	DISADVANTAGES
IMAGERY (IMINT) •satellite photos •infrared heat sensors •imaging radar •light detectors	• Graphic and compelling • Use is familiar to policy-makers • Ready availability of some targets — particularly military exercises • Can be done remotely	• Perhaps overly graphic and compelling • Still requires expert interpretation • Literally a snapshot of a moment in time; very static • Subject to problems of weather, spoofing (false signals) • Expensive
SIGNALS (SIGINT) •wire taps •radio interceptors •electromagnetic waves from radar, satellites	• Offers insights on plans, intentions • Voluminous material • Military targets tend to communicate in regular patterns • Can be done remotely	• Signals may be encrypted or encoded, requiring them to be broken • Voluminous material • May encounter communications silence, use of secure lines, spoofing via phony traffic • Expensive
HUMAN (HUMINT) •undercover agents	• Offer insights on plans, intentions • Relatively inexpensive	• Riskier in terms of lives, political fallout • Requires more time to acquire and validate sources • Problems of dangles (misleading information), false feeds, double agents
OPEN-SOURCE (OSINT) •newspapers •periodicals •government documents •online materials	• More readily available • Extremely useful as a place to start all collection	• Voluminous • Less likely to offer insights available from clandestine INTs

SOURCE: "Intelligence: From Secrets to Policy," By Mark M. Lowenthal, CQ Press. See www.cqpress.com

lutions — some of which blue-ribbon presidential commissions had clamored about for years.

After the Sept. 11 attacks, the House Intelligence Committee stressed in its report accompanying the authorization bill (HR 2883 — H Rept 107-219) that "there is a fundamental need for both a cultural revolution within the intelligence community as well as significant structural changes."

Lack of Imagination

The attacks were widely compared with the Japanese bombing of Pearl Harbor in 1941, but within intelligence circles, the analogy was made to a more cataclysmic event: the first atomic explosion in 1945.

"It was like the atomic bomb in that beforehand, nobody had the imagination to put the pieces together," said Gregory Treverton, an analyst for the RAND Corp., a national-security think tank. "The intelligence community is not great at . . . thinking outside the box. The jump from thinking about bombs on planes to planes as bombs wasn't made."

It is a divide U.S. intelligence will have to cross. The failure to foresee and detect the attacks — and the high probability of future assaults — reinforces the need for revolutionary approaches to modern-day threats.

"We need to move from a culture of guards, guns and gates to a culture of tents, terrorism and technology," said Rep. Tim Roemer, D-Ind., during House debate on the intelligence authorization bill Oct. 5. The House passed the legislation by voice vote.

Hampering the effort to combat terrorism is the way it has been viewed in many government circles.

"One reason we have not dealt effectively with terrorism is that it has been regarded almost exclusively as a law enforcement problem," former CIA Director R. James Woolsey said in a Sept. 17 interview.

Congress has taken some initial steps, with the House producing an intelligence authorization bill that addresses issues such as the lack of foreign translators and the shortfall in technology. The Senate has endorsed rescinding the restrictions on the recruitment of foreign agents to bolster the all-important human intelligence.

Precision Weapons Against Terrorism: Covert Operations and Special Forces

Osama bin Laden and his al Qaeda network are far more elusive than the conventional enemies that most U.S. combat units are designed to defeat. Moreover, a large-scale, overt U.S. attack on bin Laden's organization — and on Afghanistan's ruling Taliban militia, which hosts it — may fuel anti-American outrage in much of the Islamic world.

So, in addition to finding the targets for President Bush's war against terrorism, the U.S. intelligence community probably will have a role in striking at the terrorists and their supporters through covert operations. This will involve channeling money, weapons, supplies and information to countries and groups in the region, particularly to the Northern Alliance — a heterogenous collection of militias and ethnic contingents united in their opposition to the Taliban.

Such covert operations ran into strong opposition in Congress in the mid-1980s when the Reagan administration used the proceeds of weapons sales to Iran to provide assistance to "contras" opposed to the Marxist government of Nicaragua. But former Sen. David L. Boren, D-Okla. (1979-94), who chaired the Senate Intelligence Committee during that controversy, insists that the consultative procedures worked out then for the executive and legislative branches are sufficient for a future operation. (*1987 Almanac, p. 61*)

"In the kind of world we're in now, the tool of covert operations must be fully available to the president," Boren said. "In the aftermath of Iran-contra, there's an excellent framework in place. So now the president could utilize [covert operations] when he needs to, and he shouldn't shrink from doing it."

During the Soviet Union's occupation of Afghanistan in the 1980s, CIA assistance funneled through neighboring Pakistan to anti-Soviet guerrilla groups, or mujahedeen, was a covert operation that commanded broad support on Capitol Hill. By the late 1980s, U.S. support for the Afghan resistance movement totaled about $600 million annually. Soviet forces withdrew from Afghanistan in 1989. (*1988 Almanac, p. 467*)

Taliban Rules

Since the resistance groups had been united only in their opposition to the Soviet occupation, the country descended into chaos until 1996, when the Taliban ruthlessly imposed order on nearly two-thirds of Afghanistan's territory. Against the backdrop of the Soviet defeat, the Taliban's domination of the country gave it a fearsome reputation.

But former Rep. Charles Wilson, D-Texas (1973-96), who was a leading congressional advocate of aid to the Afghan rebels, surmises that the Taliban are more vulnerable than many observers think. "They're not as formidable as mujahedeen was, for many reasons," he said. "The country was totally unified against a Soviet invader, and apparently now they're very fragmented; even within the Taliban, they're fragmented. Secondly, they haven't got the direction and resources of the Pakistani intelligence services, which had the direction and resources of the CIA."

On the other hand, the aftermath of the Soviet exodus highlights the risks of trying to achieve U.S. goals through covert support of local governments or factions. The U.S.-supported war against Soviet occupiers turned out to have been an incubator and military training ground for thousands of anti-Western Islamic extremists, including bin Laden. Moreover, elements of the Afghan resistance, in collusion with officials in Pakistan, fostered a thriving local industry in the cultivation of poppies and the export of opium.

As Pentagon planners weigh the military options for dealing with bin Laden and the Taliban, they must take account of a potential threat to U.S. planes and helicopters: a reported 100 or so shoulder-fired Stinger missiles left over from the supply that the Reagan administration started shipping to the mujahedeen in 1986. The Stingers decimated the Soviet helicopter fleet.

Less unpredictable than covert support but possibly less provocative than a large-scale assault on Afghanistan would be the use of U.S. "special operations forces." These small, elite units of all four services include 46,000 active-duty and reserve members trained and equipped for a range of missions, including guerrilla attacks behind enemy lines and psychological warfare.

In 1980, a special operations mission to free U.S. diplomats held hostage in Iran failed largely because of ad hoc organization and jury-rigged equipment. Convinced that the services were short-changing special forces, Congress created by law in 1986 the Special Operations Command (SOCOM) to be led by a top-ranking general who would have his own budget to develop and purchase specialized equipment and to conduct training. Bush's SOCOM request for fiscal 2002 is nearly $4 billion.

Meanwhile, about 15 years of congressional prodding has produced greatly improved equipment for special operations forces. Among the items that could be useful if special forces units were sent after a target in Afghanistan are dozens of Hercules cargo planes and helicopters modified to operate over enemy territory at night. All have accurate ground-mapping radar and night-vision equipment, and at least some of the Hercules have basketball-sized turrets carrying lasers to shoot down Stingers and other heat-seeking missiles. All of the helicopters are equipped to refuel in midair, armored against bullets and given modified fuel tanks less likely to explode if hit by enemy fire.

(2001 CQ Weekly, p. 2252)

The House authorization bill would increase spending on intelligence, an amount that is classified but widely thought to be in the range of $30 billion.

The House Intelligence panel, in its report, said funding "constituted a significantly lower percentage" of the Bush administration's overall request for defense-related spending compared with previous years. Congressional sources said the committee increased intelligence spending by nearly 9 percent over the current level, excluding funds in the supplemental spending bill. *(2001 CQ Weekly, p. 2252)*

"We are redesigning intelligence for a long period of time, and it will take us a while to do it right," said Porter J. Goss, R-Fla., a former CIA agent who is chairman of the House Intelligence panel.

Boards and Commissions

Outside the committee structure, Congress is moving toward creation of special commissions, similar to the Tower Commission that investigated the Iran-contra scandal in 1987, to examine the framework of intelligence gathering. *(1987 Almanac, p. 57)*

The House authorization bill would create an eight-member bipartisan commission to be appointed by the president and House and Senate leaders. The Commission on National Security Readiness would look at existing "structural impediments" to better intelligence collection among national security agencies rather than a retroactive what-went-wrong approach, despite objections from some Democrats.

Sen. Robert G. Torricelli, D-N.J., is expected to introduce legislation as early as the week of Oct. 8 calling for a special board of inquiry to conduct a similar investigation.

The board would be modeled after panels that investigated the 1963 assassination of President John F. Kennedy and the 1986 *Challenger* space shuttle explosion.

"The idea is to make it more independent so that it can be a dispassionate look at what happened and who was involved," Torricelli said in an Oct. 2 interview.

Lawmakers have said it is unfair to place all the blame for failing to detect and deter the terrorist strikes on the spy agencies, pointing out that the FBI, the Immigration and Naturalization Service, and other agencies also were at fault.

"What went wrong Sept. 11 goes well beyond the intelligence community," Goss said.

The Bush administration had been planning in-depth reviews of intelligence before the terrorist attacks. In July, a panel of outside experts led by former national security adviser Brent Scowcroft began looking at potential ways to reorganize the 13 departments or agencies that perform intelligence. The panel is beginning to draft its report, a CIA spokeswoman said Oct. 4.

A separate internal panel of officials from several intelligence agencies has been conducting a parallel look at intelligence capabilities and reorganization.

Bush has appointed former Pennsylvania Gov. Tom Ridge to serve as chief of homeland security, overseeing the more than 40 agencies and departments that would fight terrorism.

Legislation (HR 3026) introduced in the House on Oct. 4 by Rep. Jim Gibbons, R-Nev., would give Ridge broad authority over budgets and require Senate confirmation. Ridge begins his job Oct. 8.

HUMAN INTELLIGENCE

Old-fashioned snooping, in which agents recruit foreign nationals to spy — human intelligence, or "HUMINT" — is probably the best way to detect and prevent terrorism. But such spying has fallen out of favor in recent years.

After the Cold War, the CIA substantially cut back on the number of overseas spies in its directorate of operations, according to lawmakers and intelligence experts. Those who remained often have had to assist U.S. military operations instead of focusing pre-emptively on areas where terrorism has flourished.

The recent manner in which agents have been used, combined with poor planning, "have all worked to take resources from the 'front line' field officers, thus limiting our efforts to rebuild our eyes and ears around the globe," the House Intelligence Committee said in its report accompanying the authorization bill.

In addition, many CIA agents have shied away from the difficult and dangerous work of penetrating terrorist groups, depending instead on information from intelligence gathering by foreign governments and law enforcement.

"Because we don't have robust enough human intelligence capabilities, we rely on those liaison services and, obviously, we were let down by them [on Sept. 11] as much as by our own people," Bruce Hoffman, vice president for external affairs and director of the Washington office of the RAND Corp., told the House Intelligence Terrorism and Homeland Security Subcommittee at a Sept. 26 hearing.

The CIA has failed to recruit students from top universities, said a retired high-ranking CIA official. Britain's MI-6 spy service, by contrast, has attracted numerous recruits from such prestigious universities as Oxford and Cambridge who view membership in such an elite organization as an honor.

"When I was there, we could not get a single person from the Ivy League to join the CIA," said the retired official, who requested anonymity. "To fight terrorism, we need to deal with the dregs of the Earth, and we need very bright Americans who can figure out how to go overseas and do these things."

Director of Central Intelligence George J. Tenet, acutely aware of the need for more agents, in 1998 launched the agency's largest recruiting drive since the end of the Cold War. The CIA has increased the number of new hires — it will not say how many — and résumés have poured into the agency in the past month.

Informants Wanted

The absence of direct contacts between U.S. agents and foreign nationals has resulted in fewer confidential informants. That, in turn, has made it increasingly likely that terrorists can boldly carry out their objectives without fear of being watched or tracked.

"Terrorists ought to wake up every morning . . . wondering who in their organization is informing to the Central Intelligence Agency," Virginia Gov. James S. Gilmore III, chairman of a recent commission on terrorism, told the House Intelligence subcommittee.

Former Senate Intelligence Committee Chairman David Boren, D-Okla. (1979-94), recommended doubling the budget, a classified amount, for human intelligence over the

Intelligence Highlights

The House passed, by voice vote, the fiscal 2002 intelligence authorization bill (HR 2883 — H Rept 107-219) on Oct. 5. The measure:

■ Funds intelligence activities at about 9 percent above the current appropriated level and 2 percent above the administration's request before the Sept. 11 attacks.

■ Establishes a commission to spend one year reviewing barriers to collecting, analyzing and sharing information among federal agencies on "national security threats, particularly terrorism."

■ Rescinds controversial 1995 guidelines that prohibited recruiting foreign spies who had human rights violations in their background and directs the CIA to establish new guidelines.

■ Directs the CIA and secretary of Defense to develop a plan for a foreign language training school.

next few years.

"It's not an overnight impact," Boren, now president of the University of Oklahoma, said in an Oct. 3 interview. "It takes six to eight years to develop a new American asset. They've got to be trained in the language, given in-depth cultural studies, and then they have to be on location in the part of the world they're assigned to. They can't look new in the neighborhood."

However, some in the spy business take a pessimistic view of efforts to break through the wall of terrorist groups. Former CIA agent Reuel Marc Gerecht, an expert on Middle East issues, said in a recent article in the Atlantic Monthly that it is practically impossible for U.S. agents to penetrate overseas terrorist "cells."

"Westerners cannot visit the cinder-block, mud-brick side of the Muslim world — whence bin Laden's foot soldiers mostly come — without announcing who they are," Gerecht wrote. "No case officer stationed in Pakistan can penetrate the Afghan communities in Peshawar or the Northwest Frontier's numerous religious schools . . . and seriously expect to gather useful information about radical Islamic terrorism — let alone recruit foreign agents."

But restrictions imposed on agents in establishing ties with foreign nationals may disappear in the attacks' aftermath, giving agents freer rein to work with the sources who could penetrate the shadowy world of terrorists.

Agents who have done casework in other countries often have been limited by whom they can deal with. In the mid-1990s, former Director of Central Intelligence John M. Deutch ordered the CIA to review its contacts and operations to determine if any involved links to human rights abuses.

The action stemmed from allegations of CIA complicity in the death of an American innkeeper and the disappearance of a rebel leader in Guatemala — reports that an internal CIA review concluded were "seriously flawed." (*1995 Almanac, p. 10-27*)

The spy agency subsequently developed guidelines that require field officers to obtain approval from headquarters before establishing a relationship with an individual who had engaged in disreputable activity. Although CIA officials said the guidelines have not hindered the agency's ability to recruit foreign agents, many lawmakers are certain that they have had a "chilling effect."

"Far too often, committee members have learned of field officers who have been deterred from recruiting promising assets or who have lost potential assets to competing intelligence services because of a slow and overly litigious vetting process," the House Intelligence Committee report said.

The House version of the intelligence bill and the Senate appropriations bill for the departments of Commerce, Justice and State (HR 2500) contain language that would rescind the guidelines. But the House bill also urges the CIA to develop a more flexible policy, while acknowledging human rights concerns. (*2001 CQ Weekly, p. 2252*)

Nancy Pelosi of California, ranking Democrat on the House Intelligence Committee, stressed the need for guidelines on recruiting agents because "decisions on this are too important to be made by relatively junior officers. They should be made by senior managers."

TECHNOLOGY

The challenge facing U.S. intelligence is to combine human spying with signals intelligence — information derived from satellites and other sources that intercept and analyze communications — and more extensive networking with other nations, according to RAND analyst Treverton.

"Some of the things that [Congress] will pour money at, like HUMINT, will result in us making the same old mistakes," he said. "Even if we do a lot better, most of the HUMINT will still have to come from somebody else. . . . We will need it from people who haven't wanted to deal with us, much less cooperate with us."

Meanwhile, Tenet is worried about his ability to persuade talented people to remain in the agency. Former CIA officials who have worked overseas said burnout is extremely prevalent, and the best recruits can earn far more money working for defense contractors and other private companies. "The problem is not in the recruiting; it's the retention that becomes the problem," Tenet said in an interview last year. "The mobility in this job force is very high."

Another problem facing U.S. intelligence is the lack of proficiency in foreign languages among its employees. In an effort to be efficient, agencies have tried to develop "generalists" rather than cultivate experts who are fluent in a country's language and knowledgeable about its culture.

"Thousands of pieces of data are never analyzed, or are analyzed after the fact, because there are too few analysts, even fewer with the necessary language skills," the House Intelligence report said. "Written materials can sit for months, and sometimes years, before a linguist with proper security clearances and skills can begin a translation."

The committee called for the creation of a school solely for the intelligence agencies that would train new linguists and allow current ones to maintain their proficiency. The House bill directs the CIA director and Defense secretary to develop plans for such a school by early next year.

The House bill also suggests that some proposals may warrant a "fresh look," including establishing a separate clandestine service that would oversee all human intelligence resources.

Spying and technology have long gone hand in hand. The notion of James Bond using an endless assortment of elaborate gadgets to defeat his antagonists has become ingrained in popular culture.

Nevertheless, technological improvements have not been heartily embraced by the intelligence agencies. In 1998, an advisory group to the Senate Intelligence Committee criticized the CIA as being "technophobic."

The CIA and the National Security Agency (NSA), the super-secret eavesdropping arm within the Defense Department, were faulted for their failure to predict India's nuclear weapons tests in 1998. Many lawmakers also were astonished to learn that the NSA's main computer network crashed for four days in January 2000 because of a software glitch, rendering the agency essentially deaf. (*1998 Almanac, p. 8-26*)

The NSA — which reportedly employs about 35,000 people, twice as many as the CIA — did not keep pace with rapid technological changes in signals intelligence after the Cold War. In particular, the agency's critics say it failed to adjust its satellite signal-stealing capacity to deal with the proliferation of encrypted communications over fiber-optic cables.

Intelligence experts have called NSA's situation a "crisis." It has lost ground at a time when terrorists have been able to acquire commercially available technology, such as encrypted software and satellite imagery.

Upgrading the NSA

Further complicating intelligence gathering is the reality that the communications technology used by the NSA and other agencies to share information has failed to keep pace with the technology terrorists have obtained.

"The truth is, we don't have the bandwidth we need. . . . We don't move data in pipes the way we need to. . . . The United States has to connect itself if it's going to work more efficiently," Tenet said at a Senate hearing in February.

In response to a Senate advisory group's call for change, Air Force Lt. Gen. Michael V. Hayden was appointed NSA director and assigned to oversee a major reorganization. Within the last three years, Hayden has made dramatic changes in senior management and operations.

The January 2000 computer crash "was a wake-up call to our stakeholders and us that we can no longer afford to defer the funding of a new infrastructure," Hayden said in a rare public speech at American University last year. "And the challenge doesn't stop there."

The NSA is not the only federal agency desperate for technical upgrades. The National Imagery and Mapping Agency (NIMA), which handles the dissemination of satellite and air reconnaissance imagery, has been plagued by what the House Intelligence Committee report described as "totally inadequate" planning and systems.

The House and Senate bills would provide more money to improve how NIMA and other agencies manage information and produce images.

Intelligence experts say there have been signs of improvement in some technical areas. Two years ago, Tenet announced the creation of a private, independent, nonprofit corporation, In-Q-Tel, that develops partnerships with information technology leaders on common projects.

"The world of information technology does not relate very well to the world of intelligence," former CIA Inspector General L. Britt Snider wrote earlier this year. "It thrives on transparency; we thrive on secrecy. . . . A way must be found to identify and harness the capabilities of this world to the agency's purposes without the downsides. That's why I believe In-Q-Tel simply has to succeed."

Lawmakers remain wary. The House Intelligence Committee report said members are concerned "about NSA internal management's willingness to fully understand the need for radical change and to get behind these programs."

INTERAGENCY COOPERATION

Catching terrorists is not solely the job of intelligence agencies; their employees must work with departments across the spectrum of defense and law enforcement. Despite recent advances in cooperation and coordination among government agencies, many experts said the Sept. 11 attacks point to a clear need for improvement.

One of the biggest roadblocks has been the natural tendency of agencies to guard their turf. During the 1970s, then-Secretary of Defense Donald H. Rumsfeld brusquely rejected a suggestion that the Pentagon hand over control of intelligence satellites to the CIA.

"If they're in my budgets, I'll run them," The Washington Post quoted Rumsfeld as saying. (*1996 Almanac, p. 9-17*)

The bureaucratic morass has created some forced alliances. The CIA director has the task of overseeing the intelligence community, but roughly 85 percent of the community's money comes out of the defense budget. The CIA is in charge of gathering intelligence in foreign countries, but domestic terrorism remains the province of the FBI.

Congress already has tried — without success — to impose major changes. In 1996, the Republican chairmen of the Intelligence committees — Rep. Larry Combest of Texas and Sen. Arlen Specter of Pennsylvania — sought to expand the authority of the CIA director. Their efforts came in response to the devastating 1994 espionage case involving Ames, a 31-year CIA employee who pleaded guilty to spying for the Soviet Union. (*1994 Almanac, p. 458*)

But in the face of intense opposition from the Pentagon and its congressional allies, Combest and Specter were forced to scale back their proposals. In the end, only minor changes were made to the CIA director's authority.

Some intelligence experts believe Congress should take another shot. Former CIA and Marine Corps intelligence official Robert D. Steele has developed an ambitious proposal for overhauling the intelligence community that includes developing new state and local intelligence networks.

"Without legislation, and the removal of the bulk of the intelligence program from within the Pentagon's budget, we will continue to suffer intelligence failures stemming from old mind-sets and bureaucratic gridlock," Steele said.

Nevertheless, the House and Senate Intelligence committees remain hopeful. "The only thing that has changed [in five years] is the cause for immediate emphasis," the House Intelligence Committee report said.

Bush holds a weekend meeting with Tenet, right, chief of staff Andrew H. Card, Jr., left, and national security adviser Condoleezza Rice at Camp David, Md., on Sept. 29. Tenet typically briefs the president every morning during the week.

Shaky Connections

In the absence of overhaul legislation, experts say, agencies fighting terrorism can make a tremendous difference by improving their communication and cooperation.

"The issue is coordination, it's relationships," said Mark M. Lowenthal, a former House Intelligence Committee staff director who is a senior principal at SRA International Inc., a Virginia company that contracts with intelligence agencies. "I've been speaking to members of Congress and saying that even structurally, we have what we need. It's the connections between the structures that are not working well."

In particular, experts cite the fact that three weeks before the Sept. 11 attacks, intelligence officials identified two suspected associates of Osama bin Laden and put them on a "watch list" of people to be stopped when they entered the United States. But by the time the Immigration and Naturalization Service received the names, the two men had crossed the border.

"We can probably make minimum improvements by fine-tuning the centralized, interagency capability right now," said Richard W. Bloom, director of terrorism, intelligence and security studies at Embry-Riddle Aeronautical University in Arizona. "Maybe that's some of what Tom Ridge is going to end up doing."

However, others said intelligence coordination goes well beyond Ridge's

duties as the new Homeland Security Council chief. Some suggested that the task fall to either the CIA director or a new intelligence "czar."

Coordinating homeland defense and intelligence "are two different tasks," Boren said. "If you bury intelligence under Tom Ridge, that's worse than what we've got now, where it's buried under the Defense Department."

Of particular interest to many lawmakers is fostering better cooperation between the CIA and the FBI. Although the agencies have reduced some of their frictions over counterintelligence in recent years, experts said the potential exists for them to clash on terrorism — particularly when the FBI is interested in building a criminal case using sources the CIA wants to keep secret.

The overall challenge confronting the intelligence community is reminiscent of 1947, when the National Security Act created the CIA, the core of a network of government bureaus collecting overseas information at the outset of the Cold War.

"Just as the growing Soviet menace and their developing nuclear capability gave rise to President [Harry S] Truman's re-examination of our national objectives and national security strategy, so must the attacks on New York and Washington give rise to the same type of examination," said Richard C. Shelby of Alabama, ranking Republican on the Senate Intelligence Committee. ◆

> *"Just as the growing Soviet menace and their developing nuclear capability gave rise to President [Harry S] Truman's re-examination of our national objectives and national security strategy, so must the attacks on New York and Washington give rise to the same type of examination."*
>
> —Richard C. Shelby , R-AL

Warnings and Recommendations From Recent Commissions on Terrorism

The precise method of flying hijacked jetliners into buildings may not have been predicted, but in the months — and even years — before Sept. 11, a variety of government experts clearly told Congress of the growing likelihood of some kind of strike on American civilians.

Just days before the attacks, two reports by the Congressional Research Service (CRS), which provides legislative analysis to members, issued chillingly prescient assessments of danger in America.

Kenneth Katzman, a Middle Eastern Affairs specialist at the nonpartisan CRS and a former CIA employee, updated his annual report, "Terrorism: Near Eastern Groups and State Sponsors," on Sept. 10. It singled out Osama bin Laden, whom Katzman had noted in previous versions of his report was "gunning for the U.S. mainland."

Four days earlier, Raphael F. Perl, a CRS specialist in international terrorism policy, wrote in an issue brief, "To-day a non-standard brand of terrorist may be emerging: individuals who do not work for any established terrorist organization and who are apparently not agents of any state sponsor. The worldwide threat of such individual or "boutique" terrorism . . . appears to be on the increase."

"We made some two dozen recommendations to the president and Congress in June of 2000. Until Sept. 11, none had been adopted. Since then, I can say two have. . . . We've lost 15 months, so let's get going," L. Paul Bremer III, who chaired the National Commission on Terrorism, told the House Select Intelligence Terrorism and Homeland Security Subcommittee on Sept. 26.

Several blue-ribbon commissions warned of terrorism in the United States and recommended steps to prevent attacks. Ignored in their time, these reports' observations and proposals are today at the forefront of discussion. Here are some excerpts:

Signs continue to point to a decline in state sponsorship of terrorism, as well as a rise in the scope of threat posed by the independent network of exiled Saudi dissident Osama bin Laden. . . . Based on U.S. allegations of past plotting by the bin Laden network, [these] suggest that the network wants to strike within the United States itself.

From the CRS report "Terrorism: Near East Groups and State Sponsors," Sept. 10, 2001.

The potential for terrorist attacks inside the borders of the United States is a serious emerging threat. There is no guarantee that our comparatively secure domestic sanctuary will always remain so. Because the stakes are so high, our nation's leaders must take seriously the possibility of an escalation of terrorist violence against the homeland. . . .

The lack of a national strategy results in part from the fragmentation of executive branch programs for combating terrorism. These programs cross an extraordinary number of jurisdictions and substantive domains: national security, law enforcement, intelligence, emergency management, fire protection, public health, medical care, as well as parts of the private sector.

No one, at any level, is "in charge" of all relevant capabilities, most of which are not dedicated exclusively to combating terrorism. . . . The next president should establish a National Office for Combating Terrorism in the Executive Office of the President, and should seek a statutory basis for this office. . . .

From The Advisory Panel to Assess Domestic Response Capabilities for Terrorism Involving Weapons of Mass Destruction report "Toward a National Strategy for Combating Terrorism," Dec. 15, 2000.

Today's terrorists seek to inflict mass casualties, and they are attempting to do so both overseas and on American soil. They are less dependent on state sponsorship and are, instead, forming loose, transnational affiliations based on religious or ideological affinity and a common hatred of the United States. This makes terrorist attacks more difficult to detect and prevent. . . .

In the 1990s, a terrorist incident was almost 20 percent more likely to result in death or injury than an incident two decades ago. The World Trade Center bombing in New York killed six and wounded about 1,000, but the terrorists' goal was to topple the twin towers, killing tens of thousands of people. . . .

From the National Commission on Terrorism report "Countering the Changing Threat of International Terrorism," June 7, 2000.

A direct attack against American citizens on American soil is likely over the next quarter-century. The risk is not only death and destruction but also a demoralization that could undermine U.S. global leadership. In the face of this threat, our nation has no coherent or integrated government structures.

We therefore recommend the creation of an independent National Homeland Security Agency with responsibility for planning, coordinating and integrating various U.S. government activities involved in homeland security. . . .

The [agency's] director would have Cabinet status and would be a statutory adviser to the National Security Council.

From the United States Commission on National Security/21st Century report "Road Map for National Security: Imperative for Change," Feb. 15, 2000.

Balancing Liberty and Security

Ashcroft faces uphill struggle to win certain enhancements of law enforcement powers

When Congress last debated an anti-terrorism bill, Rep. Bob Barr took a stand against expanding law enforcement's power, and a coalition of conservatives and liberals stood with him. Together, they scuttled key provisions of the 1996 bill (PL 104-132), including one that would have allowed authorities to use some illegally obtained wiretap information.

The Georgia Republican's position has not changed, and even though the political landscape has shifted since Sept. 11, many members still share his unease about giving law enforcement officials more power to peer into the lives of citizens.

"I urge you to not move hastily in recommending wholesale changes to search and seizure laws," Barr wrote Sept. 17 to Attorney General John Ashcroft. "Before we begin dismantling carefully crafted constitutionally protected safeguards and diminishing fundamental rights to privacy, we should first examine why last week's incidents occurred."

The horror of the terrorist attacks has left official Washington desperate to respond. As a result, Congress is preparing to debate new anti-terrorism legislation, proposed by Ashcroft, with provisions that just weeks ago would never have been seriously considered.

It seems certain that Congress will give Ashcroft some of the authority he seeks. But it also is clear that he faces an uphill battle to persuade lawmakers to back some of the provisions, including changes that would make it easier for law enforcement to snoop on electronic communications.

Next to authorizing the use of military force, some of the most important decisions Congress will now have to make involve striking a new balance between law enforcement powers and civil liberties.

The United States has begun to rethink fundamental questions of freedom and security, and now lawmakers

CQ Weekly Sept. 22, 2001

U.S. Attorney General John Ashcroft, left, consulted with Senate Judiciary Chairman Patrick J. Leahy, D-Vt., at a press conference Sept. 19.

will have to consider whether existing laws work in a digital world and whether law enforcement has the resources it needs to keep one step ahead of wrongdoers.

In doing so, they will have to decide such fundamental questions as whether to give government carte blanche to track e-mail and other electronic communications between individuals, and whether to make it easier for law enforcement agencies to peek over the shoulders of computer-users.

"The worst thing that could happen is we damage our Constitution," said Senate Judiciary Committee Chairman Patrick J. Leahy, D-Vt. "If the Constitution is shredded, the terrorists win."

Deliberations began in earnest on Sept. 19, when the Justice Department sent a 21-page draft of anti-terrorism proposals to Capitol Hill. Ashcroft is seeking a broad range of new authority that would make it much easier for investigators to track suspects' communi-

cations, listen to their conversations and search their dwellings.

While the Sept. 11 attacks were not computer crimes, authorities believe the prime suspect, Saudi dissident Osama bin Laden, and his associates used e-mail, messages embedded in computer files and encryption software — used to scramble electronic messages — to communicate.

The FBI and other agencies say they need to employ all existing technology to head off future threats and help them infiltrate other terrorist cells. That begins, they argue, with expanding wiretapping and other surveillance authority to the Internet.

"We need every tool available to us to curtail the potential of additional terrorist attacks," Ashcroft said after a Sept. 19 meeting with congressional leaders.

Many members were receptive to Ashcroft's plea.

"Maybe now we can get some things

Electronic Surveillance
As a Tool Against Terrorism

While the terrorist attacks on the World Trade Center and the Pentagon were not technically computer crimes, government agencies want to know how the perpetrators may have used encrypted, or scrambled, electronic communications to lay their plans.

The Department of Justice says it needs all the available tools to track and eavesdrop on suspects' communications. Privacy and civil liberties groups warn against giving government a blank check.

THE TECHNOLOGY

▶ **Packet sniffer:** With this type of computer program, investigators can monitor all the information passing over a computer network. Packet sniffers can be designed to root out specific types of data. The FBI's "Carnivore" system, for example, is a packet sniffer that lets investigators monitor suspects' e-mail.

▶ **Pen register:** This device records the numbers dialed on a telephone line, but does not allow investigators to listen to conversations. Law enforcement agencies use pen registers to track a suspect's contacts and activities. The fiscal 2002 Commerce-Justice-State appropriations bill (HR 2500) passed by the Senate on Sept.

13 would allow pen registers to be used on all electronic communication, including the Internet. Privacy advocates say the technology could allow investigators to track e-mail and files accessed on Web sites. (*CQ Weekly, p. 2155*)

▶ **Trap and trace:** A trap-and-trace device can identify the originating number of an incoming telephone call. It is similar to Caller ID. The fiscal 2002 Commerce-Justice-State bill would allow trap-and-trace devices, like pen registers, to be used on all electronic communications, including the Internet.

▶ **Wiretap:** Wiretapping allows law enforcement to eavesdrop on conversations. The technology dates almost to the invention of the telephone. The Supreme Court, in the 1928 case *Olmstead v. United States*, approved its use in police and government investigations. The 1986 Electronic Communications Privacy Act (PL 99-508) allowed the government to intercept e-mail, paging messages and other electronic communications after obtaining a court order.

▶ **Keystroke logging:** Investigators can install a hidden device in a suspect's computer to capture everything typed, allowing them to monitor electronic messages before the user

hits the send button. Keystroke logging can prove particularly useful when suspects are using encryption to protect electronic information as it is passed between computers. The FBI has kept details of its technology a secret, but law enforcement agencies say it can help them assess potential terrorist threats. Experts say keystroke logging is defensible under wiretapping laws, but federal statutes do not deal with it specifically.

THE LEGAL STANDARD

To use any of the surveillance technology, law enforcement agencies must get a court order. To get permission to use a wiretap, investigators must show "probable cause" — compelling evidence that a suspect is involved in a criminal activity.

Because trap-and-trace and pen-register devices do not monitor the content of conversations, investigators can get a court order to use them more easily than they can with wiretaps. But applying these devices to computer communication may yield more substantive information than just telephone numbers, so some lawmakers want to require that authorities meet a higher legal standard before getting permission to use them.

done that should have been done 10 years ago," said Senate Minority Leader Trent Lott, R-Miss. "Maybe if we'd done some of these things 10 years ago, we wouldn't be in the situation we're in now."

But other members, as well as civil liberties and privacy groups, say the broad authority Ashcroft seeks would compromise Americans' Fourth Amendment protections against unreasonable search and seizure.

"This has always been a controversial area," said House Minority Leader Richard A. Gephardt, D-Mo. "There will be concerns on both sides of the aisle. It won't be just Democrats or Republicans."

That Congress is willing to consider Ashcroft's package indicates how much the mood on Capitol Hill has shifted.

Only two weeks ago, it appeared Congress had a decent chance of enacting some minimal privacy standards to safeguard personal information on the Internet before year's end. Such measures would have included privacy notices and an "opt-out" box for consumers who did not want commercial Web sites sharing information they collected with other online marketers. (*2001 CQ Weekly, p. 1587*)

Now, enhanced surveillance and the ability to track suspects on the Internet or other wireless communications systems is a top priority for many. Some

lawmakers appear willing to change legal standards for surveillance and make it easier for the Department of Justice to obtain court orders to track suspects' communications on the Internet.

Even Leahy, a reliable liberal Democrat with a strong interest in protecting personal information, has endorsed the concept of "roving wiretaps" that allow law enforcement to follow suspects' conversations on any phones they might use, instead of a specific line.

But bipartisan resistance to other parts of the package show that the political atmosphere has not changed as much as Ashcroft and others may have expected.

Members, particularly in the House,

expressed concerns about other aspects of Ashcroft's proposals, including a provision to allow indefinite detention of non-citizens suspected of terrorist activities and another to allow U.S. prosecutors to use wiretap information collected by a foreign government, even if the collection violated constitutional guarantees against illegal searches and seizures.

"Parts of [Ashcroft's package] are OK; parts are off the wall," said House Judiciary Committee member Jerrold Nadler, D-N.Y. "I think among Democrats and Republicans there is some level-headedness and a determination not to allow Osama bin Laden to destroy the Constitution."

House Majority Leader Dick Armey, R-Texas, said he doubts the legislation will move as quickly as Ashcroft wants.

"What we are trying to save is our civil liberties, and they're very precious to us," Armey said.

In the House, the leadership and the Judiciary Committee have announced different game plans for handling the bill, evidence of larger disagreements about how quickly to move the bill and how broad it should be.

The bipartisan leadership of the House said Sept. 20 that they believe the Ashcroft proposals will move in two pieces: first, a few relatively non-controversial proposals, such as tougher penalties for terrorism, and later, the rest of the package. The second portion should move through the "regular order" of hearings and committee consideration before floor action, said Speaker J. Dennis Hastert, R-Ill.

That does not necessarily mean an enormous delay. Armey said he thinks work on the package will be completed before Congress leaves town for the year, perhaps at the end of October. At the same time, however, he cautioned that Ashcroft may not get all he wants.

"To the extent that Congress is going to work it out with the attorney general, the whole package will be done before we leave," he said.

The schedule announced by the House Judiciary Committee, however, is different. The panel intends to hold a hearing on Ashcroft's proposal on Sept. 24, followed by a markup of the bill the next day. And it will consider the proposal as one piece, according to its spokesman.

The Senate Judiciary Committee is expected to hold a hearing Sept. 25. The panel had not announced when it

Attorney General's Proposals

On Sept. 19, Attorney General John Ashcroft proposed a package of anti-terrorism initiatives. Following are the highlights:

SEARCHES, SEIZURES AND SURVEILLANCE

▶ **Roving wiretap authority.** Ashcroft wants to be able to link a wiretap to an individual, not a phone line, to hear all conversations. At present, authorities must get a separate court order for each phone line they want to tap.

▶ **"One-stop shopping" for court orders.** In most instances, authorities must get a warrant or other permission from a judge in each jurisdiction where they are conducting an investigation. Under the proposal, authorities would need only one warrant in nationwide investigations to proceed with searches and some electronic surveillance. Some of this authority would apply only to terrorist investigations.

▶ **Wider access to electronic information.** Ashcroft proposes a series of changes to aid law enforcement's access to information flowing over the Internet and elsewhere. Agencies would be authorized to use surveillance equipment to track e-mail and Web travel. They would be able to get more information from Internet service providers, which now are required to provide only limited information, such as a customer's name and address and how long he has used the service. Investigators, for example, could use subpoenas to gain access to credit card billing information. Authorities could seize stored voice mails with search warrants, rather than going through the more difficult process of obtaining a court order for a wiretap.

▶ **Disclosure of some Internet communication.** Service providers could decide on their own to disclose Internet communication and information about customers if they believe there is a threat of death or serious injury.

IMMIGRATION LAWS

▶ **Broader power to detain immigrants.** The federal government would be able to hold non-citizens indefinitely.

▶ **Consolidated habeas corpus appeals by immigrants.** The federal district court for the District of Columbia would handle all appeals from non-citizens challenging the government's national security deportations. The cases now go to the district closest to the plaintiff's home.

OTHER PROVISIONS

▶ **Foreign wiretap evidence in U.S. criminal proceedings.** U.S. authorities could use information obtained by foreign government wiretaps, even if the surveillance violated the rights of Americans, as long as the U.S. government was aware it was going on.

▶ **Broader definition of "terrorist."** "Terrorist" would include anyone who "affords material support to an organization that the individual knows or should know is a terrorist organization," regardless of whether the support is related to the terrorism.

▶ **Tougher penalties for terrorism.** The proposal would lift the five-year statute of limitations on terrorist crimes, and would increase both the sentences and fines that can be levied on convicted terrorists.

will mark up the legislation.

The Senate leadership seemed more interested in moving the package along in one piece.

"You're always going to have people on the far left and the far right who don't like what we do in this area," said Sen. Orrin G. Hatch of Utah, ranking Republican on the Judiciary Commit-

tee. "But I think we'll work it out."

An unusually wide variety of interest groups are anxiously watching the debate. The National Rifle Association fears the attacks will renew the demands for greater gun control. Civil libertarians and privacy groups say the focus on greater national security could compromise individual freedoms if lawmakers get caught up in the emotion of the moment.

Lawmakers feel the push and pull.

On Sept. 19, House Select Intelligence Committee member Tim Roemer, D-Ind., saw firsthand the devastation in New York and said it cannot help but influence how members approach the debate.

"Your emotions are worked up," he said. "The scene isn't breaking your heart, it's splitting your heart in half. But we have to rely not only on that, but on wisdom, accuracy and prudence."

An Old Debate

U.S. policymakers long have wrestled with civil liberties questions in times of crisis, and those seeking restraints on individual rights often have prevailed.

In 1798, not long after the country's founding, Congress passed the Alien and Sedition Acts. The Alien Act gave the president the authority to expel any foreigner considered dangerous to the public peace. The Sedition Act made it a crime to bring "false, scandalous and malicious" accusations against the president, the Congress or the government. Several newspapermen were fined and imprisoned. All later were pardoned by President Thomas Jefferson and reimbursed by Congress.

During the Civil War, President Abraham Lincoln became one of the most powerful executives the United States has seen, in part by claiming some powers traditionally reserved to Congress, such as suspending habeas corpus, the right to demand that government show why it is detaining an individual. Congress eventually ratified his actions, even though a Supreme Court justice castigated him for it after the fact.

During World War I, the military nationalized the radio industry amid security concerns. During both World War I and World War II, non-citizens from enemy countries were forbidden to own guns or fly in airplanes.

But the event most recalled by some members since Sept. 11 is the forced relocation of some 120,000 Japanese-Americans to internment camps in 1942. The action was ordered by President Franklin D. Roosevelt, and was subsequently validated by Congress. The Supreme Court ruled 6-3 that the threat to national security justified the internment.

In 1988, Congress passed a $1.25 billion reparations bill for Japanese Americans. As signed by President Ronald Reagan, the law (PL 100-383) authorized a payment of $20,000 to each of the 60,000 surviving internees. Each also received an official apology. (*1988 Almanac, p. 80*)

Rep. David L. Hobson, R-Ohio, speaking of the pending debate, said, "We should not lose sight of what's made this country great."

Hobson said the memory of what was done to Japanese-Americans is giving his colleagues pause on the current legislation. "I don't think they want to overreach, because they remember World War II," he said.

Ashcroft has tried to alleviate those concerns: "We will conduct this effort to investigate and to prosecute with strict regard for every safeguard of the United States Constitution," he said on Sept. 19. "But we will not fail to use any tool."

Modern Communications

The current debate will play out against a rapidly changing digital world, where suspects can send hidden messages buried in digital images and use off-the-shelf encryption software to scramble their cellular phone conversations or e-mail.

Ashcroft wants to be able to capture Internet e-mail addresses and Web addresses with electronic surveillance equipment. He wants to make it easier for law enforcement to get information, such as billing addresses and credit card information, from Internet service providers.

Ashcroft is proposing that law enforcement be allowed a kind of "one-stop shopping" to obtain judicial permission for portions of their investigative work. Authorities now must get a warrant or other permission from a judge in each jurisdiction where they are conducting investigations.

A draft counterproposal from Leahy shows how much work lies ahead to convince Congress to go along with the attorney general's broad plan.

While Leahy's rough draft would accommodate the Bush administration by authorizing greater surveillance on the Internet, it appears his plan would raise the legal threshold that authorities must meet for that type of surveillance, something the law enforcement community has typically opposed.

Many of the expansions of wiretap authority requested by Ashcroft are not included in the Leahy draft, and Leahy said that because of his concern over another provision allowing the indefinite detention of immigrants, he planned to stay in Washington over the weekend to work with staff and the administration.

Barney Frank, D-Mass., a member of the House Judiciary Committee, said he is prepared to give law enforcement more authority.

"I do not think you have the right to hide illegal activity from law enforcement," he said. The country does "need more electronic surveillance."

The Senate already considered a smaller form of the Ashcroft proposal during debate of the fiscal 2002 appropriations bill for the departments of Commerce, Justice and State (HR 2500). On Sept. 13, Hatch won approval of an amendment to the bill that would expand the definition of trap-and-trace devices and pen registers, technology frequently used in surveillance, to allow their use in cyberspace. (*2001 CQ Weekly, p. 2155*)

The move was more than an exercise in semantics. It would greatly expand the information the government can capture, including which Web sites suspects visit, what files they download and the e-mail addresses of people they communicate with.

Debate also likely will encompass encryption technology. Authorities have long pressed for curbs on the availability of encryption software. Although Ashcroft did not specifically request it, some observers expect Congress to be more willing to give investigators more flexibility to counter this kind of technology.

"The reality we face has changed," said Steven Aftergood, director of the Federation of American Scientists' Project on Government Secrecy. "The concerns that all of us might have had about potential government overreaching recede somewhat in the face of the all-too-real danger we witnessed."

Still, Congress will be cautious about granting law enforcement too much authority without some idea of how new rules and new technology may play out in the real world, said Adam Thierer, director of telecommunications studies at the Cato Institute, a libertarian think tank.

"It's a very delicate balancing act," Thierer said. ◆

Immigration Debate Reverses Direction

Just weeks ago, Congress was considering liberalizing immigration laws to put some illegal immigrants on the road to citizenship.

Now, the debate has flipped. The House and Senate are considering a proposal by Attorney General John Ashcroft to allow him to indefinitely detain anyone who is not a U.S. citizen. It is just one of several provisions of the anti-terrorism package Ashcroft sent to Congress on Sept. 19 that show how radically the congressional agenda has changed in just two weeks.

Pro-immigrant and civil rights groups now find themselves fighting a defensive battle to protect immigrants' existing rights, rather than going on the offensive to expand them.

"The focus has changed," said one immigration lobbyist.

It is unclear how much leeway Congress will give Ashcroft, as staff and lawmakers seek a compromise on these sensitive issues.

The changes to immigration law have a direct link to the Sept. 11 terrorist attacks: According to reports, the majority of hijackers were immigrants. Many of them had overstayed their visas and were in the country illegally.

"We're going to do everything we can to harmonize the constitutional rights of individuals with every legal capacity we can muster to also protect the safety and security of individuals," Ashcroft said Sept. 18.

Detaining Immigrants

Immigrants have faced restrictions in other times of national crisis. During both World Wars, for example, foreign nationals were prohibited from owning radios.

Ashcroft wants to be able to detain any non-citizens upon showing that there is a "reason to believe" they may pose a threat to national security. The government could hold them until they were deported or no longer considered a threat.

Millions of permanent legal residents, many of whom have lived legally in the United States for decades, would be subject to the new rules.

Traditionally, immigration law treats long-term residents differently than those who just came into the country. In general, the longer immigrants have been in the United States legally, the more rights they have. Ashcroft's proposal would ignore that distinction, which is one of the reasons House Judiciary Committee member Barney Frank, D-Mass., said he plans to oppose it.

"The indefinite detention is unacceptable," Frank said Sept. 20.

Senate Judiciary Committee Chairman Patrick J. Leahy, D-Vt., also has concerns about the detention provision, and it seems unlikely Ashcroft is going to get such broad authority in that matter.

Even if he were able to convince Congress, it is not clear the authority would be constitutional.

In *Zadvydas v. Davis*, the Supreme Court ruled 5-4 on June 28 that indefinite detention is impermissible. In that case, Kestutis Zadvydas committed a crime and was ordered deported, but no country would take him, so he was held indefinitely by the U.S. government. (*2001 CQ Weekly, p. 1576*)

Writing for the majority, Justice Stephen G. Breyer found that the underlying statute could not permit such detention because, if it did, it would be unconstitutional.

"In our view, the statute, read in light of the Constitution's demands, limits an alien's post-removal-period detention to a period reasonably necessary to bring about that alien's removal from the United States," he wrote. "It does not permit indefinite detention."

Ashcroft also has asked Congress to consolidate all national security deportation appeals to the federal district court for the District of Columbia. He argues that this would help ensure that immigrants in similar cases are treated the same.

But an immigration lobbyist said this could pose a tremendous burden on immigrants trying to prove they should not be deported. For example, they would have to find a way to bring witnesses and evidence from wherever they live to Washington, D.C.

Another provision that could have a wide-ranging impact: Ashcroft wants to be able to file terrorism charges against anyone who contributed to an organization they knew or should have known was a terrorist organization. He wants to make this retroactive.

Opponents said this could mean that someone who in the 1980s contributed to a group such as the African National Congress in South Africa, which some people have called a terrorist group, could be arrested now.

Border Controls

Ashcroft did not ask for help in beefing up border controls, but he is likely to get a lot of it.

Leahy, in a draft counterproposal, would authorize tripling the number of Border Patrol agents and Customs personnel assigned to each state along the long border with Canada. Several of the terrorists are suspected of having come into the United States across that border, which has less stringent controls than the U.S. border with Mexico.

And Leahy would give the State Department and the Immigration and Naturalization Service access to national criminal databases so agents could check whether visa applicants had criminal histories.

House Judiciary Committee Chairman F. James Sensenbrenner Jr., R-Wis., said recent events have added urgency to another longtime goal of Congress — an overhaul of the Immigration and Naturalization Service. (*2001 CQ Weekly, p. 720*)

"The terrorist attack shows that immigration service reform is more important now than ever before," he said in a Sept. 19 interview. He said one of the problems is that the service has no way to track people, like the hijackers, who have overstayed their visas. "The INS has no idea where they are," he said.

New Map of Friends and Foes

Foreign policy priorities are hastily recast as U.S. gauges support for its campaign

President Bush laid out his vision for fighting a global war on terrorism to a unified and highly receptive Congress Sept. 21. But beneath the surface, complicated questions remain for both the administration and lawmakers.

Already, there are divisions within the president's ranks over such issues as whether all terrorists should be treated equally, how to deal with longtime foes, such as Iran who have made diplomatic overtures, and the breadth of the response.

As the Bush administration wrestled with those issues, it also left Congress grappling with the diplomatic incentives under its authority to advance the war on terrorism.

Members of Congress have been divided on how far the campaign against terrorism should go. Some, such as Sen. Joseph I. Lieberman, D-Conn., a member of the Armed Services Committee, and Republican Policy Committee Chairman Larry E. Craig of Idaho, have called for a wide-ranging assault.

"It's not a question of either this kind of terrorism or that kind of terrorism, you can't pick and choose between them," said Sen. Chuck Hagel, R-Neb.

But other lawmakers, such as Senate Foreign Relations Committee Chairman Joseph R. Biden Jr., D-Del., and John W. Warner, R-Va., have preferred a more limited campaign centered largely on Afghanistan and focused more on diplomatic than military means. Biden and Warner's concerns helped guide passage of a joint resolution (PL 107-40) Sept. 14 that sought to limit any military campaign to specific retaliation for the attacks on the Pentagon and World Trade Center. (*2001 CQ Weekly, p. 2118*)

"There are a lot of options available to us, not just the military," said Sen. John Kerry, D-Mass. "No one wants to proceed in a way that we don't finish or are not prepared to finish."

White House spokesman Ari Fleischer said Sept. 18 that the administration hopes to use both economic "carrots" and military "sticks" to lure countries into cooperating against terrorism: "In different nations, the carrot may be bigger; in other nations, the stick may be bigger."

Bush's use of the stick was clear in his threats to the Taliban regime in Afghanistan. During the week of Sept. 17, the Pentagon ordered more than 100 warplanes to the Middle East to join more than 200 planes permanently stationed in the region. "The hour is coming when America will act," Bush said Sept. 20.

And he primed the American people for an attack on Afghanistan if it refuses to turn over alleged terrorist mastermind Osama bin Laden and other members of his al Qaeda organization to U.S. authorities.

Bush's military actions are largely beyond congressional control now because Congress already has given him the authority to retaliate for the Sept. 11 attacks. But Congress can be expected to play a more prominent role in the next few weeks in doling out the carrots.

"After the events of last week, I think the whole foreign aid bill is open to ways of winning this war," said Sen. Mitch McConnell of Kentucky, the ranking Republican on the Foreign Operations Appropriations Subcommittee.

Reward and Punish

After the terrorist attacks, Congress has to change the way it approaches a variety of foreign policy issues such as economic assistance, trade policy and sanctions, McConnell said.

"All of the legislation has to be viewed through the prism of the situation we find ourselves in," McConnell said Sept. 19. "We need to reward those countries that cooperate with us in fighting terrorism and punish those countries that don't."

McConnell is not alone. Prodded by Bush, lawmakers will probably cede ground on a number of international issues in an effort to present a united front with the White House and help build a global coalition against terrorism.

Washington's focus on terrorism threatens to lower the priority of concerns such as nuclear proliferation, human rights and economic development overseas. And some lawmakers are already concerned that other issues will be relegated to a back burner.

For now, though, the White House appears to have the upper hand on a number of foreign policy issues in which it had been locked in a standoff with Congress prior to the attacks. Already, Congress has yielded on a number of previously contentious foreign policy issues, including a showdown on missile defense.

Formerly controversial legislation to repay $582 million in U.S. debts to the United Nations has now won enough backing from conservative Republicans such as House Majority Whip Tom DeLay of Texas that Hill leaders are considering moving it under suspension of the rules the week of Sept. 24. That would restrict debate on the legislation and require a two-thirds vote for passage.

Senate Democrats backed off plans to amend the fiscal 2002 Treasury-Postal Service appropriations bill (S 1398) to lift a ban on travel to Cuba over White House objections.

Administration officials are looking for further concessions from Congress in the weeks and months ahead, especially on issues involving trade and economic assistance. U.S. economic power, they argue, is a crucial tool in persuading other nations to join the fight against terrorism.

"Economic strength — at home and abroad — is the foundation of America's hard and soft power," wrote U.S. Trade Representative Robert B. Zoellick Sept. 20 in The Washington Post.

Zoellick called for quick congressional action on the administration's trade agenda, particularly a pending free-trade agreement with Jordan and efforts to gain authority to negotiate trade agreements that would be subject only to an up-or-down vote on Capitol Hill.

"Congress now needs to send an unmistakable signal to the world that the

Potential Players in the U.S. Response

Longtime U.S. allies such as Britain and France immediately answered the plea for strong support following the terrorist attacks Sept. 11. As the week progressed, reliable friends continued to respond, with Australia on Sept. 14 invoking a clause in its 50-year-old military treaty with the United States, under which an attack on U.S. territory is considered an attack on Australia. But the key to President Bush's hopes of forging a global coalition against terrorism may well lie with less powerful states, including some longtime U.S. adversaries. Here is a look at a few of the new key players with which the Bush administration is exploring its options.

▶ AFGHANISTAN (1) The country's Taliban regime hosts Osama bin Laden, described as the primary suspect in the attacks. The United States helped bring the Taliban to power as part of an Islamic insurgency that forced the Soviet Union out of the country in the 1980s, but Americans soured on the regime because of its support for terrorism. U.S. officials are now threatening retaliation if the Taliban does not turn over bin Laden, and lawmakers are discussing strengthening ties to opposition groups, including granting them recognition as the country's legitimate opposition and providing military and economic assistance.

▶ PAKISTAN AND INDIA (2) Congress and the White House had already been moving toward easing sanctions that were imposed on the two countries after both tested nuclear weapons in 1998 and Pakistan's democratically elected government was deposed a year later in a military coup, but the attacks appear to have clinched the deal. Pakistan's key location — it borders Afghanistan — and its ties with the Taliban government there have made it a U.S. ally in the war on terrorism. Pakistani officials now expect not only an end to sanctions, but a resumption of the large flows of economic and military aid that the country received in the 1980s when it served as a conduit for U.S. aid to rebels battling Soviet forces in Afghanistan.

▶ SYRIA (3) This is the only one of the seven countries on the State Department's list of state sponsors of terrorism that enjoys full diplomatic relations with the United States. Despite being a key sponsor of the Hezbollah group that has carried out terrorist attacks in Israel, Syria pledged within days of the attack to join the United States in clamping down on terrorism. Syrian troops also fought alongside U.S. forces in the Persian Gulf War.

▶ LIBYA (4) Muammar el-Qaddafi's country remains listed as a state sponsor of terrorism, largely for backing several terrorist attacks in the 1980s, most notoriously the 1988 bombing of Pan Am Flight 103 over Lockerbie, Scotland. The attacks led to U.S. bombing raids in 1986, unilateral sanctions and a cutoff of diplomatic relations. Experts acknowledge that Libya's support of terrorist groups has waned in recent years, and in 1999 Libya turned over two intelligence agents believed to have carried out the Lockerbie bombing. One was sentenced to life in prison Jan. 31. That has led to suspension of United Nations sanctions on Libya, but Bush has said he will not lift sanctions until Tripoli takes responsibility for the bombings and compensates the victims. Democratic Sen. Edward M. Kennedy of Massachusetts and other lawmakers have supported putting those conditions into law. In July, Congress reauthorized and tightened 1996 legislation that punishes foreign companies that invest in Libya's oil industry.

▶ JORDAN (5) A key U.S. ally in the Arab world, Jordan has expressed strong support for U.S. actions to counter terrorism. Administration officials, such as U.S. Trade Representative Robert B. Zoellick, are pressing to reward Jordan by passing a free-trade agreement reached by the two countries. The agreement has been held up by disputes over how far such deals should go in addressing labor and environmental concerns.

▶ IRAN (6) This longtime adversary poses perhaps the trickiest dilemma for U.S. policymakers. The State Department describes Iran as the leading state sponsor of terrorism for its support of groups combating Israel, such as Hezbollah and Hamas. In June, Attorney General John Ashcroft blamed Iran for engineering the 1996 bombing of the Khobar Towers barracks in Saudi Arabia that killed 19 U.S. military personnel. During the 1990s, as part of an effort to punish Iran for its support of terrorism and its move to acquire weapons of mass destruction, President Bill Clinton banned most trade with and investment in Iran. Congress sought to further punish Iran by passing legislation in 1996 — reauthorized this year (PL107-24) — that punishes foreign companies that invest in Iran's oil industry. Clinton and Bush have waived these sanctions, however, to avoid a diplomatic row with European allies such as France and Italy, which have substantial investments there. Yet Iran, long a foe of bin Laden and Afghanistan's Taliban, has now offered strong support for the U.S. effort to punish these groups. Secretary of State Colin L. Powell said Sept. 17 that the administration took the offer seriously and wanted to learn more about it. "They may want to make cause against the Taliban, but will they make cause against other terrorist organizations that they have provided support to? . . . And so it seems to me that is an opening worth exploring, and that is as far as we go right now."

▶ ISRAEL AND THE PALESTINIANS (7) Congress annually approves nearly $3 billion in aid to Israel, giving the United States significant potential diplomatic leverage. But despite a year of violence between Palestinians and Israelis, the formidable Jewish-American lobby on Capitol Hill had helped ensure virtually unanimous support for Israel and backing for Bush's hands-off policy toward the region. It also led the House to include legislation in the fiscal 2002 foreign operations appropriations bill (HR 2506) to require the Palestinians to demonstrate "substantial compliance" with their commitments to renounce terrorism, or face possible U.S. sanctions. The tide could be turning, however. Administration officials, intent on securing Palestinian support for any retaliatory actions, have pressured Israel to pull its forces out of some Palestinian territories, while the Palestinians agreed immediately to a cease-fire, which has proven shaky.

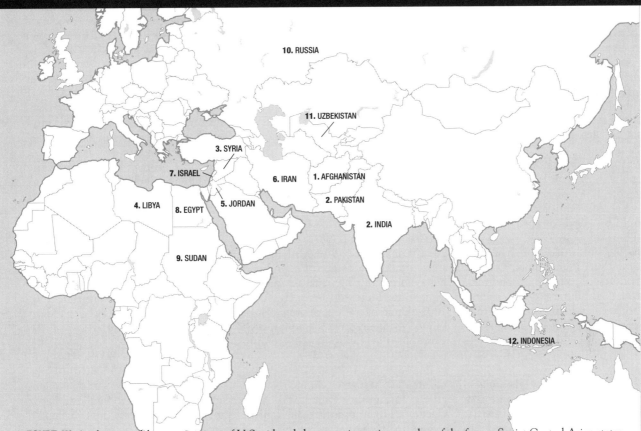

EGYPT (8) As the second-largest recipient of U.S. aid and the most populous Arab nation, Egypt will play a key role in winning Arab backing for any U.S. retaliation. But Egyptian President Hosni Mubarak, fearing Muslim militants in his own country, has been lukewarm in his support.

SUDAN (9) For months, a coalition of religious conservatives and African-American lawmakers have been pressing to impose more sanctions on Sudan, where the predominantly Muslim government has been waging a war against rebels in the country's south, most of whom practice folk religions or Christianity. The civil war has killed an estimated 2 million people and displaced 4 million. The State Department also has considered Sudan a state sponsor of terrorism, partially because it once served as a haven for bin Laden. That has led to substantial U.S. sanctions against Khartoum. In the wake of the bombings of U.S. embassies in Kenya and Tanzania in 1998, the United States launched cruise missile attacks against Sudan. But even before the Sept. 11 attacks, Powell and other administration officials had opposed additional sanctions, preferring diplomatic pressure. Sudan's actions since the attacks will likely add force to these arguments. "The Sudan has become suddenly much more interested and active in working with us on various items," Powell told reporters Sept. 17.

RUSSIA (10) Russia has sent mixed signals about how far it is willing to go in cooperating with U.S. anti-terrorist efforts. After losing a disastrous war in Afghanistan in the 1980s, Russia still feels beset by Muslim groups with ties to the Taliban, many of whom are fighting in Chechnya and the former Soviet states of Central Asia. That has led to a common front with the United States against these groups. Russia initially resisted U.S. efforts to use its territory or that of the former Soviet Central Asian states. Russian officials fear that any U.S. presence in the region could become permanent, further eroding Russian influence in its "near abroad."

UZBEKISTAN AND OTHER CENTRAL ASIAN NATIONS (11) Many of the former Soviet Central Asian states have been under siege from Islamic insurgents for years. That has helped lead to warming relations with the United States, most notably by energy-rich Kazakhstan. In 1999, Congress cleared legislation that included a provision that sought to upgrade relations with these countries, authorizing enhanced trade, economic assistance and efforts to enhance border security to guard against terrorism and proliferation of weapons of mass destruction. Aid to the region has remained quite modest, however. In an unprecedented move, two Central Asian nations, Uzbekistan and Tajikistan, have allowed the deployment of U.S. warplanes to their territory.

INDONESIA (12) As the world's most populous Muslim nation, Indonesia is a linchpin in Bush administration arguments that U.S. attacks against Islamic terrorism are intended to confront terrorism, not Islam. U.S. aid to Indonesia has increased in recent years as the country moved toward democracy after the departure of longtime President Suharto. Bush accelerated that process Sept. 19 in a meeting with Indonesian President Megawati Sukarnoputri, vowing at least $130 million in assistance and $400 million from U.S. trade finance agencies. He also lifted a ban on the export of non-lethal military items to the Southeast Asian nation. But lawmakers such as Senate Foreign Operations Appropriations Committee Chairman Patrick J. Leahy, D-Vt., continue to look warily at efforts to rebuild ties with Indonesia's military, long accused of human rights abuses.

United States is committed to global leadership of openness and understands that the staying power of our new coalition depends on economic growth and hope," Zoellick wrote.

The terrorist attacks appear to have increased Congress' desire to act quickly on the Jordan agreement, since Jordan's King Abdullah is viewed as a key ally among Muslim leaders in the anti-terrorism effort.

"Obviously, King Abdullah has been helpful," Senate Minority Leader Trent Lott, R-Miss., said Sept. 19. "I wish we could work it out and move it. It would be good for Jordan and it would be good for us."

The legislation (S 643) had been held up by Sen. Phil Gramm, R-Texas, who had vowed to block action unless controversial bilateral commitments on workplace and environmental rules were removed. But now, the Senate is scheduled to act on it Sept. 24. The House approved its version (HR 2603) on July 31.

Administration officials are also seeking to use either the imposition or lifting of trade restrictions and similar sanctions on economic aid as a tool to persuade other countries to cooperate with U.S. anti-terrorism efforts.

"We trade with countries all around the world," Commerce Secretary Donald L. Evans told CNN on Sept. 18. "If they don't want to cooperate and don't want to be on our side, there are things and measures that we can take, sanctions or other kinds of barriers to our markets here."

Pakistan: Much to Gain

One sanctions barrier, though, appears to be falling quickly: restrictions that were imposed on trade with and aid for India and Pakistan, largely because of their decisions to defy the United States and test nuclear weapons in 1998.

Even before the attacks, an attempt to repeal or waive all remaining sanctions imposed on those two South Asian countries as a punishment for those tests was gaining ground in Congress. Support for lifting the sanctions on India was particularly strong on Capitol Hill, with both Biden and Tom Lantos of California, ranking Democrat on the House International Relations Committee, calling for such a step. India's willingness to cooperate in the anti-terrorism campaign has further bolstered support.

Attitudes toward Pakistan were more mixed. The country labored under a slew of sanctions that had been imposed throughout the last decade in an effort to forestall its nuclear program and then punish Islamabad for carrying through on the tests. Most aid to Pakistan was cut off in 1999 because the annual foreign aid bills banned aid to governments in which a democratically elected leader had been overthrown in a military coup.

Even before the Sept. 11 attacks, however, attitudes toward Pakistan had been softening. Some lawmakers such as House Intelligence Committee Chairman Porter J. Goss, R-Fla., argued that Islamabad had taken new steps toward democratization and had behaved responsibly with its nuclear arsenal. A House version of the fiscal 2002 foreign operations appropriations bill intentionally gave the administration some new flexibility in applying these sanctions, aides said.

Those arguments gained force after the attacks. Pakistan's assistance became crucial for mounting an attack on al Qaeda and in confronting the Taliban regime in Afghanistan, which is believed to provide bin Laden with sanctuary. Secretary of State Colin L. Powell and other administration officials began discussing with key lawmakers the possibility of lifting the sanctions.

Their case was helped by a Sept. 19 address to his nation by Pakistani President Pervez Musharraf in which he faced down significant domestic opposition and called for helping the United States by providing overflight rights, intelligence information and logistical support. After his remarks, some pro-India lawmakers such as Benjamin A. Gilman, R-N.Y., chairman of the House Middle East and South Asia Subcommittee, said they wanted to hold off any relief for Pakistan until Musharraf proved he could carry out his promises.

But key lawmakers like Biden, House International Relations Committee Chairman Henry J. Hyde, R-Ill., and Rep. Nancy Pelosi of California, ranking Democrat on the House Intelligence Committee, said they would support lifting the sanctions, despite continuing concerns about Pakistan's nuclear program.

Musharraf, Biden said, "has taken the bold step of promising his nation's full, unstinting support to us, at the time we need it most."

Senate aides said Sept. 21 that Bush plans to use his authority to waive the remaining nuclear-related sanctions on Pakistan and Congress may give Bush the authority to waive democracy related restrictions in a fiscal 2002 continuing resolution.

"Clearly, as the relationship grows, I am sure the economic ties will grow, which could mean better market access, better treatment on debt rescheduling, and more money, both directly and through multilateral institutions," Pakistani Finance Minister Shaukut Aziz told Agence France Presse on Sept. 16.

Indeed, House Foreign Operations Appropriations Subcommittee Chairman Jim Kolbe, R-Ariz., said that lawmakers and the administration were already in initial discussions about further steps. One possibility, Kolbe said, was forgiving Pakistan's debts along the lines of what the United States provided Egypt in return for its assistance in the 1991 Persian Gulf War. In that case, the White House was able to overcome strong congressional reservations to forgiving Egypt's $6.7 billion military debt. (*1990 Almanac, p. 830*)

Kolbe also said that appropriators were studying removing proposed restrictions on aid to the Palestinian Authority, after Chairman Yasir Arafat vigorously condemned the attacks against the World Trade Center and the Pentagon and called for a cease-fire against Israeli forces. While the cease-fire is still shaky, Arafat appears to have met administration demands to try to curb the violence between the Palestinians and Israel in order to help cement its anti-terrorism coalition.

Both Kolbe and McConnell said that if Arafat sticks to his word, they are willing to look at removing conditions on aid to the Palestinian authority that the House had approved in its version of the fiscal 2002 foreign operations appropriations bill and that McConnell was championing in the Senate.

The provisions would require that the Palestinians demonstrate "substantial compliance" with their commitments to renounce the use of terrorism or face possible sanctions that could include the U.S. government closing their liaison office in Washington, designating the Palestinian Liberation Organization or one of its constituent groups a terrorist organization, and limiting aid to the Palestinians in the West Bank and Gaza to humanitarian

Authorizing Force: Between the Lines

Resolution Language	What It Means	Why It's There
To authorize the use of United States Armed Forces against those responsible for the recent attacks launched against the United States. Whereas, on September 11, 2001, acts of treacherous violence were committed against the United States and its citizens; and Whereas, such acts render it both necessary and appropriate that the United States exercise its rights to self-defense and to protect United States citizens both at home and abroad; and Whereas, in light of the threat to the national security and foreign policy of the United States posed by these grave acts of violence; and Whereas, such acts continue to pose an unusual and extraordinary threat to the national security and foreign policy of the United States,	These "whereas" clauses lay out the facts that led to the resolution and reflect Congress' concerns about the terrorist threat.	They seek to convince both domestic and international audiences of the reasons behind the U.S. determination to take military action and to argue that they hew closely to both U.S. and international law.
Whereas the President has authority under the Constitution to take action to deter and prevent acts of international terrorism against the United States. Resolved by the Senate and the House of Representatives of the United States of America in Congress assembled, **SECTION 1. SHORT TITLE** This joint resolution may be cited as the "Authorization for Use of Military Force." **SECTION 2. AUTHORIZATION FOR USE OF UNITED STATES ARMED FORCES**	This is a concession to traditional administration arguments that the president does not need congressional approval for military action, particularly retaliation for terrorism.	The Bush administration wanted to preserve the traditional administration argument over the War Powers Resolution as a precedent in future discussions and to prevent any brake on its actions.
(a) That the President is authorized to use all necessary and appropriate force against those nations, organizations, or persons he determines planned, authorized, committed, or aided the terrorist attacks that occurred on September 11, 2001, or harbored such organizations or persons, in order to prevent any future acts of international terrorism against the United States by such nations, organizations or persons.	This stops short of a declaration of war against terrorism. But the administration still has a great deal of latitude to act since it is free to define which "nations" and "organizations" were involved in the attacks.	To give the administration maximum flexibility to retaliate for the Sept. 11 attacks. The administration had originally suggested an authorization of "all necessary and appropriate force" to "deter and pre-empt any future acts of terrorism or aggression against the United States."
(b) War Powers Resolution Requirements (1) Specific Statutory Authorization — Consistent with section 8(a)(1) of the War Powers Resolution, the Congress declares that this section is intended to constitute specific statutory authorization within the meaning of section 5(b) of the War Powers Resolution. (2) Applicability of Other Requirements — Nothing in this resolution supersedes any requirement of the War Powers Resolution (PL 107-40).	These sections mirror language in the resolution authorizing the Persian Gulf War (PL 102-1). The 1973 War Powers Resolution (PL 93-148) insists that Congress, not the president, has the power to initiate military hostilities.	Lawmakers, led by Sen. Joseph R. Biden Jr., D-Del., continue to insist the administration is bound by the War Powers Resolution as a way to ensure that Congress is included in future deliberations on use of military force overseas.

assistance. Bush has requested $75 million in aid for the Palestinians.

Sen. Richard G. Lugar, R-Ind., a senior member of the Foreign Relations Committee, said that Central Asian nations such as Uzbekistan and Tajikistan — which Pentagon officials said have broken with their Soviet past and permitted the deployment of U.S. warplanes to their territory — should be rewarded for their cooperation. Those countries "might well become much bigger recipients" of U.S. assistance, he said.

The anti-terrorist campaign will also probably further stall House-passed legislation (HR 2052) to impose tough sanctions on Sudan. That bill differs sharply from a Senate-passed bill (S 180) that calls for using diplomatic pressure to force the predominantly Muslim Sudanese government to seek peace with rebels in the country's south, most of whom practice folk religions or Christianity. The civil war has killed an estimated 2 million people and displaced 4 million others.

The administration has long favored the Senate's approach. But the anti-terror campaign makes administration officials even more inclined to favor diplomacy over sanctions. Sudan once served as a haven for bin Laden and is on the State Department's list of state sponsors of terrorism.

But Powell told reporters Sept. 17 that "Sudan has suddenly become much more interested and active in working with us on various items." That day he spoke to Sudanese Foreign Minister Mustafa Osman Ismail about antiterrorism, the first high-level contact between the countries in years. ◆

Regrouping With A Common Purpose

CQ PHOTO / SCOTT J. FERRELL

They spoke words of anger. They called for war. They vowed to unite, Democrats and Republicans, to find a way forward in a world changed forever. But as evening fell on the day after the worst attack ever on American soil, the men and women of Congress gathered in the vast silence of the Capitol Rotunda, beneath statues of the nation's heroes, and they prayed for guidance.

Sen. Barbara A. Mikulski, D-Md., reached back millennia to the writings of the prophet Job to express the nation's anguish and her own: "The thing which I feared greatly has

come upon me and that which I was afraid of is come to me."

They had all known this might happen, could happen. Witnesses at countless hearings had told them that. The country is vast, open, trusting, vulnerable. Few believed it would happen, at least not like this — airliners seized and turned into suicide bombs to attack the symbolic centers of U.S. military and commercial might. Terror is the weapon of the weak, and America's strength had been turned against it.

Washington had not felt so exposed since perhaps the Civil War, when Abraham Lincoln set the Capitol's iron dome in place as a defiant sign of the strength and endurance of the United States of America.

CQ Weekly Sept. 15, 2001

At the prayer vigil, Republican Sen. Jon Kyl of Arizona told of waking up at 4 a.m. the day after the attacks to smell smoke from the Pentagon still smoldering across the Potomac. "It made me feel sick," he said. "It made me feel powerless."

Congress and the nation are far from powerless, but they were knocked reeling by the terrorist assault on Sept. 11, 2001. The shock waves now are rippling through government, society, commerce, diplomacy and culture. America's view of the world will change, with friends and enemies more sharply defined. Americans will debate fundamental questions of freedom and security.

The entire agenda of the president and Congress, all the usual political plots and calculations, has been swept aside. Issues and arguments that a week ago seemed crucial now seem almost insignificant. For the present, there is only one issue, one agenda.

It is for the president to set that course, as in all times of national crisis, and it is for Congress to close ranks behind him. After months without a mandate, President Bush has almost universal public support to do what he considers necessary, and, with a few reservations, lawmakers seem ready to agree.

"Their role at the moment is to cheer him on, to show unity and give him what he wants," said Stephen J. Wayne, a professor of government at Georgetown University. "They're reflecting a unified public right now, and the public wants that because they are frightened."

Ultimately, however, it is through Congress, the nation's deliberative and law-making assembly, that America must define the shape and limits of a changed world and strike a new balance between trust and safety.

It is in Congress, in committees, that the long-term war on terrorism will be fashioned, said James A. Thurber, director of the Center for Congressional and Presidential Studies at American University in Washington. The war against terrorism, he said, will be a great deal like the war to contain communism, but even more complicated.

Defining the response will take time and congressional deliberation, Thurber said. Congress will be called upon, for example, to work out all the details of making America feel safe again, balancing increased security measures with civil liberties. Congress will need to determine whether to expand the intelligence-gathering powers of government and how to protect privacy rights in the process.

"This first stage, getting funding, went quickly," Thurber said. "But the next stage, over the coming months and years, will be more difficult — getting the evidence of what will be needed to contain terrorism. It's going to be hard work in committees."

The First Wave

In the wake of the attacks, members of Congress quickly resolved to get their footing and play their parts.

At first, there was confusion and fear, as they fled their of-

Congress twice gathered for prayer services; at a prayer vigil, above, in the rotunda Sept. 12 and at the National Cathedral on Sept. 14 for a memorial.

fices on Capitol Hill after the attacks began. Top leaders were spirited away to undisclosed locations, while rank-and-file members and their staffs flooded into the streets, uncertain where to go, frantically scanning the sky. To some, it was a scene from Hitchcock, with crowds running and traffic snarled. Hundreds fleeing the Longworth House Office Building froze in horror at the sight of a plane passing overhead.

"We heard, and believed, that the Capitol had been hit, that the Mall was on fire, that the Sears Tower [in Chicago] had been hit," said Rep. Jack Kingston, R-Ga.

By afternoon, however, lawmakers were clamoring to get back into their offices. They returned in the early evening to join their leaders on the Capitol's east steps, facing the Supreme Court and the Library of Congress, as daylight faded at their backs.

Helicopters clattered overhead. Police stood at checkpoints on the surrounding streets, their barricades lit by red flares. It was surely not business as usual, but — as many members noted — Congress stayed open for business.

"There was a strong feeling that we needed to be at this Capitol tonight to let people know we're not going to be run out of this place," said Sen. Jeff Sessions, R-Ala.

Democrats mingled with Republicans, senators with representatives, arrayed on the steep marble steps like an extended family posing for a photograph, with Lincoln's dome rising behind them as a backdrop. They sang "God Bless America," unaccompanied.

They were determined to send a message to the American public and to the world, both friend and enemy, that

Lott, left, emerged from a closed-door briefing held Sept. 12. A day earlier, Hastert and Daschle, above, arrived at the Capitol for a press conference during which they announced Congress would reconvene.

Congress was standing tough.

The next day, senators quietly sat at their individual desks on the blue-carpeted floor, as they do on rare solemn occasions, then rose one by one to vote "aye" on a resolution of condolence to victims of the attacks and support for the president in a war to eradicate terrorism.

"The world should know that the members of both parties in both houses stand united," Majority Leader Tom Daschle, D-S.D., said from the floor. "We will rebuild, and we will recover."

Minority Leader Trent Lott, R-Miss., echoed those words.

"We must put ourselves on a war footing," Lott said. "We must make up our minds we're going to fight this scourge of the world. We will. . . . There are moments in history when in the past the people of this country have set aside their prejudices and passions and have come together. We'll do it now. We've already done it."

Especially striking were the joint appearances by House Minority Leader Richard A. Gephardt, D-Mo., and Speaker J. Dennis Hastert, R-Ill. The two men rarely talk, let alone stand together before the public with a common purpose. Both said they would put aside partisan differences and divisive issues to work together.

Gephardt said he and Hastert had been in nearly continuous meetings since the attacks Sept. 11. He pledged to work so closely with the president and Hastert that there would be "no air and no light" between them.

"We are shoulder to shoulder," Gephardt said at a press briefing Sept. 13. "We are in complete agreement, and we will act together as one. There is no division between the parties, between the Congress and the president."

Despite the displays of unity, however, difficult questions were already emerging. Some were old, some new. All came spinning out of the week's terrible events, blowing apart the agenda and assumptions that had stood before.

And fissures were showing, too. Some members expressed frustration at the lack of information from the Bush administration and intelligence agencies.

"The briefings we've gotten have been absolute pap," said Rep. Nita M. Lowey, D-N.Y. "We learn more from CNN."

Some spoke of a failure of American intelligence and demanded an accounting.

Others warned against finger-pointing in the face of such a dramatic outside threat.

"That's a circular firing squad for our country," said Rep. Zach Wamp, R-Tenn. "This was a surprise attack by design."

A Call for Trust

Gephardt called for trust between the parties and between the president and Congress.

"I said to the president the other day, and I've said to the other leaders, 'Look, we've got to trust one another. We've got to find a way to really trust one another,'" he said. "And to get trust, you have to have collaboration, you have to have communication and you have to have respect of one another and one another's motivation to get the job done for the American people."

Congress may find that its present role chafes, but it is inescapable, said Charles O. Jones, a political scientist at the University of Wisconsin at Madison.

"As effective as Congress is at the work it does and as much as Congress in the last 30 years has geared itself up to play an increased role in the policy process, when you get something like a domestic Pearl Harbor right here, that crisis calls out for leadership," Jones said. "Congress is not one thing. It's at the very least two — two parties. It has leaders, but no single leader. . . . It can

Capitol Police established a wide perimeter around the Capitol immediately after the hijacked jetliners crashed into the World Trade Center and the Pentagon.

AP PHOTO / DENNIS COOK

only gravitate to the president.

"Congress' role in the process is to be consulted and lend support. But [it is] not structured to manage a war."

It is an old dynamic for the United States, Jones said. But it is bound to be a wrenching shift after years when the political landscape had no dominant, commanding issue to truly coalesce power around the president.

"This one just sweeps through everything," he said.

What the president needs now, besides money, is a united Congress backing him up as he stands before the world, political scientists said. To get it, he must involve Congress, as well as show leadership and compassion, they said.

Meanwhile, Congress plays an important role on two fronts: deciding how new defense money should be spent and ensuring that civil liberties do not get eaten away, said David T. Canon, a political scientist at the University of Wisconsin at Madison.

Each of those roles contains its own set of questions, all of which Congress must wrestle with. Did the attacks strengthen the case for a missile-defense shield, as Republicans say? Or did it prove it would be useless, as Democrats say?

A Delicate Balance

On the issue of civil rights, delicate and longstanding debates about the tensions between government's intelligence-gathering capabilities and privacy rights have taken on new urgency. So have worries about air-port security.

Congress will be called upon to strike a delicate balance.

"You can't have a police state that protects you from terrorists and still have the kinds of freedoms we're used to," Canon said.

And there were other issues, large and small: Should the U.S. government lift its ban on political assassinations? How will insurance companies handle claims for damage in New York City if the attacks are declared an act of war?

How to help New York rebuild? How to care for the children orphaned?

Members of Congress said they were still trying to take it all in, sort through the hundreds of details, like a family in mourning.

"There's a shock to all this," said Sen. Christopher J. Dodd, D-Conn. "The body just wants to move. We have hearings, the body is moving. But our heart isn't in it."

In the midst of outraged speeches and calls for war Sept. 12, Dodd hurried off the Senate floor, then took an elevator down to his car outside, parked by the Senate's east steps. He was on his way to join his wife, Jackie Marie Clegg, at the hospital. They were expecting a child.

Dodd's wife, in fact, had been due to give birth the day before at an Arlington hospital, but the doctors stopped her labor and sent her home in the turmoil after the attack on the Pentagon.

Life, as well as work, on Capitol Hill, was moving on. But there were reminders everywhere of the attacks — and the threshold that America had been pushed so violently across.

In one hand, Dodd held pages listing the companies with employees in the World Trade Center. It spoke to the financial implications of the attacks, but most of all, to the human toll.

"Have you seen this?" he said in disbelief, leafing through the pages of names.

From the Senate floor, Dodd had said, "The human dimension of all this is something I haven't been able to get my hands around."

Outside, as Dodd climbed into his car under a painfully sunny sky, the Taft Memorial carillon just off the Capitol grounds played "God Bless America."

In the distance, sirens wailed. ◆

Congress and the President: A Recalibration of Powers

Hill tries for a balance between wartime unity and protecting constitutional prerogatives

As Congress has rethought its institutional relationship with the president, it has settled on this rule of thumb: Wartime deference will not extend beyond proposals to combat terrorism. Gephardt, with other House Democrats on Sept. 25, has made this clear to the White House.

Two weeks after the terrorist attacks on the United States, the Democrats warned the Bush administration that it was pushing its wartime agenda too aggressively. On the afternoon of Sept. 25, House Minority Leader Richard A. Gephardt of Missouri telephoned Andrew H. Card Jr., the White House chief of staff, to alert him that one member of the Cabinet was overplaying the president's newly strengthened hand — threatening to squander Bush's good will with Congress and causing lawmakers to question how much political and procedural latitude they could still give the president.

The cause of Gephardt's warning was a speech the day before by U.S. Trade Representative Robert B. Zoellick. In pressing the case for reviving presidential "fast-track" negotiating authority, Zoellick suggested that trade expansion was integral to winning the war on terrorism because it would allow the United States to spread worldwide "the values that define us against our adversary." Zoellick also suggested that the proposal's opponents were too often basing their view on political, rather than policy, considerations.

Democrats, who are the main opponents of fast track, said the inference they took from the speech was that their patriotism was being questioned. "There's no question but that Zoellick crossed the line," fumed Rep. Robert T. Matsui of California, a pivotal Democrat in the trade debate. "We all know what's related to this crisis situation."

The flare-up was a clear signal, Gephardt told Card, that now was not the best time to push the trade legislation — particularly if the White House wants to keep tucked away for as long as possible the formidable array of disagreements between Bush and most Democrats. (*2001 CQ Weekly, p. 2186*)

But the incident also illustrated an additional point about the reconfiguring of the relationship between Bush and the 107th Congress: At most, the legislative branch appears to be inclined to acquiesce in the executive branch's wishes only on matters that directly relate to combating terrorism.

Although lawmakers have been overwhelmed by a series of new legislative priorities since Sept. 11, they also have been confronting institutional questions of long-lasting import: How forceful can they be in asserting their own powers and prerogatives without appearing to be obstructionist — not just in these weeks, but once the promised military campaign begins and beyond that? Do they run any risks — in the eyes of voters, or in the eyes of history — if they respond to Bush's entreaties by saying, in effect: "Yes, *but* . . ."?

The early answers to these questions suggest that Congress is willing to allow at most an only slightly revised tipping point on these balance-of-power questions, fearful that otherwise it will cede powers it might not be able to reclaim once the focus on terrorism has subsided. The last thing either end of Pennsylvania Avenue wants right now is a turf war, but neither side is willing to abandon its current turf, either.

The most prominent current example of this delicate positioning concerns the creation of a new Cabinet-level office to oversee the domestic campaign against terrorism. While members of Congress appear uniformly enthusiastic about the idea, they are insisting that they must write the legislation to make it happen — not simply allow Bush to establish the job on his own authority and give it to Tom Ridge, now the Republican governor of Pennsylvania.

"We're not in surrender mood. We're in a cooperative mood . . . and that's where we need to be," said Sen. Pat Roberts, R-Kan. Added Henry J. Hyde, R-Ill., the chairman of the House International Relations Committee: "We don't want to slow things up, but we've got to show we're not potted plants."

Preserving a Delicate Balance

At almost every public appearance, the president thanks Congress for its cooperation thus far and vows to keep "working with" Capitol Hill on his agenda. But the proposals he has outlined would embody a robust expansion of his powers. Members of Congress in both parties generally say they are happy to follow the lead of their president — especially at the outset of this war — but they are unwilling to give up their legislative, let alone constitutional, responsibilities and allow the president to go unchecked.

The Democrats, especially, are attuned to any move by the president to take advantage of wartime congressional deference to push priorities of his that have at best only a tangential connection to combating terrorism. In addition to the contretemps over the trade legislation, the Democrats' drawing of those distinctions the week of Sept. 24 led to continued standoffs on energy policy, on the components of an economic stimulus package and on how to allocate billions of dollars in additional spending in order to write a smooth ending to the fiscal 2002 appropriations process.

"Many of us want to make sure that, as we unify behind the president, we don't set legal and policy precedents that in the end alter the separation of powers," Ron Wyden of Oregon said as he emerged from a Sept. 25 caucus of Democratic senators where the question was discussed.

All sides say this recalibrating is an outgrowth of a unique situation in Washington. Unlike wars of the past, where enemies were defined and confined, the current target has many faces and it inhabits many nations — including the United States. The effort to recover from the most severe foreign attack ever on American civilians is of unprecedented size. And the demands of protecting the nation from additional assaults are of unprecedented scope.

Bush has made clear he is setting no deadline for the coming military campaign, and that much of it will be conducted out of public view. For now, Congress is accepting that, partly because lawmakers have been satisfied with the effort the White House has made to make them feel they are being consulted — even if much of the information passed along has been less informative than what newspapers and television networks have reported.

"They're dealing with a brand-new animal," said Alcee L. Hastings, D-Fla., a member of the House Intelligence Committee. "Clearly this administration recognizes that loose lips sink ships. The president has an exceptional category of responsibility that will allow for certain actions to be taken that you can't even run the risk of telling 535 members of Congress."

Already, however, efforts are under way in both the House and Senate to write legislation that would establish a board of inquiry to determine why U.S. intelligence agencies failed to prevent the Sept. 11 attacks. Such investigations have accompanied or followed almost every military conflict in American history.

Taking the Middle Ground

Ninety hours after hijacked commercial airliners tore into the World Trade Center and the Pentagon, Congress had — with almost complete unanimity — given Bush the pair of tools he said he wanted first to launch his war on terrorism. But in both cases, the lawmakers sought to stand on the middle ground of power sharing. While they wrote an emergency appropriations measure (PL 107-38) that gave the president the unprecedented carte blanche authority he sought to spend $20 billion immediately to recover from and retaliate against the attacks, they added the additional proviso that Congress itself would have the primary responsibility for allocating another $20 billion. And while they cleared a resolution (PL 107-40) putting the seal of approval on Bush's plans to use the armed forces to find those responsible for the attack, its authority was narrower than the president sought — and included language making it clear that Congress reserves the right to review the effort's merit in the future. (*2001 CQ Weekly, pp. 2128, 2118*)

Those compromises were written when Congress was under intense pressure to take immediate, concrete actions to show the world that it was behind the president as the nation began to react to its historic wound. But with those immediate needs satisfied, a return to the more measured and deliberate pace of the exercise of power is the order of the day.

In several cases, Bush has exercised his presidential powers in ways Congress has found no reason to criticize. Most notably, on Sept. 24 he issued an executive order freezing all the assets in the United States of 27 individuals and organizations suspected of having links to Islamic terrorist organizations, particularly Osama bin Laden and his al Qaeda network, which Bush has described as the primary suspects. The order was unusually broad — under it, foreign banks that do not cooperate could have their transactions blocked in the United States as well — but it raised no discernible hackles

Investigating Wars

For now, Congress is expressing little skepticism about President Bush's quest to curb terrorism, but in the long run it will almost certainly ask pointed questions about the coming military campaign — and about administration actions before the Sept. 11 attack on the United States. That is because throughout American history the legislative branch has exercised its investigatory powers over almost every such conflict, often before they are finished.

"Congress has always looked into these situations," noted Donald A. Ritchie, an associate Senate historian, because "Congress would like to be in on the takeoff, not just the landing."

The review of foreign, defense and intelligence policies surrounding military engagements has focused not only on militarily unsuccessful or politically unpopular engagements. A year after the Persian Gulf War ended Iraq's occupation of Kuwait, Congress pressed an inquiry of the George Bush administration's prewar policies with Iraq. (*1992 Almanac, p. 545*)

That conflict, the nation's last full-scale military campaign, was fought just after the Cold War ended. Since then, some scholars of the balance of power in the federal government contend that Congress has not done enough to preserve its war-making powers.

Truman inspects Missouri's Fort Leonard in 1942.

"Our main concern then was what do we do in a nuclear attack; the Constitution didn't prescribe congressional actions in a surprise attack," said former Rep. David E. Skaggs, D-Colo. (1987-99), now the executive director of the Center for Democracy and Citizenship at the Council for Excellence in Government.

"There's now such a practice of deferring to the executive, it now becomes odd for Congress to raise questions," said Skaggs, who had constitutional objections when President Bill Clinton considered invading Haiti without advance congressional approval. "These are the times when it is most important for Congress to raise questions. That's what we're supposed to be fighting for." (*1994 Almanac, p. 449*)

Of all major U.S. military engagements through the Vietnam War, only the Spanish-American War of 1898 escaped congressional scrutiny. President William McKinley forestalled a legislative inquiry by naming a commission to conduct that investigation. The very first congressional investigation sought to understand why 600 troops under the command of Maj. Gen. Arthur St. Clair had been massacred by Indians in 1791. Congress explicitly rejected the idea of having President George Washington conduct the inquiry. The first joint House-Senate committee, created in 1861, was charged with investigating the Civil War. It is remembered for one of the longest and most partisan inquiries in congressional history: Under the control of radical Republicans opposed to President Abraham Lincoln, it spent four years critiquing almost every element of the war effort.

What is widely regarded as the most effective investigating group in congressional history was the special Senate committee created in March 1941 to study preparations for the expected U.S. entrance into World War II. The committee kept operating throughout the war, but its initial chairman, Harry S Truman, D-Mo. (1935-45), aware of the excesses of the Civil War panel, scrupulously avoided any attempt to judge military policies or operations.

on Capitol Hill.

More routinely, the president has started to propose legislation and, as the civics textbooks say, Congress has started to dispose of it.

In the only outright rejection the week of Sept. 24, the Senate brushed aside a Bush administration request that it be granted broad authority to waive sanctions on nations in return for their participation in the anti-terrorism coalition the president is trying to establish. Rather than putting the idea to a vote, senators sympathetic to Bush's cause agreed on a much more narrow course.

Attorney General John Ashcroft spent two days in the hearing rooms of the House and Senate Judiciary committees trying without success to build a head of steam for the administration's anti-terrorism package. The House panel's markup was postponed at least until the week of Oct. 1, because lawmakers on both sides of the aisle have expressed an array of concerns about the administration's proposed expansions of its own surveillance authority.

Lawmakers say the package will be severely trimmed, and there is discussion of putting a sunset provision in it — another indication of a Congress unwilling to create broad new powers that the executive branch could exercise outside the scope, and beyond the duration, of the war on terrorism.

"This is a tougher area for us to look at than areas that involve money," said House Majority Leader Dick Armey, R-Texas, noting the difference between administration requests for appropriations — which are revisited annually — and requests to expand the federal government's power.

"This really was the first initiative to have legislative legs to it," Mark Peterson, a University of California at Los Angeles political scientist, said of the Ashcroft package. "It's a domestic, non-military issue that requires legislative action. It's the first time the consensus [between Congress and the White House] is being tested."

While Ashcroft's package may be the first legislative initiative to test that balance, a more direct test may emerge from Bush's declaration that he will sign an executive order establishing an Office of Homeland Security — and that by Oct. 8 Ridge will have arrived in Washington to become its first director.

In the Capitol, the idea came as one of the biggest surprises out of the Oval Office since Sept. 11. There was only cursory reference to it in the text that the White House gave reporters in advance of Bush's address Sept. 20 to a joint session of Congress, and the announcement was known to only some of the lawmakers who have long been pressing for the creation of a counterterrorism czar.

The initial astonishment was soon replaced by a cool insistence that Congress use its legislative authority to define and launch the office — all in the name of giving its new director the appropriate budgetary and other statutory powers to carry out his mandate. Chairman Dan Burton, R-Ind., of the House Government Reform Committee went to the White House on Sept. 25 to inform administration officials that the panel would soon hold hearings on the proposal. "They said they would cooperate," Burton reported afterward.

Democrats Preserving Power

Most lawmakers agree that the unprecedented situation the country is responding to — more than 6,000 civilians killed in a single morning by a well-coordinated group of terrorists, who have left behind evidence that their attacks are not over — will bring into question the current balance of power between Congress and the president. "This is being made up as we go along," said Rep. Neil Abercrombie, D-Hawaii, a member of the Armed Services Committee. "The issue of the executive versus the legislative is not an issue right now."

And there appears to be a unanimous view that, for now, the president has done nothing irreversible to overstep his boundaries. More Democrats, predictably, say they are on the lookout for an inappropriate move, but Republicans say this is not the time to play watchdog.

"We'll know if a president is overstepping his authority given to him by Congress," said Sen. John McCain, R-Ariz., a leader of the move for Congress to legislate the creation of the domestic counterterrorism office. "This is a time to rally around the president, not to start worrying about our turf."

During their weekly lunchtime caucus, Senate Democrats on Sept. 25 briefly discussed the importance of ensuring that congressional authority is not usurped in the interest of preserving the appearance of unity during the coming conflict.

"There's a delicate balance here,"

said Richard J. Durbin of Illinois. "There is cooperation with the president in a way I've never seen before, yet we understand we have responsibilities under the Constitution. . . . When there is an honest disagreement, it should be aired in an open debate."

Asked in particular what Senate Democrats are wary of, Max Baucus of Montana reached for a poetic image. "It's like beauty," he said. "You can't define it, but you know when it's there."

The Next Expected Struggle

If there is a consensus, it is that the onset of military strikes will be the next occasion when balance-of-powers issues come to the fore. But those issues will turn controversial, many say, only if the administration discontinues its current practice of having at least some communication almost daily with the leadership of Congress.

"It's a very important concern we're all wrestling with right now," said Tim Roemer, D-Ind., a member of the House Intelligence Committee.

Administration officials say they are well aware that even in times of crisis lawmakers can turn fickle if they are not made to feel that they are at least privy to the decision making, if not always a part of it.

"What Congress gives, Congress can take away," said former Rep. Pete Geren, D-Texas (1989-97), who recently signed on as a special assistant to Secretary of Defense Donald H. Rumsfeld.

Geren was among the administration officials who came to the Capitol on Sept. 25 for a classified security briefing in the House chamber, the third such event since Sept 11. Senators also have been invited to a series of classified briefings in the soundproofed suite of the Senate Intelligence Committee, which is tucked under the Capitol dome.

Those who have attended these sessions say they offer little insight on the state of the world that is not available in the mass media. "There was no need to sweep the room" for listening devices, Rep. Christopher Cox, R-Calif., said as he left one session. But others say the gatherings do give members the opportunity to voice their opinions to the executive branch.

"There was a good-faith effort to exchange views. They are making it clear they are wide open to suggestions," Abercrombie after the Sept. 25 briefing, where he said Rumsfeld and Secre-

tary of State Colin L. Powell generally listened as several dozen members expressed their views. Abercrombie gave them a copy of George Orwell's "Shooting an Elephant," a novel using that incident as a metaphor for cultural conflict between East and West.

Along with the classified meetings, members also receive regular updates from their leaders, who are in constant contact with the White House. House Speaker J. Dennis Hastert, R-Ill., talks with administration officials several times a day and with the president at least once a day, the Speaker's aides say. Gephardt's aides say the House's top Democrat has spoken with Bush about a half-dozen times since the attacks and talks with administration officials almost every other day. On the Senate side, both Majority Leader Tom Daschle, D-S.D., and Minority Leader Trent Lott, R-Miss., have a similar level of communication with the president and his top advisers.

"The way to do it is to keep their arms around each other," Bob Dole, the former Kansas senator (1969-96) and 1996 Republican presidential nominee, said when asked how Congress and the White House should deal with each other during this time of war. "No one makes a move without each other."

Holding Public Opinion

Along with regular consultation and an agreement to concentrate on a legislative agenda in which all items can in some clear way be connected to the war effort, another key element to maintaining unity between the White House and Congress is public opinion. As long as the country continues its patriotic rally behind the president, Congress is likely to follow.

"A president that has 90 percent approval ratings gets some deference from Congress," said Peter Shane, a professor of law and public policy at Carnegie Mellon University in Pittsburgh. "Nobody wants to be seen as opposing something the overwhelming majority of America say they want to happen."

Ninety percent of the 1,005 respondents to a Sept. 21-22 Gallup Poll said they approved of the way Bush was handling his job —the highest approval rating Gallup has recorded for any president.

That "has not been a bump for George W. Bush per se," UCLA's Peterson said of the poll numbers, "but a bump for patriotism and unity." ◆

Congress Maintains its Right To Remain in the Loop

Bush softens edict restricting classified briefings after Lantos cites 1956 law

President Bush's attempt to curb congressional leaks collided with an unexpected obstacle: a congressman brandishing a 45-year-old law. And it may not be the last time that the president and Congress lock horns over the control of the flow of sensitive information.

Hours after Bush announced Oct. 9 that he was restricting classified briefings to a handful of senior lawmakers to try to stop news leaks, Rep. Tom Lantos, D-Calif., told the president he was obligated to keep the International Relations Committee in the loop. At a White House meeting with other lawmakers that had been intended as a discussion of foreign policy, Lantos showed Bush a section of the State Department Basic Authorities Act of 1956 (PL 84-885) that said the State Department must keep Congress' foreign affairs committees "fully and currently informed" about all activities within the panels' scope.

"My impression was, they realized a mistake was made and that it had to be rectified," Lantos, International Relations' ranking Democrat, recalled in an interview after the meeting.

A chastened White House agreed the next day to expand the closed briefings to include members of the Armed Services, Foreign Relations and Appropriations committees, in addition to Lantos' panel. Lawmakers also said the administration would resume holding after-the-fact sessions for all members on military and diplomatic actions. Members said they, too, would be more sensitive.

"I think we all got the lesson here," House Minority Leader Richard A. Gephardt, D-Mo., told reporters after the administration announced its about-face. "Everybody's on notice now that if you're going to get secret information, you better keep it secret."

But with a war that is being conducted largely in the shadows, a public hungry for information and an administration intent on controlling its message, a battle over the flow of information was probably inevitable — and is likely to continue. It is not surprising that Congress has asserted itself forcefully in this fight.

Since Sept. 11, members had been complaining that the briefings they were getting from the White House were of little value. After Bush's announcement, lawmakers said restricting information even more would impair the oversight role of Congress and damage the mutual trust between Capitol Hill and the White House. Some suggested more immediate repercussions.

"When they put it in writing that they're not going to brief the committee that funds them, that's pretty stupid," said John P. Murtha of Pennsylvania, the House Defense Appropriations Subcommittee's ranking Democrat.

Sources of Friction

Despite the uproar, many lawmakers acknowledged they do not rely on the briefing sessions as their only source of critical military information.

"I've never been too concerned [about briefing restrictions], because I get information from other places," said John McCain, R-Ariz., a member of the Senate Armed Services Committee. "I've never gotten much information from [the briefings]."

Quick Contents

Congress' need to know and the Bush administration's desire to control the flow of information were certain to set the two branches at loggerheads over classified briefings. Several lawmakers, however, say they have other channels for staying informed.

AP PHOTO / HILLERY SMITH GARRISON

Lantos, left, and Biden emerge from an Oct. 9 meeting with President Bush in which Lantos cited a law requiring that the administration keep relevant panels informed.

Murtha noted that in the week before Bush's edict he spent four hours at CIA headquarters and two hours with Defense Secretary Donald H. Rumsfeld discussing military and intelligence operations.

But even those who said they did not rely on the briefings for information were concerned about the precedent and principle of limiting information given to Congress.

"Let's take, for example, the Armed Services Committee," said Senate Majority Leader Tom Daschle, D-S.D. "They have to make some very serious judgments about public policy, much of which is involved around intelligence. Clearly, they can't make those judgments, they can't conduct themselves in their proper oversight role without access to intelligence data."

Appropriators said classified material about the use of weapons systems and intelligence tools is essential in knowing exactly how money should be spent in those areas each year.

Bush's decision Oct. 5 to issue a memorandum to limit the information to eight members of Congress — the four leaders and chairmen and ranking members of the House and Senate Intelligence committees — struck many lawmakers as either a monumental overreaction or a warning to lawmakers that would later be rescinded.

"You can come out with guns blazing, but you don't do it with nuclear weapons," said Tim Roemer, D-Ind., a member of the House Intelligence Committee.

Congress, members said, has had a far better track record than the Pentagon or the rest of the executive branch in keeping secrets.

"Every time a president complains about leaks, it backfires on him," said Rep. Rob Simmons, R-Conn., a former CIA agent and staff director for the Senate Intelligence Committee. "We all know that the ship of state leaks from the top."

Mostly Anger

Administration officials based their decision on an article in The Washington Post on Oct. 5 that said intelligence officials believed there was a "100 percent" chance of retaliatory terrorist attacks after U.S. bombing of Afghanistan. The story cited a closed congressional briefing among its sources.

Word of Bush's action did not reach

lawmakers, away for the Columbus Day holiday, until Oct. 9. While some lawmakers were sympathetic to the White House's cause, most were furious.

At a news conference that day with German Chancellor Gerhard Schroeder, Bush defended his decision.

"These are extraordinary times — our nation has put our troops at risk," Bush said. "I felt it was important to send a clear signal to Congress that classified information must be held dear."

The House Appropriations Defense Subcommittee abruptly and angrily canceled its markup of the fiscal 2002 spending bill after learning of the order. It approved the legislation after Bush's change of heart.

Appropriations Committee Chairman C.W. Bill Young, R-Fla., spoke with White House Chief of Staff Andrew H. Card Jr. about the need to keep his committee informed. Young characterized the flap over the briefings as "a little blip" and predicted it would not jeopardize relations with the White House.

It was clear that in the Senate, however, it would take longer to smooth over the hard feelings. After the White House promised it would allow members to receive classified briefings, it reversed itself and instructed Director of Central Intelligence George J. Tenet to cancel a planned Oct. 11 briefing for all senators.

The cancellation enraged senators who wondered if the administration was being true to its word. By the end of the day, however, Bush again changed his mind and cleared Tenet to brief senators at an unspecified later date.

"I think cooler heads prevailed today," said Democratic Policy Committee Chairman Byron L. Dorgan of North Dakota, who had set up the joint briefing weeks ago.

Some Sympathy

Leaks of sensitive material were a concern to Congress and the White House well before the Sept. 11 terrorist attacks. Earlier this year, the Senate Intelligence Committee pushed to revive a controversial proposal that would have made almost all unauthorized and willful disclosures of classified information a felony. (*2001 CQ Weekly, p. 2081*)

News organizations and many Democrats vigorously opposed the idea, saying it would silence whistleblowers and violate the First Amendment. A similar provision prompted President Bill

Clinton to veto the fiscal 2001 intelligence authorization bill last year; legislation without the provision was subsequently enacted into law (PL 106-567). (*2000 Almanac, p. 11-17*)

The Bush administration declined to support the Senate Intelligence proposal, prompting senators to delete it from their fiscal 2002 authorization bill (S 1428).

However, administration officials have become increasingly upset over leaks. Last month, Rumsfeld and Secretary of State Colin L. Powell took Orrin G. Hatch, R-Utah, to task after the senator told reporters that intelligence officials had intercepted communications between associates of suspected mastermind Osama bin Laden claiming they had struck targets in the United States. (*2001 CQ Weekly, p. 2147*)

Many lawmakers said they sympathized with the administration's attempts to keep a lid on classified information. For example, Senate Foreign Relations Committee Chairman Joseph R. Biden Jr., D-Del., told reporters Oct. 9 that if he were president, he "would be mad as hell" about the recent leaks.

"We have to have access to that [classified] information," Pat Roberts, R-Kan., a member of the Senate Armed Services and Intelligence committees, told reporters Oct. 10. "But on the other side, we also have a responsibility to keep our damn mouths shut."

The House Committee on Standards of Official Conduct, in an Oct. 12 memorandum, reminded lawmakers, staff and employees that disclosing classified information violated the House's secrecy pledge and could result in punishment.

"At all times — and especially in this time of our country's war on terrorism — the Committee on Standards takes the obligations imposed by the Classified Information Oath with the greatest seriousness," the committee said in a statement accompanying a copy of the oath.

Some House members have clamored for action to be taken against lawmakers who had leaked information. Rep. J.D. Hayworth, R-Ariz., began circulating a letter Oct. 10 calling for the committee to investigate the source of the leak that led to Bush's directive.

"This is a serious matter that cannot be swept aside with pledges that it won't happen again," Hayworth said in his letter. ◆

Hill Clears Aid for Airlines

Lawmakers move quickly on package of loans, guarantees and liability limits

After days of negotiations between congressional leaders and the White House and a struggle over liability and labor issues, Congress on Sept. 21 cleared a $15 billion package to help the nation's airlines recover from the Sept. 11 terrorist attacks.

The bill (HR 2926) would provide $5 billion in cash for airlines and freight carriers and up to $10 billion in loan guarantees for airlines, which is $2.5 billion less than airline executives requested. The legislation would offer the companies some liability protection.

The House passed the bill, 356-54, and the Senate cleared it by voice vote. The Senate earlier passed an identical measure (S 1450), 96-1.

The bill did not include provisions sought by Democrats and organized labor to help as many as 100,000 airline employees who face layoffs in the aftermath of the attacks.

House Speaker J. Dennis Hastert, R-Ill., and Minority Leader Richard A. Gephardt, D-Mo., said that legislation to address labor issues would be on the floor the week of Sept. 24.

Florida Republican Mark Foley told his House colleagues that by saving the airlines from possible bankruptcy, Congress would be helping to rescue the nation's economy. "The economic pain is real, not imagined," he said.

Some members of both parties said they would return the week of Sept. 24 with proposals to help airline workers who are laid off and to improve aviation security.

"If we don't address airport security, we're not going to get people back on the planes," Gephardt said Sept. 21. (*Aviation security, p. 2215*)

Not a Bailout

Lawmakers have been emphatic that the bill not be considered a bailout for an industry that was suffering financially long before the terrorist attacks.

"We ought to respond to events from Tuesday [Sept. 11] forward, not the underlying problems that the air-

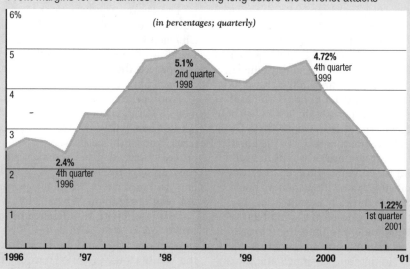

Hard Times in the Air
Profit margins for U.S. airlines were shrinking long before the terrorist attacks

(in percentages; quarterly)

5.1% 2nd quarter 1998

4.72% 4th quarter 1999

2.4% 4th quarter 1996

1.22% 1st quarter 2001

Note: Figures are for 98 large, certified air carriers and include domestic and foreign operations

SOURCE: Department of Transportation, Bureau of Transportation Statistics

line industry may have created for itself prior to that," said Sen. Christopher J. Dodd, D-Conn.

Airlines would have to document their losses since the attacks to qualify for a share of the $5 billion in federal

> "We ought to respond to events from Tuesday [Sept. 11] forward, not the underlying problems that the airline industry may have created for itself prior to that."
> —Sen. Christopher J. Dodd, D-Conn.

cash. The $10 billion in low-cost loans and loan guarantees would be managed by a four-member board consisting of the secretaries of Transportation and

Treasury, the Federal Reserve chairman and the comptroller general of the General Accounting Office. To be eligible for loans, airlines would have to freeze compensation for their top executives.

The bill affirms President Bush's announced decision to improve aviation security with $3 billion of the $40 billion in emergency appropriations enacted Sept. 18 (PL 107-38). (*2001 CQ Weekly, p. 2128*)

The package also includes a provision that would limit airlines' liability so they do not lose insurance coverage. It also would give the president authority to extend the War Risk Insurance Act of 1917 to cover acts of domestic terrorism. If Bush extends the program, the Transportation Department will effectively become the airlines' insurer.

Those injured in the attacks or families of those killed could seek compensation either by filing suit in federal court in New York or by filing a claim with a special master appointed by the Justice Department. The special master would determine whether an applicant was eligible for compensation and the appropriate level. Claims awarded by the Justice Department would not be tax-free.

Negotiators on the bill — Rep. Roy Blunt, R-Mo., the House Republicans' chief deputy whip; Senate Majority Leader Tom Daschle, D-S.D.; Senate Commerce Committee Chairman Ernest F. Hollings, D-S.C.; and Office of Management and Budget Director Mitchell E. Daniels Jr. — set out to write a bill that would give only financial aid to airlines. But negotiators faced pressure from Republicans to include liability protection for the carriers — particularly American and United, whose aircraft were hijacked — and pressure from Democrats to protect airline workers.

A number of Democrats took the House floor to complain that the bill omitted aid for laid-off workers. "The airline industry is taking advantage of us. We're chumps," said Corrine Brown, D-Fla.

Supporters of Amtrak had sought extra money to help the railroad deal with additional riders, and the U.S. Conference of Mayors said Congress should help workers in airport shops who lost business in the crisis.

Blunt and House Transportation Committee Chairman Don Young, R-Alaska, himself a longtime labor supporter, said Congress should first help to stabilize the airline system before addressing labor and other issues. "We have to get this done as soon as possible or we will not have an aviation system," Young said Sept. 19.

Negotiations were difficult. A deal reached the night of Sept. 20 collapsed the next day after some lawmakers had second thoughts about protecting the airlines from liability.

The administration originally proposed giving $5 billion to the airlines but without loan guarantees. Blunt said in a Sept. 21 interview that the administration offered a compromise proposal that included the board to oversee the loan guarantees and to ensure that the loans did not go to airlines that were financially insolvent.

Two Rough Days

With their stock values tumbling and lines of credit drying up, the airlines were clearly in deep trouble. For the two days that airports were closed, the carriers had to feed and house thousands of stranded travelers. Untold numbers are now afraid to fly, and companies tightening their belts are

Key Provisions of Aid Bill

The idea was to help the airlines weather financial losses following terrorist attacks Sept. 11 that forced the government to close the aviation system for two days and frightened away travelers. The White House and many lawmakers did not want the bill to look like a bailout for an industry that was in financial trouble anyway. Here is what they came up with:

▶ $5 billion in direct cash payments to the airlines and cargo carriers from the Treasury's general fund. Payments would be based on the lesser of either actual losses or a pro-rata share based on a carrier's percentage of industry mileage multiplied by its seats or cargo tonnage.

▶ Up to $10 billion in loan guarantees for the airlines. A four-member board — the secretaries of Transportation and Treasury, the Federal Reserve chairman and the comptroller general of the General Accounting Office — would make all decisions. Airlines could receive the guarantees only if they froze compensation for top executives.

▶ United Airlines and American Airlines would be liable for deaths on the ground and property damage from the Sept. 11 attacks only to the limit of their insurance.

▶ Those injured in the attacks and the families of those killed could seek compensation either by filing a claim with a special master at the Justice Department or by suing in federal court.

▶ The Transportation Department could limit the liability of U.S. airlines in any terrorist attacks within the next six months to $100 million, with the government taking responsibility for the rest.

▶ For the next six months, the Transportation Department could use the "war risk" insurance program to reimburse airlines for higher insurance premiums as a result of the Sept. 11 attacks.

▶ The Transportation secretary is urged to protect essential air services to small communities.

canceling travel.

The Air Transport Association, the main trade group for the nation's airlines, estimated that its members would lose $4.7 billion between Sept. 11 and Sept. 30.

"The airlines are hemorrhaging cash, and [congressional] policy should prevent widespread bankruptcy," said Steven A. Morrison, a professor at Northeastern University and an authority on aviation issues.

Morrison said that in addition to federal cash, he favors suspending the airline ticket tax. "My concern is to get the aviation system back up to as high a level as it can be," he said, "and that takes lower fares."

In a Sept. 19 letter to Treasury Secretary Paul H. O'Neill, Morgan Stanley directors Gerry Pasciucco and Nelson Walsh said the attacks had virtually closed U.S. capital markets to airlines. They said the source of funds would remain closed unless Congress helped the airlines recover. "Even then, access is likely to be severely limited until the path to a more normalized airline sys-

tem becomes clearer," they wrote.

An effort in the early morning hours of Sept. 15 to pass an airline aid bill failed after one House member, Democrat Lloyd Doggett of Texas, objected, saying the bill set a bad precedent. "It sends a signal to others who will stand at the door of the Treasury and ask for their subsidy," Doggett said.

House leaders then designated Blunt to manage the recovery bill. Blunt, who is from southwestern Missouri, has several times come to the aid of airlines, who are important to his state. Earlier this year, he backed American Airlines' acquisition of Trans World Airways, a move that would preserve some of the 33,000 TWA jobs in his state. (2001 CQ Weekly, p. 290)

The airlines initially asked Congress for a $24 billion aid package, but trimmed that amount a day later to $17.5 billion.

"We are looking for a recovery to the sorry state our industry was in before these events occurred," said Tom Horton, chief financial officer for American Airlines. ◆

Shaken Congress Confronts Bio-Terrorism Here and Now

Chambers' disparate reactions to mailed anthrax add to Capitol Hill tensions

For the past month, Congress has been gradually insulating itself from outside intrusions. Concrete barriers across driveway entrances. Wire fences lining the sidewalks. Police in black uniforms in the Capitol hallways, now empty of tourists. All of it was set up to prevent the next physical attack, allowing senators and House members to start to return to their normal routines for writing legislation, making partisan charges and raising money for the next campaign. Doing that, lawmakers said, would reassure the world that the nation's business goes on.

And then the newest threat showed up in one small envelope — and it turned out to pose a challenge far more mental than medical.

Congress has now had its first anthrax scare. The opening of a letter to Majority Leader Tom Daschle exposed perhaps two dozen Senate aides and Capitol Police to the potentially deadly bacteria. Thousands of other nervous staffers and lobbyists formed long lines to get themselves tested. All six congressional office buildings and half of the Capitol were cleared out over the weekend so federal authorities could make sure no stray spores were in the air. And the House, for the first time in history, postponed its deliberations in the face of danger and sent its members home.

By the end of the week of Oct. 15, the biological damage did not appear to be remotely as serious as everyone feared: Nearly 1,400 anthrax tests came back negative, and the 28 people who had tested positive were on antibiotics, which would almost certainly prevent them from becoming infected. Even that figure may drop in the coming days. The real damage was psychological. Nobody in the 107th Congress

has any experience with an invisible threat, and few are confident that they know how it can be spread. Suddenly, bio-terrorism was no longer one of those futuristic and disturbing topics for half-empty committee hearing rooms. It was real — and it was happening here.

Even some of the lawmakers themselves said it was not Congress' finest hour. House leaders told their members and aides to go home, believing that their Senate counterparts were doing likewise. They were not. Facing a rebellion within their ranks when they tried to send their colleagues home, Daschle and Minority Leader Trent Lott, R-Miss., announced with a defiant tone that the Senate would remain at work and that its half of the Capitol would not be shuttered.

The perception was that, at a time of potential crisis, the two halves of Congress could not stick to a unified plan — in fact, could not even agree on whether they had a plan. That left House Speaker J. Dennis Hastert, R-Ill., and Minority Leader Richard A. Gephardt, D-Mo., to absorb the grumbling derision of House members and senators alike — and the humiliation of their picture above this Oct. 18 New York Post headline: "WIMPS: The leaders who ran away from anthrax."

The basic decision on which Congress could not agree — whether to stay or go — will not soon disappear. The leadership must decide how to strike the right balance between keeping Congress in town this fall, appearing resilient and unfazed in the face of attacks, and making sure lawmakers and their employees feel safe at work.

Congress has weighed in once this fall, on Sept. 11, choosing determinedly to convene the next day in the shadow of a national crisis. But as the danger has grown in the

CQ Weekly Oct. 20, 2001

Those who were tested for anthrax exposure by the attending physician's office in the Capitol were given a six-day supply of antibiotics to take prophylactically. House members streamed down the Capitol steps the afternoon of Oct. 17 after their last vote of the week. The next morning's New York Post headline offered a stinging rebuke to the decision by Gephardt and Hastert to send the House home. The Senate met and cleared a spending bill Oct. 18, but the southeast quarter of the Hart Building was closed and guarded by the Capitol Police.

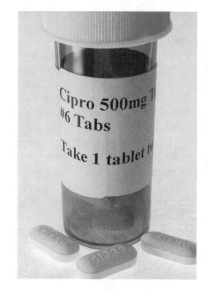

Capitol and across America, so too, has an urgent legislative agenda. For every domestic program that has slid to the bottom of the priority list is a once-esoteric security decision that must be dealt with right away.

Many lawmakers say they must simply increase the amount of personal risk with which they are willing to live. "When the U.S. is a target, political leaders are more of a target. That's just something you have to accept," said Sen. John Ensign, R-Nev.

"Anybody who works in a high-visibility place must take extra precautions," said Rep. Robert T. Matsui, D-Calif. But "we're not shutting down the airlines, we're trying to make them safer. We need to do the same with the Capitol."

Doing that is getting harder these days. When a mentally disturbed man shot and killed two Capitol Police officers on the Capitol's ground floor in 1998, bag searches became more thorough, for a while, and lawmakers began talking about the long-stalled visitor center's security benefits as much as its tourist benefits. When the Capitol was evacuated the morning of Sept. 11, many were convinced — and still are — that the hijacked airliner that crashed in Pennsylvania was intended to hit the Capitol. That prompted more moves to make the complex look less like a bustling campus and more like a military base. The trend makes members feel more safe, but they worry about the public perception.

Now, everyone with business on Capitol Hill has the shared experience of a week in which "Have you been tested?" was the most common question asked.

"This is the first time the legislative business was interrupted" by a threat to lawmakers' security, said former Rep. Ronald Sarasin, R-Conn. (1973-79), now president of the U.S. Capitol Historical Society. But then, he added, "We've never had a biological threat to the complex." Lawmakers had gone home for the year four months before the Capitol was burned by British troops in the War of 1812, forcing Congress to seek other quarters for five years.

Tense Times

Still, by the end of the week there was growing evidence that the letter to Daschle was part of a coordinated terrorist campaign. Its postmark was from the same Trenton, N.J., post office as an anthrax-spiked letter sent to NBC News anchor

Tom Brokaw. And both letters apparently contained the same strain of anthrax that caused the only death from the disease so far this fall: an editor at the Florida tabloid publisher American Media Inc.

The connections were enough to rattle the most hardened members of Congress. All tough talk aside, the level of tension was obvious from the conflicting decisions of the House and Senate leaderships about whether to stay in session, and in the long lines of people waiting for their nasal swabs and preventative antibiotics at the four testing centers opened during the week. By Oct. 18, when the Centers for Disease Control and Prevention said there was no further need for such testing, 3,900 people had been through the doors — many who had been nowhere near the Hart Senate Office Building, where the letter to Daschle was opened.

That building was almost abandoned at midweek, even though only the dozen senators' offices in the southeast tower had been quarantined. Capitol Police patrolling the balconies easily outnumbered the few aides who stayed behind. Yellow tape blocked off the elevator banks, a vivid reminder that this was a crime scene.

"It's very stressful and a little scary" for the staffers, said Rep. Jack Quinn, R-N.Y. "When you come to work in the morning and you have to go past three security checkpoints, you've really got to love your job to come to work. . . . People are stressed out and nervous, and they should be."

Still, lawmakers know they will not be able to put congressional business on hold during every scare. This time, the incident was mysterious enough that lawmakers accepted a wide "environmental sweep" to make sure the danger was contained. The next time, some said, Congress will have to calm down.

"After Sept. 11, we went through a period where we were evacuating the buildings every time we got a threatening phone call. Now we don't evacuate the buildings anymore, and we still get phone calls," said Sen. Joseph R. Biden Jr., D-Del. "I can't imagine that somebody else won't send another letter. I think we just get used to it."

There does not appear to be any magic formula. Most lawmakers and analysts believe Congress will simply set up more precautions — physical barriers, police patrols, mail inspections — and then lean toward staying in session, rather than leaving town as quickly as the House did.

"We're not stupid. We're going to have things checked the way the experts say they should be checked. But after that, we're going to keep working," said Sen. Mike DeWine, R-Ohio.

"This is new. We've never faced this before, so it will take people a while to get their bearings," said Thomas Mann, a senior fellow in governmental studies at the Brookings Institution. "I think you'll see them finding their footing. No great damage was done."

Senate vs. House

The initial response to a bio-terrorist attack may leave some lingering resentment between the House and the Senate. Hastert and Gephardt believed they had a deal with Daschle and Lott that both chambers would recess one day early for the week — on the afternoon of Oct. 17. To many, the Senate's decision to stay in town left the impression that House leaders were being overly cautious.

"We have to stand a little bit in amazement," said Bill Frist, R-Tenn., whose standing as the Senate's only physician catapulted him into the role

of spokesman for the bipartisan Senate leadership. "The scare was here — and not there."

The lasting import of the incident, however, may be that it is yet another illustration of how easy it is for House leaders to impose their will upon the rank and file, compared with their Senate counterparts. Far more cajoling and consultation is required of the Senate leaders, because senators never perceive themselves as members of the rank and file.

Many House members in both parties said they were no more eager to leave than the senators were, arguing that it would send the wrong signal to the country. But they were never offered an opportunity by Hastert and Gephardt to decide the question; it was presented as a fait accompli. "If we'd voted on that, it might have changed," said Republican Roy Blunt of Missouri, the chief deputy House majority whip. "We can't tell the country to go about their business if we don't set an example for them."

Daschle and Lott, however, were effectively shouted down when they presented the idea of going home early to a joint caucus of all senators.

Congressional analysts say the conflicting decisions are not surprising, given the differences in the cultures of the two chambers. "The House organizations are pretty disciplined in a party

sense. There's more of a comfort level" with following leaders, said Christopher J. Deering, a professor of political science at George Washington University. "Senators are less likely, both individually and collectively, to go along."

But there was also a notable difference in tone all week.

In describing the initial response to the situation in Daschle's office, the House Speaker said after one meeting Oct. 17 that "there was a flume that came out from that office and the ventilation system was not closed down for half an hour." After receiving another briefing the next day, Gephardt reported that those who had examined the contents of the Daschle letter "believe that it is a higher-grade, weapon-grade kind of anthrax." He warned that people who had been in Hart could have brought anthrax on their clothing to the Capitol, where the spores "can replicate themselves" and "live for 100 years."

Senators consistently endeavored to sound more reassuring. Frist went on television to say there was no evidence of anthrax in the ventilation system; to remind people that exposure to a disease is different than infection; and to declare that antibiotics taken at the right time are "100 percent effective."

Daschle, the man at the center of the drama, sought to sound like a consoling father figure. "I'm concerned for my staff. I'm angered that this has happened. But I feel very confident about those steps and about the fact that everyone will be okay," he said.

The House had its defenders. Lott said Hastert and Gephardt did not have the benefit of the regular updates from

federal officials that senators were getting, and he offered that the Senate needed the extra day of work to act on legislation that the House had already considered. "I think far too much is being made of all this," he said Oct. 18.

Rep. Richard M. Burr, R-N.C., said there would have been little point in keeping the House in session during the sweeps of the office buildings because staffers would have been too nervous to be productive. But in the long run, he said, "if we're going to worry every time we see a plane landing at National Airport and wonder if it's going to turn and hit the Capitol . . . that's just not something we can spend a lot of time on."

Back to Business

Just as they did after Sept. 11, members insisted that their legislative agenda would be unaffected by the apparent terrorist attack. And, this time, partisan fighting took no break; all week, Senate Republicans were sniping over whether Democrats were moving fast enough to confirm President Bush's judicial nominations.

Still, it was clear that some debates will be put off, if for no other reason than the time Congress has lost as it has dealt with this fall's events. Besides the obligatory appropriations bills, there is a consensus that the counterterrorism bill (HR 2975), the airline security measure (S 1447) and the economic stimulus package (HR 3090) must be cleared by the end of the first session of the 107th Congress.

Other domestic priorities, however, may slip. Negotiations over the education overhaul bill (HR 1), which has

been mired in a House-Senate conference committee since July, have slowed to a crawl, and some congressional leaders are now saying it is not absolutely necessary to finish the bill this year. *(2001 CQ Weekly, p. 2271)*

Once their office buildings were shut, senators and House members showed they know how to wing it.

The Senate Judiciary Committee held a hearing on judicial nominations in the Capitol. Majority Whip Tom DeLay, R-Texas, and Bob Ney, R-Ohio, chairman of the House Administration Committee, briefed House Republicans on new Capitol security procedures at the National Republican Congressional Committee headquarters. A House Democratic task force discussed bioterrorism at a townhouse a block south of the Longworth Building.

Some lawmakers and staffers simply worked the phones and bounced e-mails back and forth. In the midst of the near-chaos Oct. 17, DeWine said he was on the phone to House Education and the Workforce Committee Chairman John A. Boehner, R-Ohio, trying to work out acceptable language for a provision of the education overhaul bill. "I'm not missing any meetings," said DeWine. "The way this place works is, people talk to each other."

Dealing With the Unknown

Still, some lawmakers acknowledged that the brave public face has its limits. "I'm not in favor of cutting the agenda short just yet," said Quinn. However, he added, "I don't think there's anything we do here that can't be postponed when people's safety is a concern. . . . If you can't safely, reason-

ably conduct your business, maybe it's time" to cut it short for the year.

For some, the public face was never truly brave to begin with. Until the threat was better understood, some of them would have been just as happy following the House's lead and close the entire Capitol.

As word spread about the staffers who had tested positive, the demand for anthrax tests took on ever-rising levels of urgency. Some staff members waited for more than three hours to get checked out, and wondered why it had taken so long to shut the office buildings down. "They don't know how much stress they're putting on people by not closing the whole building," said Joan Lee, a congressional liaison to the Department of Veterans' Affairs who works in the Hart Building. "You never know what's affected."

Gradually, Daschle and other senators spread the word that positive test results are not the same as infections and that infections are treatable. That took some of the mystery out of the experience for the staffers, as did the reports Oct. 18 that hundreds of tests had come back negative.

But what most staffers need at such times, experts say, is to hear their bosses say that their courage is appreciated. Daschle gave it his best shot in a floor speech Oct. 18 as the Senate wrapped up its unsettling week. "This attack was meant to undercut [their] spirit," he said. "And what I have seen in the past three days is all I need to know that that attack has missed its mark."

It may not be the last time he has to give that speech. ◆

The anthrax that spilled into Daschle's Hart Building mailroom Oct. 15 arrived in a letter bearing a fictitious return address, but in other ways it was linked to anthrax letters sent to the media in New York and Florida. Two days later, Lott and Daschle were surrounded by police as they announced that the Senate would not adjourn early for the week, as the House was. The next day, the Senate Judiciary Committee packed into the Appropriations Committee's small but ornate room for a hearing. Meanwhile, aides and others waiting to have their noses swabbed could read the paper or consider Alexander Calder's sculpture, "Mountains and Clouds."

Controversial Add-On To Be Revisited After Senate Unanimously Passes Bill Funding Commerce, Justice and State

Senate leaders wanting to send a message that Congress had resumed its work after the tragedies of Sept. 11 used the fiscal 2002 spending bill for the departments of Commerce, Justice and State to make their point.

The Senate passed its $41.5 billion version of the bill (HR 2500) on Sept. 13 by a vote of 97-0 after a day of behind-the-scenes negotiations and little actual debate.

But dramatizing the reality that it will be impossible to return to anything like normal, the Senate was interrupted during its only roll call vote on an amendment by a bomb threat. In addition, the bill they chose to consider involved funding for agencies whose responsibilities spanned the spectrum of law enforcement and international affairs, allowing for amendments on issues with direct implications for combating terrorism.

Work on the bill itself also was not routine or typical. In the Senate on Sept. 13 there were no policy battles on the measure and no lengthy debates.

The only real disagreement came at the end, late on Sept. 13, on a last-minute amendment offered by Judiciary Committee ranking Republican Orrin G. Hatch of Utah, that would make it much easier for law enforcement officials to obtain phone numbers and track Internet communications.

Despite significant concerns about the broad authority in the amendment, Democrats conceded to the heightened anxiety of the moment and allowed it to become part of the bill by voice vote. They vowed to spend significant time over the coming weeks exploring the scope of the amendment, which was not part of the bill the House passed on July 18.

It was perhaps fitting that the first substantive piece of legislation considered by the Senate following the attacks was the CJS bill, which would create a deputy attorney general for counterterrorism. That provision had

been included in the bill long before Sept. 11.

Judd Gregg, R-N.H., ranking member on the CJS Appropriations Subcommittee, noted the difficulty of confronting an enemy "that basically seeks martyrdom as its cause." He told colleagues, "We as a nation are going to

> *"American values require that we choose our enemies specifically and never use race or ethnicity."*
> —Orrin G. Hatch, R-Utah

have to be more aggressive in the use of human intelligence."

The Senate also approved, 98-0, a sense-of-the-Senate amendment by Tom Harkin, D-Iowa, condemning violence against Americans of Arab descent.

According to Senate Republicans, the bill would appropriate about $485.3 million for counterterrorism investigations, foreign counterintelligence and other related national security activities.

The CJS bill now heads to conference with the House, whose version would spend $41.5 billion. In addition to Hatch's controversial provision on communications tracking, there are deep differences between the two measures that could take time to work through.

The House bill, for example, includes $4.3 billion for law enforcement grants to state and local governments; the Senate measure includes $4.1 billion, and the Bush administration requested $3.7 billion.

The Senate bill does not include funding for a planned renovation of the

Supreme Court; the House bill includes $63.5 million for the first year's construction costs.

The Senate bill includes a provision authorizing a pay raise for federal judges and justices, something not included by the House, but with which members are likely to agree.

In action on the bill before Sept. 11, the Senate included provisions designed to block U.S. funds from being spent to establish an International Criminal Court that is under way through the United Nations. Another amendment also would prevent the U.S. government from getting involved in lawsuits against Japanese companies filed by U.S. citizens for reparations from World War II.

Trap and Trace

The FBI and other law enforcement agencies have for years wanted Congress to update the laws that govern their ability to obtain phone numbers using special "trap and trace" devices. Law enforcement agencies want it made easier for them to use the devices on modern communications, such as those involving computer modems.

Traps and traces allow law enforcement personnel to get phone numbers as they are dialed, but the equipment does not capture the content of the communication as a wiretap does.

The amendment, which was sponsored by Hatch, Jon Kyl, R-Ariz. and Dianne Feinstein, D-Calif., would make it easier for law enforcement officials to put traps and traces in place to track Internet communication. Currently, a separate judge must approve a trap in each jurisdiction, making the process difficult because Internet communications can cross multiple state lines.

"We are talking about giving the tools to law enforcement it needs to stop further terrorist acts," said Hatch. "This is a tool that absolutely has to be had now."

Before he relented, Leahy said the broadly written amendment did more than was necessary. "I thought we were here to give help to our anti-terrorism effort," he said. "What does this do to help the men and women who were injured or killed?"

It is unclear what the fate of the provision will be. The speed with which opposing Democrats dropped the fight Sept. 13 suggests they may plan to resume their argument later in the process. Leahy said his staff would review the amendment over the next few weeks and try to answer questions from other members about just how broad the new authority would be.

The amendment also would rescind a 1995 CIA regulation that prohibited the recruitment of intelligence sources on terrorism who have human rights violations in their backgrounds.

And it would require the Comptroller General to study whether U.S. National Guard troops should play a primary role in the prevention of and response to attacks with weapons of mass destruction. The administration would be required to come up with a program of research and development in technologies to combat terrorism.

The amendment also would require the administration to enhance the physical security of biological pathogens located at hospitals and research facilities across the country.

Amid all the money for anti-terrorism and enhanced law enforcement authority, the Senate also took note of another result of the terrorist attacks: a rash of violence against Americans of Arab descent. A bipartisan group, led by Harkin and Hatch, said it was critical for the Senate to speak to the violence that was taking place, from desecration of mosques to hate-filled messages painted on the walls of Arab organizations in America.

"We cannot afford hate, divisiveness or prejudice, or we become like the terrorists," Harkin said after reading a litany of attacks on Arab-Americans or Muslims that have occurred since Sept. 11. Added Hatch: "American values require that we choose our enemies specifically and never use race or ethnicity."

International Court Dispute

The Senate began work on the CJS spending bill by considering an amendment that would prohibit U.S. money from going to the creation of the International Criminal Court or to the commission behind it.

Sen. Larry E. Craig, R-Idaho, offered the amendment, which was adopted by voice vote, saying the proposed court poses a "fundamental threat to American sovereignty and civil liberties." He said countries hostile to the United States could use the court to try U.S. military personnel or U.S. allies — such as Israel — for crimes against humanity.

The court will not be established until 60 countries agree to its creation, but more than 30 countries have signed on so far. However, there is disagreement in Congress over whether the United States should ratify the treaty authorizing the court or continue participating in the drafting process.

Craig said the court is another example of the U.N. trying to usurp countries' sovereignty. "Are we ready to trust the United Nations to tell us who should be prosecuted and who should not?" he asked.

Craig said that although court supporters contend that it would be used to prosecute leaders in Sierra Leone and other nations accused of such crimes as genocide, the treaty is broadly worded. "Nothing in the treaty requires them to respect us and to respect our Constitution and our citizens' rights," he said.

The court amendment was adopted with little opposition, although Arlen Specter, R-Pa., later said he was concerned about it.

President Bill Clinton signed the treaty in order to allow the United States to participate in ongoing discussions about the court. But he told the Senate not to ratify it until pending concerns were worked out.

Harkin and New Hampshire Republican Robert C. Smith teamed up to offer an amendment that would prohibit both the State and Justice departments from spending taxpayer dollars to file briefs or motions that challenge the validity of slave-labor claims against Japanese companies.

The amendment, which was adopted by voice vote on Sept. 10, is in response to a 50-year old government policy stating that because the United States signed the 1951 San Francisco Peace Treaty, U.S. citizens who were prisoners of war in Japan during World War II cannot win reparations from Japan or private Japanese companies.

There are about 5,300 surviving veterans of the war who were interned by the Japanese and who worked under horrific conditions for companies like Mitsubishi Electric Corp. and Nippon Steel Corp.

In recent court cases, the State and Justice departments have filed briefs arguing against allowing the POW reparations cases to proceed because their claims are moot under the treaty.

The Senate approved a series of amendments to the bill by voice vote with no debate.

One amendment would change a provision in the bill that established a user fee for cruise line passengers. As approved by the Senate Appropriations Committee, the bill would have imposed a $3 per person inspection fee on cruise ship passengers and increased the airline passenger inspection fee from $6 to $7.

The amendment, offered by Ted Stevens, R-Alaska, would cut the cruise ship fee to $1.50 per passenger and to $6.50 per passenger for airline travelers. The House-passed version of the bill has the $3 and $7 levels.

Also by voice vote, the Senate attached another bill (S 1084) to the CJS measure. It would prohibit the importation of diamonds into the United States unless the country exporting them can show it has export controls on rough diamonds. It is an attempt to shut off funding to rebel groups in several African countries.

The Senate also amended the bill to set aside $2 million in the bill for grants to improve the election process, subject to authorization. ◆

Congress Fearful of Ceding
Too Much Foreign Policy Control

Members warn White House against pushing agenda unrelated to anti-terrorism effort

Congress is increasingly resisting the Bush administration's pleas that it surrender much of its control over foreign policy to give the White House more diplomatic leverage in its attempts to build a global coalition against terrorism.

While continuing to support the thrust of the administration's diplomatic efforts, lawmakers are making clear that they are not willing to give the administration a free hand to conduct foreign policy. They are quickly yielding to the administration on issues that appear to have a direct tie to international efforts to respond to the Sept. 11 terrorist attacks, but they are digging in their heels on matters with less obvious connections.

"We want to make sure that we are not giving the store away," said House International Relations Committee Chairman Henry J. Hyde, R-Ill.

During the week of Sept. 24, those tensions played out over several issues, including repayment of U.S. debts to the United Nations, as well as how much authority Congress was willing to surrender on trade and aid sanctions imposed on foreign governments because of nuclear proliferation and human rights abuses.

"You've got to be careful that you're not taking advantage of the events of Sept. 11 to advance an agenda you had before," said Christopher J. Dodd, D-Conn., a member of the Senate Foreign Relations Committee.

During the week of Sept. 17, Bush administration officials floated a series of proposals for gaining more power over a slew of existing sanctions in order to have diplomatic "carrots" to offer countries such as Iran, Syria and China that it wanted to entice into the anti-terrorism coalition.

In particular, officials suggested that Congress agree to waive all existing restrictions on U.S. military assistance and weapons exports for the next five years to any country if the president determined that the aid would help the anti-terrorist campaign.

Almost immediately, Senate Armed Services Committee Member James M. Inhofe, R-Okla., moved to turn the proposal into law, drafting an amendment to the pending fiscal 2002 defense authorization bill (S 1438) that would have granted the administration broad authority to waive sanctions including those on military aid.

"We need to give the president more leverage," Inhofe said.

Limited Support

Inhofe's proposal won some support from top lawmakers, such as Sen. Mitch McConnell of Kentucky, ranking Republican on the Foreign Operations Appropriations Subcommittee. Even liberal Sen. Barbara Boxer, D-Calif., a member of the Foreign Relations Committee, said she was willing to take such a step, arguing that building the anti-terrorist coalition was by far Congress's top foreign affairs priority.

"Congress should just step back and see what we can do to make things easier," Boxer said. "I want to get this coalition built — the last thing I want to do is stand in the way."

But the proposal ran into opposition from key lawmakers in both parties who worried that their authority to shape foreign policy would be severely limited if such a waiver were to take effect.

"People started wondering, 'if this goes through, why don't we just get rid of the foreign assistance act?'" said one aide, referring

Pakistani women and their children pay homage to the victims of the Sept. 11 terrorist attacks. The headband on the boy at right reads "Peace Forever."

House Clears Payment of Debt to U.N. As Anti-Terrorism Effort Takes Priority

Longstanding congressional resistance to paying $582 million in U.S. debts to the United Nations melted away in the heat of efforts to build a global coalition against terrorism.

The House on Sept. 24 easily cleared legislation (S 248) to pay a portion of the arrears. U.S. debts to the United Nations have mounted sharply since the mid-1990s, and both the Clinton and Bush administrations have called for Congress to take steps to pay. But the White House had only limited success until the Sept. 11 terrorists attacks sparked a stunning turnaround.

Within days of the attacks, House leaders had agreed to not only tackle the debts, but to place the measure on the suspension calendar, where it was subject to limited debate and needed a two-thirds majority to pass. It passed by voice vote.

"Meeting our financial obligations to the United Nations will help to ensure that our policymakers can keep the focus on broad policies that unite the members of the [United Nations] Security Council in the fight against global terrorism," said International Relations Committee Chairman Henry J. Hyde, R-Ill.

The U.N. Security Council was close to adopting a resolution that would call on countries to prosecute suspected terrorists and to have the legislation in place to do so. It would seek to block funds for clandestine groups and punish those assisting terrorists.

In a separate move, the Bush administration said it planned to submit to the Senate for ratification U.N. conventions against terrorism adopted in 1997 and 1999.

Hyde originally had opposed the stand-alone bill, arguing that the debts should be repaid only if the repayment was coupled with legislation (HR 1794) by Majority Whip Tom DeLay, R-Texas, to prohibit cooperation with a proposed International Criminal Court, which was fiercely opposed by GOP conservatives.

The court would handle war crimes and other human rights violations, but U.S. military leaders and

> *"Meeting our financial obligations to the United Nations will help to ensure that our policymakers can keep the focus on broad policies that unite the members of the [United Nations] Security Council in the fight against global terrorism."*
>
> —Henry J. Hyde, R-Ill.

many lawmakers worry that it would expose U.S. troops to politically motivated accusations and trials.

The House had included both measures in a pending State Department authorization bill (HR 1646) it passed May 16. But that measure is not likely to be taken up soon by the Senate, which is unwilling to tackle many sensitive foreign policy issues while President Bush is seeking to build a global anti-terrorism coalition.

The Senate had passed the stand-alone U.N. measure in February, and under pressure from the White House, DeLay and Hyde agreed to take up that bill. *(2001 CQ Weekly, p. 2118)*

At the same time, State Department officials said they would be willing to accept a modified version of DeLay's bill in separate legislation. The department is now supporting an amendment by Jesse Helms of North Carolina, ranking Republican on the Senate Foreign Relations Committee, which incorporates some changes it requested to the Senate version of DeLay's bill (S 857). The amendment is to the pending fiscal 2002 defense authorization bill.

Helms will face a battle, however, from fellow Foreign Relations Committee member Christopher J. Dodd, D-Conn., who will seek to counter with legislation (S 1296) that permits significant U.S. cooperation with the court to try war criminals.

Last year, President Bill Clinton signed the Rome Treaty that would establish the court and allow the United States to continue to participate in negotiations on its implementation. But citing "significant flaws," he did not submit the treaty to Congress for ratification. The Bush administration has said it does not intend to submit the treaty.

Still, once the treaty comes into force, even troops from countries that did not sign or ratify the accord would be subject to prosecutions if they were accused of massive human rights violations on the territory of one of the parties to the pact.

As a protest, DeLay's measure would block U.S. funds and intelligence-sharing for the court, restrict U.S. participation in U.N. peacekeeping operations if U.S. troops are not exempted from prosecution by the court, and bar U.S. military aid to countries (other than NATO members and other key allies) unless they sign agreements to shield U.S. troops from being handed over to the court.

A key change accepted by Helms would water down a provision that blocked the sharing of classified intelligence with the proposed court and restricted the flow of information to nations that have signed the Rome Treaty. Bush, eager for intelligence-sharing to combat the terrorist attacks, would be largely unimpeded in doing so, but would be required to notify Congress when he does.

to Congress's primary law for influencing foreign policy.

In talks with administration officials, Jesse Helms of North Carolina, ranking Republican on the Senate Foreign Relations Committee, voiced opposition to the move. Helms is a strong supporter of many existing sanctions such as those on Cuba and Iran.

Also voicing opposition were panel chairman Joseph R. Biden Jr., D-Del., Hyde and Patrick J. Leahy, D-Vt., chairman of the Senate Foreign Operations Appropriations Subcommittee, who worried that it would undermine U.S. efforts to promote human rights overseas.

"I don't like blankets," Biden said, adding that he wanted the administration to justify any changes it needed to make to existing law.

"I would prefer a case-by-case analysis," agreed Hyde. "A blanket waiver eliminates any assessment of the costs of accepting their conduct which has proven so deleterious in the past. We need some review of their eligibility."

Members were particularly wary that endorsing the proposal would allow the administration to provide aid to Iran, Syria and China. Iran and Syria are barred from such assistance because they are described by the State Department as state sponsors of terrorism. China has been largely cut off from U.S. military aid since the 1989 Tiananmen Square massacres.

"I'd have a heck of a threshold for countries like that," said Sen. George F. Allen, R-Va., a member of the Foreign Relations Committee. "There would have to be a high burden of proof to sell military equipment to Iran, Syria or China. I think we should only provide that kind of assistance to countries that share our values."

'Pandora's Box'

Even lawmakers who generally oppose sanctions and support the administration's approach saw the proposal as a non-starter.

Sen. Pat Roberts, R-Kan., a leading sanctions opponent, said he feared that surrendering power to the administration could actually lead the White House to tighten some unrelated sanctions such as those on Cuba.

"You can use it either as an inducement or a threat," Roberts said.

Jim Kolbe, R-Ariz., chairman of the House Foreign Operations Appropriations Subcommittee, said the White House already had substantial powers

to waive most laws — and that Congress would be willing to back other moves that could be directly tied to the Sept. 11 events.

"You proceed with one country, then another country. They can wait to get into line," Kolbe said.

With that view widespread on Capitol Hill, Inhofe dropped the proposed amendment Sept. 24.

The same day, Bush backed away from the suggestion as well, telling reporters that "where the law allows, I will do it case by case. But we don't intend to ask Congress for a blanket waiver."

Said a top Senate aide: "They realized they were opening a Pandora's box and dropped it."

But Bush did take advantage of existing authority to waive sanctions on India and Pakistan, two key allies in the anti-terrorism campaign. Bush's Sept. 22 executive order lifted remaining sanctions imposed against the countries for testing nuclear weapons in 1998.

Those sanctions originally had been imposed — without a presidential waiver — under the Arms Export Control Act contained in the 1994 State Department authorization bill (PL 103-236). But Congress, under pressure from farmers and other business groups, passed a law in 1999 (PL 106-79) granting the president permanent authority to waive the sanctions. (*1999 Almanac, p. 23-24*)

President Bill Clinton then waived some sanctions against the two countries. But partly to convince them to sign the Comprehensive Test Ban Treaty and accept other arms control measures, he chose to retain limits on the export of military technology and products with both civilian and military uses. The United States also continued to restrict its support for loans for non-humanitarian purposes from the World Bank and other international financial institutions. (*2000 CQ Weekly, p. 578*)

Additional sanctions remain on Pakistan, because the annual foreign aid bills banned or restricted many forms of aid to governments in which a democratically elected leader had been overthrown in a military coup.

Sam Brownback, R-Kan., a member of the Senate Foreign Relations Committee, noted that overall aid to Pakistan was limited to $50 million per year, and that the sanctions block any major bilateral aid for rescheduling of Pakistan's massive foreign debt, as well as prevent

any balance-of-payment support to help Pakistan bolster its foreign reserves.

After the terrorist attacks, lawmakers showed widespread support for giving the administration the power to waive those sanctions as well.

"Pakistan is helping us against this battle of terrorism. We need to lift all sanctions to work with them," Brownback said. "We are going to need to help them economically during this very difficult time for them and for us."

Brownback introduced legislation (S 1465) Sept. 25 that would codify Bush's order and waive the remaining sanctions on Pakistan for two years. Brownback said he plans to attach the legislation as an amendment to either the defense authorization bill or to the fiscal 2002 foreign operations appropriations bill that the Senate is expected to consider in the next few weeks.

Citing the terrorist attacks, Brownback also plans to try again to lift restrictions on U.S. aid to energy-rich Azerbaijan.

Azerbaijan and neighboring Armenia have been locked in a bitter dispute for more than a decade over the enclave of Nagorno-Karabakh. Armenian-Americans have considerable influence on Capitol Hill, and their lobbying has blocked efforts to repeal section 907 of the Freedom Support Act (PL 102-511). That provision bars direct U.S. government assistance to Azerbaijan until that country lifts its war-related embargo on trade with Armenia. (*2001 CQ Weekly, p. 1173*)

The Senate narrowly defeated a previous Brownback attempt to lift the sanctions in 1999, but Brownback said, "It's a new day in that region of the world." (*1999 Almanac, p. 2-62*)

Unlike Pakistan, Azerbaijan does not border Afghanistan. But it is one of several former Soviet states with large Muslim populations that the United States has taken more interest in as it seeks to build its coalition.

Brownback also said he could foresee the U.S. stepping up aid, particularly the provision of military equipment, to several former Soviet republics in Central Asia that have pledged to help the U.S. anti-terrorism effort. Previous support to Uzbekistan, Tajikistan and Kazakhstan had been limited because of their lack of democratic governments.

"We could have a better relationship with the Uzbeks, Kazaks, and Tajiks," Brownback said. " This could really be a new era of cooperation." ◆

Unhurried Pace of Judicial Confirmations Is Typical of a President's First Year

Republicans point to the hundred-plus vacancies in the federal court system as proof of foul political play, but Democrats say they won't be rushed

Listening to the latest rhetoric, it sounds as if the fight over confirming President Bush's judicial nominations could soon shut down the Senate.

And maybe it will. But even with control of the Senate switching hands midyear and partisanship on the issue raising tensions, the pace of hearings and confirmations of Bush's nominees to the federal bench is just about the same as it has been in the first year of the previous three presidents.

That is not to say that it has been fast. So far, four of Bush's picks for the federal courts have won confirmation: two appeals court judges and two district court judges. Only one of those, Roger L. Gregory, was among the first 11 appeals court nominations Bush sent to the Senate on May 9. (*2001 CQ Weekly, p. 1071, 898*)

But by the beginning of August in his first year, President Bill Clinton had won confirmation of none of his judicial nominations. In fact, Clinton did not send his first 13 nominees to the Senate until Aug. 6, 1993, just prior to the August recess.

President George Bush, father of the current president, had won confirmation of only four of the first eight nominations he sent the Senate by early August in 1989. And in 1981, President Ronald Reagan had won confirmation of two judges of the 11 he had sent the Senate before the summer recess.

The difference now is that the new Bush administration quickly ramped up its selection process for judges, which it made significantly shorter by dropping the traditional evaluation of the American Bar Association (ABA). By Aug. 3, Bush had sent 48 judicial nominations to the Senate, far more than his predecessors, and four of them were confirmed. Only a few of Bush's nominees had a hearing before the August recess. (*2001 CQ Weekly, p. 640*)

Democrats say the delays can be attributed to the strange year in the Sen-

ate, which had trouble organizing as an institution split 50-50 between the parties, and then abruptly flipped into Democratic control in June.

In addition, the White House decision on the ABA has played a significant role in causing delays, Democrats argue. They will not act on a nominee without the ABA evaluation, which now does not begin until after the nomination is sent to the Senate, rather than before. As a result, Democrats said, a two-month lag has been built in between submission of a nomination and the ability of the committee to hold a hearing on the candidate.

The ABA has a special committee that conducts interviews with the nominee and those who know him, then evaluates the candidate's integrity, competence and judicial temperament. It rates each judge as "well-qualified," "qualified" or "unqualified."

Partisanship, Old and New

But conservatives charge that Senate Democrats are deliberately delaying the process to keep Bush from putting his stamp on the federal judiciary.

"Senate Democrats obstruct Republican nominees," said Tom Jipping, the head of the conservative interest group Free Congress Foundation's Judicial Selection Monitoring Project. He said the delays follow a "long-term, committed, partisan pattern that Democrats have followed for the last 20 years."

"They're on track to set a record low" in the number of judges confirmed this year, Jipping said.

By the end of his first year, Clinton had won confirmation of 27 judges, Bush had won 15 (out of the 19 nominated), and Reagan had won 41.

In an Aug. 14 interview with CNN, White House Counsel Alberto R. Gonzales was pessimistic about the number of Bush's picks likely to be confirmed by the end of the year, saying he expected no more than five.

But Gonzales blamed the situation on what happened in the years before

Bush became president, when Democrats say Republicans unfairly blocked Clinton's nominees and denied him his right to place judges on the bench.

"We are trying to work through some of the logjams, but there is a lot of bitterness," Gonzales said. "This is a bit of a payback. I can't argue with some of [the Democrats'] perceptions."

Talking about what had happened in the past, when nominees were held up for months, Gonzales said it was wrong and noted that in the current situation, "part of this is based on the conduct of the Republican senators in the past. We had nothing to do with this problem. But it does affect us."

So far, Democrats have worked only on the least controversial of Bush's nominees, holding rare recess confirmation hearings on one current and one former Judiciary Committee staffer, both of whom are virtually unopposed in their bid for judgeships.

But the road ahead will almost certainly be more difficult.

For one thing, there is a technical problem. Because of a squabble in the Senate on Aug. 3, the administration must resubmit all of the nominations that were pending when the Senate recessed. Traditionally, just before a recess the Senate approves a motion to hold over all pending nominations; otherwise they are returned to the president.

When Democrats made the motion this year, however, the list did not include two troubled nominations: Mary Sheila Gall, the administration's pick to head the Consumer Product Safety Commission, and Otto J. Reich, the nominee to be assistant secretary of State for Western Hemisphere Affairs. (*2001 CQ Weekly p. 734*)

Gall's nomination was defeated in the Senate Commerce Committee on Aug. 2. And it is unclear whether Senate Democrats would have allowed the Foreign Relations Committee to take up Reich's nomination. (*2001 CQ Weekly, p. 1927*)

With Gall and Reich omitted from

Where the Nominations Stand

Before President Bush nominated his first group of judges to federal appeals courts on May 9, it was clear that Republicans and Democrats in the Senate would clash over the issue of filling the federal bench. The chart below will track Bush's first batch of nominees through to Senate confirmation or rejection. The categories include the American Bar Association rating, which was split for some nominees, and the 'Blue Slip' evaluation of senators from the nominees' home states.

NOMINEE	CIRCUIT COURT	ABA RATING	BLUE SLIP	HEARING	COMMITTEE VOTE		FLOOR VOTE	
Terrence W. Boyle	4th	Qualified	Jesse Helms, R-N.C. - yes John Edwards, D-N.C. - not returned					
Edith Brown Clement	5th	Well-Qualified*	John B. Breaux, D-La. - yes Mary L. Landrieu, D-La. - yes					
Deborah L. Cook	6th	Qualified	Mike DeWine, R-Ohio - yes George V. Voinovich, R-Ohio - yes					
Miguel A. Estrada	D.C.	Well-Qualified	Not applicable					
Roger L. Gregory	4th	Qualified	George F. Allen, R-Va. - yes John W. Warner, R-Va. - yes	7/11/01	7/19/01	19-0	7/20/01	93-1
Michael W. McConnell	10th	Well-Qualified	Orrin G Hatch, R-Utah - yes Robert F. Bennett, R-Utah - yes					
Priscilla Richman Owen	5th	Well-Qualified	Phil Gramm, R-Texas - yes Kay Bailey Hutchison, R-Texas - yes					
Barrington D. Parker	2nd	Well-Qualified	Christopher J. Dodd, D-Conn. - yes Joseph I. Lieberman, D-Conn. - yes					
John E. Roberts Jr.	D.C.	Well-Qualified	Not applicable					
Derris W. Shedd	4th	Well-Qualified*	Ernest F. Hollings, D-S.C. - yes Strom Thurmond, R-S.C. - yes					
Jeffrey S. Sutton	6th	Qualified *	DeWine - yes Voinovich - yes					

* Means a majority of the ABA committee voted for this rating. All other ratings were unanimous.

the list, Minority Leader Trent Lott, R-Miss., objected, so the motion failed. The White House must now renominate each name on the list when the Senate is back in session. The Senate returns the week of Sept. 3.

Qualified, and Conservative

Senate Democrats still have not figured out how to handle the Bush nominees, especially those chosen for appeals courts that render decisions on matters of constitutional law.

Most nominees have strong conservative backgrounds, which has the liberal interest community up in arms. "This administration has thrown down the gauntlet by nominating people that are so out of step with mainstream American values," said Nan Aron, president of the Alliance for Justice, a liberal interest group that monitors ju-

dicial selection.

Charles E. Schumer, D-N.Y., chairman of the Senate Judiciary Subcommittee on Administrative Oversight and the Courts, held a hearing on whether the Senate should consider ideology when evaluating judicial nominations, and Democrats were roundly criticized by Republicans for even considering the question.

But Aron said nominees "need to be considered in light of the composition and direction of the circuit [court]" to which they would be appointed. Currently, half of the 12 regular courts of appeal are dominated by GOP nominees. Three courts have a majority of Democratic nominees, and three are split.

Jipping and other conservatives, meanwhile, are fighting Democrats by using remarks they had made while complaining about delays for Clinton

nominees. Jipping's group is keeping a database of such comments.

One of his favorites is a quote from Judiciary Committee Chairman Patrick J. Leahy, D-Vt., saying in 1998 that "any week in which the Senate does not confirm three judges is a week in which the Senate is failing to address the vacancy crisis."

When Leahy made that statement there were about 80 vacancies in the courts. As of early August this year, the number reached 107.

Jipping said Bush and Republicans must make an issue of the need to confirm judges. "The necessary ingredient is Senate Republican activity, and they're being fairly inert on this."

No one disputes that Bush has chosen qualified people. The ABA gave its highest rating of "well-qualified" to seven of his first 11 nominees. ◆

High Court Again Shows a Taste For Limiting Lawmakers' Reach

Justices Kennedy and O'Connor remain crucial 'swing' votes as court sets another record for 5-4 decisions

In its nine-month session that ended June 28, the Supreme Court continued whittling away at Congress' power, though in different ways than in previous terms.

The court in several cases ventured beyond its traditional role of interpreting legislation and chose instead to effectively rewrite portions of law. At the same time, the court broke from its cautious past by stepping into the political realm and deciding the contested presidential election, a job the Constitution assigns to Congress.

Taking on Congress is nothing new for this court, which has gradually reduced legislative authority over the last several years with decisions that restricted Congress' ability to use federal courts to settle social problems and sharply curtailed Congress' ability to use the Commerce Clause to justify legislation.

"The court has not been altogether kind to Congress," said University of Virginia law professor A.E. "Dick" Howard.

The latest term of the Supreme Court will be remembered most for its controversial 5-4 decision in *Bush v. Gore*, which ended the presidential election recount in Florida and, in effect, decided the race for Republican George W. Bush over Democrat Al Gore. Otherwise, the court considered cases on the fringes of congressional authority that did not provide the chance to impose sweeping restrictions on what Congress could do, such as when the court in 1998 struck down the line-item veto authority lawmakers tried to give the president. (*1998 Almanac, p. 6-21*)

"There has been no 300-pound elephant of a case this time around," said Dennis J. Goldford, political science professor at Drake University in Des

The Supreme Court chose to be the venue for deciding the disputed presidential election, which drew protests last December.

Moines, Iowa.

The court issued 75 signed opinions, a case load similar to last term's but still far less than 10 years ago. And for the second year in a row the court set a record for the number of cases decided by 5-4 votes: 26, which is five more than last year.

The frequency of split decisions highlights the importance of the court's two "swing" justices, Anthony M. Kennedy and Sandra Day O'Connor, as well as the intense attention interest groups have begun paying to future Supreme Court nominees. On the close decisions, Kennedy was on the prevailing side 21 times, O'Connor 19.

The court concluded its session without the announcement some had expected. Chief Justice William H. Rehnquist was thought to be considering retirement with a Republican now in the White House to choose his replacement. Justices typically announce their retirement at a term's end.

In its final week, the court issued 10 decisions, among them three significant rulings in immigration cases. By a 5-4 vote, the court ruled on June 25 in two related cases that immigrants who are about to be deported for committing crimes have the right to make their case in federal district courts. Al-

so by 5-4, the court on June 28 ruled that immigrants who have committed crimes but have nowhere to be deported to cannot be held indefinitely.

The landmark moment for this court was the case of *Bush v. Gore* — if not for the ruling itself, for the court's decision to hear an appeal of the Florida Supreme Court's ruling that mandated recounts of ballots in several counties. The Supreme Court could easily have declined to hear the case, but it chose to become involved.

"The significance of *Bush v. Gore* is the constitutional role the court played," said Douglas Kmiec, Pepperdine University law professor. Kmiec said there was no inherent reason for the court to intervene — in fact, the Constitution intends for Congress to handle contested presidential elections.

There was a "sense of, 'Oh, how messy it would be if Congress had to solve it,' " echoed Howard. The court seemed to be asserting, he said, that "we are the better forum for deciding this case."

It was a decision the public seemed to accept. "For whatever reason, we have more faith in most outcomes from the court than from Congress," said Kmiec. "It does signify that we're not willing to trust sometimes political actors to do what the Constitution said they had a right to do."

The case has established a political precedent for the Supreme Court to get involved in presidential election disputes, which could have implications about Congress' role in settling similar disputes in the future.

Scholars disagree on the legal precedent the court's ruling set. On Dec. 12 the court found that the differing methods used by Florida counties to determine what constitutes a vote violated the Constitution's Equal Protection Clause. (*2000 CQ Weekly, p. 2854*)

While Kmiec believes that the "law decided in the case is very inconsequential," Goldford believes it may be difficult for the court to get around the new idea that equal protection can be applied to voting methods. "Can they contain that yawning chasm they've opened up there?"

Howard said the decision was another example of how self-confident — and activist — this court has become. "People assume that conservatives will do less, but in this case, conservatives do more," he said.

Not as Congress Intended

The trio of immigration decisions seemed certain to provoke renewed debate in Congress, even though the court ostensibly upheld the laws at issue. In both sets of decisions, the court ruled in favor of the federal law, but pointedly arrived at the decisions using its own interpretation of the law rather than the one offered by the government. The court said that following the government's argument of what Congress was trying to do might have rendered the laws unconstitutional, which provoked the dissenting justices to say the resulting laws are not necessarily what Congress had intended.

In the first pair of cases, *Immigration and Naturalization Service (INS) v. St. Cyr* and *Calcano-Martinez v. INS*, both decided by identical 5-4 votes, the court clarified the consequences of a pair of 1996 laws that changed immigration rules.

Before passage of the Anti-Terrorism and Effective Death Penalty Act (PL 104-132) and the Illegal Immigration Reform and Immigration Responsibility Act (PL 104-208), legal immigrants who committed crimes and faced deportation could challenge their status in court and apply to the attorney general for a waiver. The new laws prohibited courts from getting involved in the decision and severely restricted the attorney general's authority to waive deportation.

In the first case, Enrico St. Cyr pleaded guilty to a crime in 1996, but the government did not begin deportation proceedings until April of 1997, after the new laws took effect. Because of those laws, then-Attorney General Janet Reno said she could not consider St. Cyr's deportation waiver request.

In the second case, the defendant was not allowed to argue his case in federal court because the government interpreted the immigration law to prohibit any court review of his case.

The Supreme Court found that Congress did not repeal the habeas corpus authority of the federal district court because the language in the immigration laws did not explicitly do so. Habeas is the legal theory used by those detained by the government to show that they are being held unfairly.

"For the INS to prevail, it must overcome both the strong presumption in favor of judicial review of administrative action and the longstanding rule requiring a clear statement of congressional intent to repeal habeas jurisdiction," wrote Justice John Paul Stevens for the majority, which also included Justices Kennedy, David H. Souter, Ruth Bader Ginsburg and Stephen G. Breyer.

Stevens concluded that the only way to avoid the problem was to find that Congress did not intend to repeal the habeas jurisdiction. The court also found that it was improper to go back and retroactively change the rules on St. Cyr, who pleaded guilty with the expectation that he could ask for a waiver.

Justice Antonin Scalia wrote a scorching dissent. "The Court today finds ambiguity in the utterly clear language of a statute that forbids the district court (and all other courts) to entertain the claims of aliens such as respondent St. Cyr, who have been found deportable by reason of their criminal acts. It fabricates a superclear statement, 'magic words' requirement for the congressional expression of such an intent, unjustified in law and unparalleled in any other areas of our jurisprudence."

Similar reasoning prevailed in the 5-4 decision on indefinite detention that involved two cases that were consolidated: *Zadvydas v. Davis*, and *Ashcroft v. Ma*. Kestutis Zadvydas and Kim Ho Ma are immigrants who committed crimes and were to be deported, but no country will accept them, so they have been held by the government.

Writing for the majority, Breyer said that if the court were to read the law to allow indefinite detention, it would pose a serious constitutional question.

"In our view, the statute, read in light of the Constitution's demands, limits an alien's post-removal-period detention to a period reasonably necessary to bring about that alien's removal from the United States. It does not permit indefinite detention," he wrote.

Kennedy's dissent said the court overstepped its bounds, noting that the other branches of government have historically had wide discretion on immigration law. "Far from avoiding a constitutional question, the Court's ruling causes systemic dislocation in the balance of powers, thus raising serious constitutional concerns not just for the cases at hand but for the Court's own view of its proper authority."

Congress' Limits

Although most cases were not stark disputes with Congress, the court did tackle a few legislative decisions. Barbara A. Perry of Sweet Briar College said the rulings were "almost evolutionary" in building on previous cases.

In *University of Alabama Board of Trustees v. Garrett*, the court held, 5-4, that Congress exceeded its power when it included in the Americans With Disabilities Act (PL 101-336) a provision allowing state employees to sue in federal court. State employees, the court held in February, could sue only in state courts. (*2001 CQ Weekly, p. 422*)

On June 25, the court threw out a 1990 law that required mushroom handlers to contribute to a fund for generic pro-mushroom advertising. In *United States v. United Foods*, the court held that because the fund was not part of a "broader regulatory scheme," it violated First Amendment free speech rights.

In *Legal Services Corporation v. Velazquez*, also decided 5-4, the court struck down a restriction Congress had placed on legal service lawyers, which prohibited them from suing the state or federal government over welfare laws. The court said the restriction denied agency clients their rights to full legal representation. (*2001 CQ Weekly, p. 488*)

But it was not all bad news for Congress. The court unanimously ruled in *Whitman v. American Trucking Associations* that Congress can delegate rulemaking authority to agencies. And the court upheld, 5-4, Congress' right to impose more conditions on fathers seeking to transfer their U.S. citizenship to their children born abroad out of wedlock than imposed on mothers. (*2001 CQ Weekly, pp. 1448, 484*)

On June 28, the court ruled, 5-4, in *Lorillard Tobacco Co. v. Massachusetts* that only Congress has the authority to regulate cigarette advertising and marketing. The court threw out Massachusetts' tobacco advertisement rules. ◆

Committees Taking a Critical Look At Ashcroft's Request for Broad New Powers

Proposals for secret searches, use of foreign wiretap information and indefinite detention of non-citizens are likeliest to be rejected or heavily rewritten

When Attorney General John Ashcroft rolled out his anti-terrorism proposal on Sept. 19, he called on Congress to pass it that same week. He will be lucky now to get even some of what he wants by the end of October.

Members have deep concerns about the scope and constitutionality of Ashcroft's package, and despite the extraordinary times and pressure from the Bush administration, they have made it clear that they will not rush it through.

At least for now, the House and Senate Judiciary committees — not the Bush administration or congressional leadership — are in control. Committee leaders are picking critically through Ashcroft's request for broader authority to track Internet communications, seize property and tap phones in the battle against terrorism.

Where the attorney general wanted urgency, he has gotten "regular order" and plenty of skepticism. Leaders have refused to short-circuit the usual committee process in the interest of moving quickly and decisively, as they did with an airline bailout and other legislative responses to the Sept. 11 terrorist attacks. (*2001 CQ Weekly, p. 2206*)

The House and Senate are working on separate tracks, but several of the attorney general's proposals, including wider authority to conduct secret searches, already seem certain to be rejected. Others, such as changes in the law that would make it easier to seize voice mail, will be rewritten.

"The Justice Department was throwing a lot of things out there," said a House Republican leadership aide, and that made members nervous. It fell to the Judiciary Committee to "shake out" the package, the aide said.

Ashcroft made two public appearances on Capitol Hill the week of Sept. 24 to defend his sweeping proposal, which would make it easier for law enforcement agencies to track e-mail and allow them to obtain "roving wiretaps"

Utah Sen. Orrin G. Hatch, the Judiciary Committee's ranking Republican, left, and Chairman Patrick J. Leahy, D-Vt., hear from Attorney General John Ashcroft at a Sept. 25 hearing.

that would follow suspects to any telephone lines they use.

President Bush made his only substantive plea for the package in a speech Sept. 25 at FBI headquarters.

"I want you to know that every one of the proposals we've made on Capitol Hill, carried by the attorney general, has been carefully reviewed," Bush said. "They are measured requests. They are responsible requests. They are constitutional requests. . . . But we're at war, a war we're going to win. And in order to win the war, we must make sure that the law enforcement men and women have got the tools necessary, within the Constitution, to defeat the enemy."

Many members were not convinced. "Hastily drafted measures could backfire," House Republican Policy Committee Chairman Christopher Cox of California wrote in the Oct. 15 edition of Forbes Magazine.

It would be ironic, Cox wrote, if the government had to free a suspected terrorist because the gathering of evidence thought to have been "authorized" by Congress was found to violate Fourth Amendment guarantees against unreasonable searches and seizures.

One proposal that might help ease the provisions through Congress would

be to "sunset" any new authorization, automatically ending it after a specified period. That idea was rejected by Ashcroft, but endorsed by some committee members.

The real work the week of Sept. 24 took place behind closed doors, where staff and members reviewed and revised Ashcroft's request. Participants said they made progress, but much remained undecided. The negotiations were to continue through the weekend.

Contentious Provisions

At least two of Ashcroft's most controversial proposals seem likely to fall off a final bill. One would allow agencies to conduct more secret searches without notifying suspects. The other would allow the government to use information from foreign governments' wiretaps of U.S. citizens, even if the wiretaps were unconstitutional.

Other contentious provisions, such as one to allow the attorney general to indefinitely detain all non-citizens he deems risks to national security, will be extensively rewritten to curb the far-reaching scope of the power requested. (*2001 CQ Weekly, p. 2210*)

It is unclear just when the full House

Ashcroft's Counterterrorism Requests

Following is a look at how Attorney General John Ashcroft's proposals are faring on Capitol Hill:

SEARCHES AND SURVEILLANCE

▮ "Roving" wiretaps: Grant court orders to wiretap any phones that suspects might use, rather than requiring separate permission for each line.
Outlook: Members are receptive but worry investigators might tap into too many unrelated conversations.

▮ Voice mail: Allow agencies to seize voice mail with search warrants instead of going through the lengthier process of getting a wiretap order.
Outlook: May pass, but limited to voice mail under control of suspects.

▮ "One-stop shopping" for court orders: Grant one warrant or court order in nationwide investigations to proceed with searches and some electronic surveillance, rather than requiring separate orders in each jurisdiction.
Outlook: This has raised constitutional concerns. Rep. Jerrold Nadler, D-N.Y., noted that the Fourth Amendment requires warrants "particularly describing the place to be searched and the persons or things to be seized."

▮ Secret searches: Allow more searches without notice to the suspect.
Outlook: Dead on arrival, according to House Judiciary Committee Chairman F. James Sensenbrenner Jr., R-Wis.

▮ Customer information: Allow investigators to get credit card numbers and other customer information from Internet service providers with a subpoena, rather than requiring more time-consuming court orders.
Outlook: Uncertain. Privacy advocates oppose it.

▮ Internet tracking: Expand the reach of high-tech surveillance tools to Internet communications.
Outlook: Members seem to agree that law enforcement needs better access to some information, but they may find it difficult to write legislation narrow enough to satisfy privacy advocates and others.

IMMIGRATION

▮ Definition of "terrorist": Include anyone who supports terrorist groups, even if the support is unrelated to terrorism. The broader definition would apply retroactively, and the government could try non-citizens with secret evidence.
Outlook: Unlikely to pass without substantial revisions narrowing its reach.

▮ Detention for non-citizens: Authorize the attorney general to indefinitely detain any non-citizen believed to be a national security risk.
Outlook: Dead. Ashcroft has backed away from this request, although he may get some additional authority to detain non-citizens.

SEIZURE

▮ Enemy property: Authorize the president to seize the property of "enemies" during armed hostilities or attacks on the United States.
Outlook: Members on both the right and left have called this an unreasonable expansion of presidential power.

▮ Terrorist property: Authorize the seizure of a "terrorist organization's property," even if it is not linked to terrorist activities.
Outlook: Significant opposition from members on the left and right.

▮ Advance seizures: Authorize the seizure of suspected terrorists' property after a grand jury indicts them, but before they have been convicted.
Outlook: Unlikely to pass. Among those objecting is Rep. Henry J. Hyde, R-Ill., who, as Judiciary chairman last year, helped push through a bill limiting government's power to seize property.

DISCLOSURE

▮ Wiretap information: Authorize the disclosure of wiretap information to any officer or employee of the United States.
Outlook: Members on the right and left oppose this, arguing that it blurs the line between criminal and intelligence information. It is easier to get

permission to gather intelligence information, which is related to national security.

▮ Foreign wiretaps: Authorize the use of wiretap information from foreign governments against U.S. citizens.
Outlook: Unlikely to be included. Opponents say it would allow the government to get around Americans' constitutional protections.

▮ Internet information: Allow Internet service providers to voluntarily disclose information about a subscriber if they believe there is imminent danger of death or serious bodily injury.
Outlook: Likely to pass, despite some opposition.

▮ Student records: Open student education records to investigators.
Outlook: Some opposition. The House Education and the Workforce Committee is studying it.

▮ Grand juries: Authorize disclosure of secret grand jury information to various authorities.
Outlook: Unlikely to pass unless it is significantly narrowed or judges are given oversight.

▮ Tax information: Allow disclosure of tax information from the Internal Revenue Service to local, state and federal law enforcement during terrorist investigations.
Outlook: The House Ways and Means Committee will study it.

TERRORISM

▮ Statute of limitations and other legal provisions: Drop the five-year statute of limitation on prosecution of terrorist crimes and add terrorism to the list of crimes that can trigger racketeering investigations; broaden prohibitions on assisting terrorists; allow the collection of DNA evidence of convicted terrorists.
Outlook: Likely to pass.

▮ Penalties: Increase maximum penalties for terrorism and extend the period of post-release supervision for terrorists.
Outlook: Likely to pass, despite some opposition.

and Senate committees will meet to consider the proposals. Both want to be able to introduce a consensus bill, one with broad support. The House Judiciary Committee may be on track to take up such a bill sometime during the week of Oct. 1, but the Senate panel may not follow suit until the week of Oct. 8.

The Senate Judiciary Committee has scheduled a second hearing for Oct. 2, when Ashcroft may be asked to return to answer more questions. The chairman of the panel's Constitution Subcommittee, Russell D. Feingold, D-Wis., also will chair a hearing on Oct. 3 entitled, "Protecting Constitutional Freedoms in the Face of Terrorism."

Different Tracks

Unlike many of the other congressional responses to the terrorist attacks, such as the quick approval of a $40 billion supplemental spending bill (PL 107-38), the law enforcement package is receiving full legislative scrutiny, including hearings and intense committee debate. (2001 CQ *Weekly*, p. 2126)

While the leadership staff in both chambers is following the negotiations, the Judiciary committees and their staffs are making the key decisions.

The two committees, however, are pursuing different negotiating strategies.

In the Senate, Democrats and Republicans, lawmakers and their staffs, negotiated together, along with representatives from the White House and Justice Department. Their definition of a consensus bill is one that can pass the Senate with White House support.

"Well, it won't be the Ashcroft anti-terrorism bill until it's the Ashcroft-Leahy-Hastert anti-terrorism bill," Senate Majority Leader Tom Daschle, D-S.D., said Sept. 25, referring to Senate Judiciary Committee Chairman Patrick J. Leahy, D-Vt., and House Speaker J. Dennis Hastert, R-Ill. "We really want to bring a terrorism bill to the floor that has the kind of cohesive support that we've been able to demonstrate on other issues."

In the House, the negotiations were confined to the bipartisan Judiciary Committee leadership and its staff, with less input from the Bush administration. Their definition of a consensus bill is one that could get through the tough territory of the Judiciary Committee and the full House, without much concern over whether the Bush administration has signed off first.

Of greater importance to House Ju-

diciary Chairman F. James Sensenbrenner Jr., R-Wis., is maintaining his committee's jurisdiction and preventing the House leadership from taking the bill away — something the leadership so far does not seem eager to do.

"I am very fearful that if this bill is put on a slow roll, all of the sudden we will lose as a committee our right to make improvements and to attempt to reach a bipartisan process to present to the House of Representatives," he said Sept. 24. ". . . That means that everybody who is a participant in this process, whether it's the Justice Department, the majority party, the minority party and the bipartisan leadership, is going to have to bend a bit, because a compromise by definition is something that gets the job done but doesn't make everybody completely happy."

Neither the House nor the Senate committee seems terribly concerned about coordinating its efforts with the other chamber. Both sides seem to agree that the administration is more likely to get more out of any deal the Senate committee reaches than the House. House Republican conservatives tend to be far more leery of expanding law enforcement authority than their Senate counterparts.

Unknown, at least now, is how much public contention the leadership will be comfortable with on the bill. Will leaders in the House, for example, be willing to allow an extended and intense debate over controversial provisions? Or will those provisions be jettisoned in the name of unity and bipartisanship?

A GOP aide said Hastert and other leaders are not pursuing "bipartisanship for the sake of bipartisanship."

"We're not trying to do this to make the nation feel better," the aide said. "We're doing this to get things done."

In the Senate, Leahy called Ashcroft on Sept. 26 to ask him to urge his staff to work harder to find compromises on several of the sticking points, according to a Democratic aide.

One of those is Ashcroft's request for broad authority to share secret grand jury information with law enforcement officials. More troubling to some members is his request for a provision that would allow law enforcement to capture e-mail addresses with electronic surveillance. The concern is that investigators might be able to get more information than intended unless the legislation is written carefully.

So far, Ashcroft has failed to per-

suade many members that they need to pass his package quickly.

During Ashcroft's appearances before the House and Senate Judiciary committees, members asked him if the new authority he has requested would have prevented the attacks.

"There is absolutely no guarantee that these safeguards would have avoided the Sept. 11 occurrence," Ashcroft said. "We do know that without them, the occurrence took place. And we do know that each of them would have strengthened our ability to curtail, disrupt and prevent terrorism. But we have absolutely no assurance."

Pointed Questions

Skeptics such as Rep. Bob Barr, R-Ga., asked whether Ashcroft is trying to take advantage of the situation to get authority Congress previously rejected.

"If we are interested in proposing here changes to criminal law and criminal procedure to attack international terrorism, why is it necessary to propose a laundry list of changes to criminal law generally and criminal procedure generally to cast such a wide net?" Barr asked Justice Department representatives after Ashcroft left the Sept. 24 hearing.

"Does it have anything to do with the fact that the department has sought many of these authorities on numerous other occasions, has been unsuccessful in obtaining them and now seeks to take advantage of what is obviously an emergency situation to obtain authorities that it has been unable to obtain previously?" he asked.

Barr and four other members of the House Judiciary Committee sent a letter Sept. 21 to Sensenbrenner and ranking Democrat John Conyers Jr. of Michigan in which they divide Ashcroft's requests into four categories, from those they would readily approve to those that were "unacceptable as written."

Included in the "unacceptable" category are requests for nationwide authority for e-mail search warrants and authorization for agents to seize terrorist suspects' assets before the suspects have been convicted of a crime.

It is unclear at this point just how problematic Barr and his allies will be for Ashcroft. If the House leadership decides it wants to prevent heated debate on the floor more than it wants an extensive bill, a decision that has not yet been made, that could hand Barr's group significant power. ◆

Defense Debate Redrawn

Both sides on anti-missile issue see vindication; 'two-war' strategy may lose backers

Congressional debate over contentious military issues, such as missile defense and the decade-old policy of keeping U.S. forces ready to win two wars, was forever altered by the terrorist attacks in New York and Washington.

While the Sept. 11 assaults erased one sticking point between the Bush administration and Congress — the president's $343.5 billion national defense request for fiscal 2002, including $18.4 billion that he tacked on to his initial proposal late in June — the landscape took on new dimensions for President Bush's most controversial proposal, speeding up deployment of a nationwide anti-missile defense, and Defense Secretary Donald H. Rumsfeld's decision to drop the Pentagon's two-war policy.

The attacks and the likely proposals to give the Defense Department a larger role in counterterrorism also may trigger a debate over the historic ban on the use of military forces in domestic law enforcement.

"We've been tiptoeing around that issue for some time," Air Force Gen. Richard B. Myers told the Senate Armed Services Committee on Sept. 13. "My view is that this tragedy will crystallize our thoughts and we'll have a productive debate."

Myers, current vice chairman of the Joint Chiefs of Staff, was appearing before the Senate panel as Bush's nominee to succeed Army Gen. Henry H. Shelton as chairman of the Joint Chiefs. The Senate approved the nomination by voice vote Sept. 14.

House action on its version of the defense authorization bill (HR 2586), which had been scheduled for Sept. 12-13, now may begin Sept. 20. Senate action on its counterpart bill (S 1416) also may occur the week of Sept. 17.

The House Defense Appropriations Subcommittee's markup of the companion defense spending bill, which was just getting under way Sept. 11 when the Capitol was evacuated, has not been rescheduled.

A military helicopter takes off near the damaged area of the Pentagon, which was hit Sept. 11 when hijackers commandeered a commercial airliner and crashed into the building.

In the aftermath of the attacks, the surge of support for beefing up defenses suggests that Bush's overall spending request may be the floor, rather than the ceiling, for funding.

"It's a wake-up call to the nation," said House Armed Services Committee member Duncan Hunter, R-Calif. "It's clear that this is as dangerous a century as the one we just left."

Moreover, members' overwhelming desire to rally behind Bush as a demonstration of national unity has fostered a desire by many to avoid, for now, contentious debates, particularly on national security issues.

Missile Defense

Senate Armed Services Committee Chairman Carl Levin, D-Mich., and senior committee Republican John W. Warner, R-Va., are trying to craft compromise amendments to the defense authorization bill that would bridge deeply rooted disagreements over national missile defense and base closings. Failing that, Levin said, he hoped to simply defer action on contentious issues while the Senate acted on the rest of the bill.

"The differences we focus on now

seem unimportant in the short term," said House Armed Services member Tom Allen, D-Maine.

Members of Congress on both sides of the missile defense debate found in the Sept. 11 attacks new evidence to buttress their cases.

Bush has proposed speeding up deployment of a nationwide anti-missile defense that could fend off a small number of missiles that might be launched by a radical state such as North Korea or Iraq. That would require the United States to abrogate the anti-ballistic missile (ABM) treaty of 1972, a step that Levin and many other Democrats oppose on grounds that it may trigger a new arms race.

Among critics of Bush's anti-missile program, the chief concern is that it would provoke military and diplomatic responses by Russia, China and other countries that would make the world more dangerous. But in the political debate on the issue, the critics place heavy emphasis on the argument that it would be much easier for a radical regime or terrorist group to smuggle a nuclear, chemical or biological weapon into a major U.S. city in a shipping container than to attack the city with a long-range ballistic missile.

In prescient remarks Sept. 10, Senate Foreign Relations Committee Chairman Joseph R. Biden Jr., D-Del., a critic of increased spending on missile defense, said, "We'll have diverted all that money to address the least likely threat, while the real threat comes to this country in the . . . belly of a plane."

Opponents of Bush's proposal contend that the $8.3 billion request for the Ballistic Missile Defense Organization (BMDO), a 57 percent increase over the fiscal 2001 appropriation, is excessive.

Many of the critics insisted that the Sept. 11 attack vindicated their view that the country faced far more probable threats than missiles: "It's clear that we don't need money for 'star wars,' " said Sen. Tom Harkin, D-Iowa, using its critics' derisive nickname for the anti-missile program. "Whatever we were going to spend on that, we should use for counterterrorism and rebuilding," he insisted.

Anti-missile proponents contend that the attacks highlight the fact that there are groups eager to inflict the massive, indiscriminate destruction to which U.S. cities are vulnerable.

"We shouldn't pinpoint the last [attack] that happened and just address that," said Senate Appropriations Committee member Kay Bailey Hutchison, R-Texas. "We should look at our range of vulnerability and address it so that the world knows you can't do this."

Senate Armed Services member Joseph I. Lieberman, D-Conn., one of the Democrats most supportive of missile defense, doubts that the critics will be able to force a trade-off between anti-missile funding and counterterrorism. "The net effect will be that we will authorize and appropriate more money to defend against terrorism, but it will not diminish the amount of money we'll spend on BMDO," Lieberman said.

In an extraordinary departure from Senate Armed Services' typical pro-defense bipartisanship, the panel split along party lines, with only the majority Democrats voting to approve the defense authorization bill. But the split was due only to a Levin-sponsored provision that would bar Bush from conducting any anti-missile tests during fiscal 2002 that would violate the ABM Treaty, unless Congress approved them. The prohibition would not apply if the U.S. and Russian governments had agreed to changes in the pact that would allow the tests in question.

President Bush and Defense Secretary Donald H. Rumsfeld tour the damaged area of the Pentagon the day after the attacks.

Pentagon officials have said that planned tests might "bump up against" the treaty's limits as early as next spring. (*2001 CQ Weekly, p. 2079*)

The Senate committee bill also would slice $1.3 billion from Bush's $8.3 billion missile defense request, but those cuts were not focused on the projects deemed likely to conflict with the ABM Treaty soon.

Democrats on House Armed Services made no effort to include in the committee's version of the authorization bill a provision limiting Bush's ability to break the ABM pact. However, they did try, unsuccessfully, to slice $984 million from the anti-missile request, with most of the cuts intended to stop projects that might violate the treaty. (*2001 CQ Weekly, p. 1931*)

While Bush insists that he will abrogate the ABM Treaty unilaterally if Russia does not agree to replace the pact with a new strategic framework, he also insists he wants Russia to concur in getting rid of the treaty. Russian officials have insisted on many occasions since Bush took office that an end to the ABM Treaty would knock the props out from under an array of other arms control agreements.

Russian President Vladimir Putin's expressions of support for the United States in the wake of the Sept. 11 attacks could be a harbinger of significant support from Russia in U.S. action against the Taliban, a Muslim fundamentalist militia that runs Afghanistan. That nation hosts Osama bin Laden, the suspected mastermind of these and other terrorist attacks against the United States. The Russian government is locked in a brutal battle with Islamic fundamentalists in the breakaway province of Chechnya, a group that gets support from the Taliban.

The prospect of Russian help in hunting down bin Laden might offer Bush an incentive to defer, for now, a clash with Putin over the ABM Treaty.

However, on Sept. 11, after a meeting between high-level U.S. and Russian defense officials to discuss Bush's plans, a senior Russian general reportedly indicated that his government was reconciled to Bush's decision to pull out of the treaty.

"The U.S. side is proposing to abandon the ABM [Treaty] and build a new strategic relationship," Deputy Chief of Staff Yuri Baluyevsky said. "We propose to make movement to this goal safer. . . . U.S. withdrawal from the ABM pact will not affect these relations of trust."

Two Wars

A new focus on counterterrorism could simplify future defense debates by stifling opposition to the decision by Rumsfeld to drop the Pentagon's decade-old goal of keeping U.S. forces ready to win two, nearly simultaneous regional wars in widely separated parts of the globe.

Although the Clinton administration embraced that goal, it also deployed forces in an array of other missions which, while individually much less demanding than a major war, added up to enough of a burden that the force could not meet its two-war goal. That shortfall provided ammunition for GOP critics, who contended that Clinton was frittering away the forces on peripheral missions.

However, Rumsfeld's new standard endorses the significance of less-than-war missions, calling for U.S. forces to be able to conduct several of them and defend the U.S. homeland while being able to win one major war and fend off a major attack on a U.S. ally in a second region. The new salience of homeland protection may undercut nascent opposition by some defense hard-liners to dropping the "two-war" goal. ◆

53

Arms for a New Kind of War

House, Senate tweak defense bill to make military more agile, effective against terrorists

The terrorist attacks bolstered Defense Secretary Donald H. Rumsfeld's argument that the defense establishment must retool to wage war against a wider variety of threats, but Congress had already started down that road.

Rumsfeld has tried to make the defense establishment focus more on non-traditional threats such as an attack on U.S. cities with chemical or biological weapons or an electronic assault on the nation's cybernetic nervous system.

The respective versions of the fiscal 2002 defense authorization bill, which the House took up Sept. 20 and the Senate began considering Sept. 21, made hundreds of changes to President Bush's $343 billion defense budget request.

Among the changes are accelerating efforts to make the combat forces more agile and beefing up work aimed at countering terrorist attacks, particularly those that might involve the use of chemical or biological weapons.

For example, the Senate bill (S 1438) includes $13 million to speed production of modular command posts that could be rolled into a transport plane and used to plan an attack while U.S. forces were en route to their target.

It also added $77 million to the $128 million requested to beef up security at Army bases, and it added $14 million to the budget for counterterrorism training for special forces. It also added $6 million to accelerate the purchase of hand-held explosive detectors that could screen people approaching a ship.

The House Armed Services Committee has proposed similar initiatives in its version of the bill (HR 2586). They included an addition of $19 million to the $20 million requested to develop a small, fast patrol boat and an addition of $9 million to develop a mobile chemical weapons detector to be used by Marine Corps teams trained to respond to chemical or biological terror attacks.

To be sure, neither committee proposed scrapping major existing weapons systems to free up funds for reshaping the force. But such tradeoffs may be less essential in the new budget environment. House Armed Services

> *"Because of the end of the Cold War, and because of the Gulf War which told people not to compete with armies, navies and air forces, countries do look for asymmetrical ways they can threaten the United States and Western countries."*
>
> —Donald H. Rumsfeld

Research and Development Subcommittee Chairman Duncan Hunter, R-Calif., has called for adding as much as $50 billion to the fiscal 2002 defense budget.

Budget Numbers

Both chambers aim to pass the defense authorization bill the week of Sept. 24, before agreement can be reached on a significant budget increase. But Hunter noted that a higher total could be incorporated into the subsequent House-Senate conference report on the bill. The real test will be whether the budget is increased in the companion defense appropriations bill, for which a markup has not yet been scheduled.

Among the contentious issues members jettisoned from the congressional agenda to close ranks behind Bush was a provision of the Democratic-sponsored Senate bill that would have let Congress block anti-missile tests that would violate the 1972 Anti-Ballistic Missile (ABM) Treaty.

Bush's budget request included $8.3 billion for missile defense, a large chunk of which was earmarked to accelerate development of a system intended to protect U.S. territory from a small number of missiles that might be launched by a radical state such as North Korea or Iraq.

Such a defense would abrogate the ABM Treaty, which Russia insists is the linchpin of strategic stability. Bush says he wants Russia's concurrence in supplanting the treaty with a new "strategic framework," but that he will pull the United States out of the pact rather than let it interfere with anti-missile tests, some of which the administration expects to "bump up against" the treaty within the next several months.

Senate Armed Services Chairman Carl Levin, D-Mich., and other Democrats contend that scrapping the treaty may provoke military and diplomatic responses by Russia, China and other countries, which would reduce U.S. security.

By a party-line vote, the Senate panel included in the version of the authorization bill approved Sept. 7 a Levin-sponsored provision that would bar anti-missile tests during fiscal 2002 that would violate the treaty, unless Congress approved them or the U.S. and Russian governments agreed to changes in the treaty that would allow the tests. Republicans threatened to veto the bill over the provision.

On Sept. 19, after Democrats agreed to drop the anti-missile test restriction, Levin introduced a bill (S 1416) that was identical to the committee-approved bill, with that provision removed. He also introduced the anti-missile test restriction as a free-standing measure (S 1439).

Levin insists that the current crisis may persuade Bush to slow the missile defense program so there will be more time to work with the Russian government on changes in the ABM Treaty that will allow robust testing while accommodating Russia's view that the treaty remains the linchpin of U.S.-Russian strategic relations.

"In this setting, when they realize how important it is that we be part of a coalition," Levin said in an interview Sept. 21, "I think they're going to be a little less likely to break that treaty quickly."

Democrats in both chambers also scaled back their efforts to cut Bush's $8.3 billion anti-missile budget.

The Senate committee had cut $1.3 billion from that amount. But on Sept. 21, leaders of the two parties agreed to allow Bush to decide how to allocate the $1.3 billion between missile defense and counterterrorism.

In the House, the Armed Services Committee had trimmed $135 million from the request in its version of the authorization bill (HR 2586). Democrats led by John M. Spratt Jr. of South Carolina and Ike Skelton of Missouri had planned to offer an amendment to transfer $918 million from missile defense work to other parts of the defense budget. But on Sept. 20, Republican and Democratic leaders agreed on a compromise amendment that would reduce the total missile defense authorization to $7.8 billion.

Rumsfeld's Review

Rumsfeld has pressed the military to make conventional combat units more mobile and agile by using networks of sensors, computers, robot weapons and precision-guided munitions that could supplant some of the 70-ton tanks, $5 billion aircraft carriers and fighter planes that are the centerpieces of the current force. (*2001 CQ Weekly, p. 1054*)

The terrorist attacks altered the politics of the defense debate by making far more money available for defense than had seemed remotely possible only a day before. But Rumsfeld also is using the incident to buttress his more fundamental argument that the military must change.

The attacks highlighted the country's susceptibility to the catastrophic damage that could be caused by a wide range of non-traditional attacks.

"Because of the end of the Cold War, and because of the Gulf War which told people not to compete with armies,

Levin Drops Missile Test Curb

Even before the terrorist attacks prompted Congress to drop contentious issues and back President Bush, Democrats hoping to block anti-missile tests that would violate the 1972 ABM Treaty faced an uphill battle. But Senate Armed Services Committee Chairman Carl Levin, D-Mich., gave them a shot by including a provision in the defense authorization bill that would require congressional approval for any anti-missile test that would violate the treaty.

Because the administration has not produced a promised description of which scheduled tests would conflict with the treaty, Levin framed the issue as an effort to protect Congress' right to know how money it appropriated was being used.

Armed Services Chairman Carl Levin

All that changed on Sept. 11 after which national unity trumped a rancorous fight over the ABM Treaty, in Levin's mind:

"We have a wartime Congress here now," Levin said in an interview Sept. 21. "That means we've either got to come together on issues, or we've got to defer them."

Levin's decision to shelve the treaty fight is accepted as realistic by prominent liberal activists who laud his blend of principle and pragmatism. "There are a lot of liberals whose idea of legislation is to stand up on the Senate floor, offer an amendment, give a 15-minute speech, and that's it," says John D. Isaacs, president of the Council for a Livable World. "Levin has always been a legislator who wants to win."

Back home, GOP leaders have been beating the bushes for months to find a candidate to run against the popular incumbent in 2002, hoping as recently as this summer to enlist Michael Skupin, a contestant in the reality TV show "Survivor II." While solidly in the liberal Democratic mainstream on most issues, Levin typically has operated within the Armed Services Committee's pro-defense consensus, which fractured untypically this year on the treaty issue.

Levin's stance on missile defense and other national security issues may come under more scrutiny than usual next year if the state GOP nominates State Representative Andrew Raczkowski, an Army reservist who may volunteer for active duty in the current crisis. However, Bill Ballenger, publisher of the newsletter "Inside Michigan Politics," speculated that Levin's strong support for Bush since the Sept. 11 attack would insulate him, politically: "It's a potential problem, but I doubt that it's an actual problem," Ballenger said in an inteview. "He's pretty much snuffing it out right now."

Given the extraordinary degree of party unity on both sides of the ABM Treaty issue, the likelihood that the restriction would become law was slim from the outset. Defense Secretary Donald H. Rumsfeld promised to recommend that Bush veto the authorization bill if it included the test restriction.

navies and air forces, countries do look for asymmetrical ways they can threaten the United States and Western countries," Rumsfeld said in a Sept. 20 news conference.

"We have to recognize the magnitude of the threat," he said, "and the extent to which people are willing to give their lives, as these pilots of these airplanes did, and impose damage on us." ◆

Embracing Homeland Defense

Congress moves to put its stamp on new security office and affirm Ridge's powers

Congress has been clamoring for years to have a single person in the federal government lead the fight against terrorism. Now that President Bush has tapped Pennsylvania Republican Gov. Tom Ridge as his point man, lawmakers promised to move quickly to ensure that Ridge has effective tools to defend against terrorism.

As the focus has shifted fundamentally to counterterrorism and U.S. intelligence-gathering following the Sept. 11 attacks, the Bush administration and Congress have stepped up their efforts, with once-dormant ideas revived and leaders taking charge.

"I've said a million times that the only thing that's changed [since the attacks] is not my message, it's my audience," said Porter J. Goss, R-Fla., chairman of the House Intelligence Committee and a former CIA agent. "It's now broader and deeper."

Bush announced Sept. 20 that he was creating a new, Cabinet-level post to centralize and coordinate the counterterrorism efforts of 40 agencies and departments.

Ridge, a Vietnam veteran and former House member (1983-95), will head the Office of Homeland Security — a post several in Congress have sought for years.

"He will lead, oversee and coordinate a comprehensive national strategy to safeguard our country against terrorism and respond to any attacks that may come," Bush said in a speech to a joint session of Congress.

Lawmakers who have pressed for such an appointment said it is important to pass legislation putting a congressional imprimatur on the Cabinet post as well as to ensure that Ridge has the power to carry out his formidable job.

"I'm not sure that without legislation he would have all the authority he needs to do all the things that might be necessary, such as changing the budget components for various agencies," Fred Thompson, R-Tenn., the ranking member on the Senate Governmental Affairs Committee, said Sept. 21.

Reflecting that concern, Senate Intelligence Committee Chairman Bob Graham, D-Fla., introduced legislation Sept. 21 that would make the head of the new office subject to Senate confirmation and ensure that the office has the authority to put together counterterrorism budgets.

"We want to build on what the president has done," Graham said.

Governmental Affairs Chairman Joseph I. Lieberman, D-Conn., also plans to introduce his own legislation in the coming weeks to establish a homeland security office.

Lieberman said Ridge's appointment was "a very good first step, but we're still not clear on what the content of the agency is, or his authority."

The White House appeared resistant to congressional action, saying the president had the authority to create a Cabinet-level position without Senate confirmation.

Streamlining Legislation

The legislative activity on the new security office was just one reflection of the congressional imperative to combat terrorism and improve intelligence gathering after the World Trade Center and Pentagon attacks. House and Senate leaders grabbed the initiative with an eye on maximizing cooperation with the White House and reducing the likelihood of institutional turf battles.

Counterterrorism has been the subject of countless committee hearings and several high-level commission reports, but relatively little recent legislative action. Lawmakers expressed the hope that they could eventually find unanimity as the United States faces down a non-traditional and stealthy adversary. (*2001 CQ Weekly, p. 2145*)

"Again and again, we have seen this problem rear its ugly head, and I think again and again, we have not mounted an adequate response," said House Minority Leader Richard A. Gephardt, D-Mo. "This is the time for us to respond."

In the House, Speaker J. Dennis Hastert, R-Ill., took a working group on terrorism that he had formed earlier this year and made it a subcommittee of the House Intelligence Committee, with the power to subpoena witnesses. Members of the nine-member panel of Intelligence Committee members planned a series of public hearings beginning Sept. 26 for the purpose of developing legislation later this year.

The panel will coordinate all committees of jurisdiction in the House, said Rep. Saxby Chambliss, R-Ga., the new subcommittee's chairman.

"We're not going to limit, but we need to coordinate the direction in which they go . . . and avoid duplication as much as possible," Chambliss said Sept. 20.

In the Senate, Majority Leader Tom Daschle, D-S.D., and Minority Leader Trent Lott, R-Miss., were poised to create a "super committee" that would minimize possible friction among the six Senate panels with a piece of the issue, with the likelihood that the two leaders would be in charge.

"Tom and I may have to do it ourselves," Lott said Sept. 19. "There's clearly a need for some better coordination."

In addition to improving coordination within the federal government

Relevant Committees

Complicating the congressional effort to aid the U.S. fight against terrorism is the number of committees with oversight responsibility. Here is the list of the panels with a say on the issue:

SENATE	HOUSE
•Appropriations	•Appropriations
•Armed Services	•Armed Services
•Foreign Relations	•Government Reform
•Governmental Affairs	•International Relations
•Judiciary	•Judiciary
•Intelligence	•Intelligence
	•Transportation & Infrastructure

and Congress, lawmakers stressed the need for comprehensive legislation to revamp U.S. intelligence-gathering and counterterrorism efforts, from improving electronic eavesdropping to easing restrictions on recruitment of spies with questionable backgrounds.

Graham introduced a second bill Sept. 21 that would change several laws, including the Foreign Intelligence Surveillance Act (FISA) of 1978, in an attempt to enhance the ability to infiltrate terrorist "cells" and collect information.

The bill would try to close legal loopholes that allow spies and terrorists to escape wiretaps by switching phones.

It also would seek to make it easier to wiretap suspected terrorists who were using computers and would establish a national center for foreign-language translators to help in the investigation of terrorist acts.

Intelligence Committee member Dianne Feinstein, D-Calif., a co-sponsor of Graham's bill, said intelligence agencies are not properly set up to share information rapidly among themselves.

"Now is the time to give our intelligence effort the coordination, the structure, the ability to really develop intelligence and communicate it properly and rapidly," said Feinstein, chairman of the Senate Judiciary Subcommittee on Technology, Terrorism and Government Information.

Senate Ready for Action

In a reversal of their traditional roles, the Senate appeared more eager than the House to pass comprehensive anti-terrorism legislation quickly. House leaders indicated that they will deal with the issue in stages, with the most popular provisions handled immediately and more controversial items put off to a later date.

"The counterterrorism package is something we need to weigh and to do a regular order on as much as possible," Hastert said. "And if we can get agreement on a good part of the package, we

ought to do it. If there's some things we don't have agreement on, we need to take them through the process."

Several Senate committee chairmen, by contrast, looked to move rapidly. Judiciary Committee Chairman Patrick J. Leahy, D-Vt., exchanged legislative proposals Sept. 19 with Attorney General John Ashcroft on expanding law enforcement's ability to fight terrorism.

In an interview, Daschle promised that Democrats "are going to try to work in concert with the administration before we [senators] take any unilateral action on terrorism."

However, lawmakers remained eager to act. In the House, the Transportation and Infrastructure Committee's Subcommittee on Economic Development, Public Buildings and Emergency Management did move on terrorism-related legislation Sept. 20, working in concert with the White House.

Initially, the measure (HR 525) would have created a President's Council on Domestic Terrorism Preparedness to coordinate federal, state and local anti-terrorism efforts and to develop a national strategy on terrorism.

Responding to the Bush administration's request, the panel adopted a substitute amendment by voice vote that would have the council draw up a national strategy and set policies but leave the coordination to an Office of National Preparedness within the Federal Emergency Management Agency.

The subcommittee's action, however, may have suddenly been rendered moot by creation of the Cabinet-level post.

The next terrorism-related legislation on the House agenda is the fiscal 2002 measure authorizing spending and setting priorities for the CIA and other intelligence agencies. The House Intelligence Committee plans to mark up the authorization bill the week of Sept. 24.

Goss said the legislation would closely follow the Senate Intelligence Committee's authorization bill (S 1428

— S Rept 107-63) approved earlier this month.

The Senate committee focused on four areas that many lawmakers agree need an infusion of cash: hiring more spies; improving electronic eavesdropping; increasing research and development; and improving the analysis of intelligence data. (*2001 CQ Weekly, p. 2081*)

One area Goss said he hopes to address is the recruitment and use of foreign agents with questionable backgrounds. During the mid-1990s, former Director of Central Intelligence John M. Deutch ordered the CIA to review all its contacts and operations to determine if any involved links to human rights abuses.

The spy agency subsequently developed guidelines that require field officers to obtain approval from headquarters before establishing a relationship with an individual who had engaged in disreputable activity.

Many lawmakers say those guidelines must be removed to gain better intelligence. Senate Intelligence member Jon Kyl, R-Ariz., won approval Sept. 13 of an amendment to the fiscal 2002 spending bill for the departments of Commerce, Justice and State (HR 2500) that rescinds the guidelines. (*2001 CQ Weekly, p. 2155*)

However, other lawmakers and the CIA said the guidelines have not been a hindrance to obtaining information.

"They do not prevent us from engaging people in services that are useful to us," said Nancy Pelosi of California, the House Intelligence Committee's ranking Democrat.

Goss said the Intelligence Committee still needs to discuss other volatile issues to fight terrorism.

"This is a time where we need to talk about things like psychological warfare, disinformation operations — is that something we do? What do we do about encryption now? What do we do about international banking transactions?" ◆

Deal Clears Way for Final Passage Of Anti-Terrorism Legislation

Conferees agree to include money-laundering and sunset provisions

Quick **C**ontents

The House paved the way to a deal on anti-terrorism legislation by agreeing to include money-laundering provisions similar to the Senate's in a final bill. The Senate, in turn, agreed to a "sunset" on some provisions.

The already dwindling list of differences holding up a deal on anti-terrorism legislation all but evaporated amid the anthrax scare the week of Oct. 15, clearing the way for Congress to grant Attorney General John Ashcroft many of the broad new investigative powers he asked for a month ago.

Votes on a House-Senate compromise bill, which would expand law enforcement's power to eavesdrop on suspects, search property and track Internet communications, could come early the week of Oct. 22, with the legislation going to President Bush for his signature by the end of the week. The final breakthrough came with agreements by top negotiators to include language aimed at strengthening money-laundering laws, as well as a sunset provision that would end some of the new powers in 2005 unless Congress reauthorizes them.

For a time, the House and Senate seemed headed for a showdown over the legislation, with House members on the right and left warning that Ashcroft's proposals could threaten civil liberties. But faced with pressure from the Bush administration and FBI warnings of further terrorist attacks on U.S. soil, the House and Senate now are poised to give final approval to legislation that closely tracks the Senate-approved bill (S 1510) and the Bush administration's proposals.

The threat of anthrax added even more urgency to the push to get the anti-terrorism legislation through, said Orrin G. Hatch of Utah, ranking Republican on the Senate Judiciary Committee and one of the cosponsors of the Senate bill.

"We can't wait another week for this," Hatch said on Oct. 18. "Look what's happening. We need to use whatever tools are available to counter terrorism."

The House will take up the anti-terrorism legislation early in the week, said John Feehery, spokesman for Speaker J. Dennis Hastert, R-Ill.

"There's a lot of cases that could be closed and people arrested if we make these changes," Feehery said. "It's of critical importance that we move expeditiously."

Even members of the House Judiciary Committee who had said that Ashcroft's proposal overreached now support the bill. Among them is Christopher B. Cannon, R-Utah, who said he stands behind the compromise legislation.

"There are many people who are committed to our destruction," he said. "We need to find these people and we need to stop them."

Without the anti-terrorism legislation, Cannon said, he fears law enforcement agents will not have the arsenal they need to identify and deter terrorists.

Senate and House leaders, as well as chairmen and ranking members of the House and Senate Judiciary committees, met the week of Oct. 15 with the goal of passing final legislation before the weekend. House and Senate aides continued to draft the final language even after the closure of the House on Oct. 17, although the abrupt end to the work week killed any chance of a final vote on the bill until at least Oct. 23. Negotiators announced Oct. 18 that they had reached a deal.

"We're now at the point simply where we're drafting," said Patrick J. Leahy, D-Vt.,

The Makings of a Deal

Here are highlights of the agreement on anti-terrorism legislation:

What's In:

• **Sunset:** Some search and surveillance powers would end in 2005 unless Congress reauthorized them. Ongoing investigations could continue under the expanded powers. The sunset would not apply to provisions expanding the reach of some surveillance tools to the Internet.

• **Money-laundering provisions:** The final money-laundering language would be nearly identical to provisions in the Senate-passed anti-terrorism bill. House leaders had wanted a separate bill.

• **Secret searches:** The House and Senate agreed to allow investigators to conduct more searches without notifying the suspect.

• **Bio-terrorism:** It would be a crime for certain people, including non-resident aliens, to possess harmful biological agents and toxins. No one could have such materials unless "reasonably justified by a peaceful purpose." These provisions were not in the House bill.

What's Out:

• **Changes to the McDade law:** The Senate dropped a provision that would have made federal prosecutors subject to ethics laws of federal districts rather than states, as now required by the McDade law. The law is named after former Rep. Joseph M. McDade, R-Pa. (1963-99), who was investigated by the FBI but acquitted at his 1996 bribery trial. (*1996 Almanac, p. 1-35*) chairman of the Senate Judiciary Committee. "It's not the easiest thing in the world with all the offices closed down."

Among the biggest differences between the House bill (HR 2975) and the Senate's was the sunset provision. The House included a sunset; the Senate did not. Negotiators ultimately agreed to make some search and surveillance provisions expire after four years. Officials with the Bush administration, which had opposed a sunset of any kind, signed off on the deal, according to a Democratic aide to the Senate Judiciary Committee.

Staff aides drafted language late in the week that would exempt or grandfather ongoing investigations, allowing them to continue under the expanded surveillance authority even if Congress opted to change any of the provisions in 2005. The grandfather clause will be narrow enough to ensure that ongoing investigations could not go on indefinitely, a House Republican aide said.

At least as significant for the final deal, however, was the agreement to roll money-laundering provisions into the final anti-terrorism bill.

Money Laundering

The last real obstacle to finishing the talks was officially removed Oct. 17 when the House passed a money-laundering bill (HR 3004) with provisions matching ones the Senate had included in its broader anti-terrorism bill. The overwhelming House vote, 412-1, belied the complexity of bringing the bill to the floor or the controversy associated with it.

The measure had emerged from the Financial Services Committee on a 62-1 vote Oct. 11, but its potential to curb profitable banking practices and impose new recordkeeping requirements kept industry support lukewarm at best. House GOP leaders — who had prevented a similar bill from reaching the floor last year — had kept the money-laundering bill separate from the anti-terrorism bill that passed Oct. 12. *(2001 CQ Weekly, p. 2399)*

On the other side of the Capitol, however, Senate Majority Leader Tom Daschle, D-S.D., was adamant that the provisions would be included in the final anti-terrorism bill. In the end, the lopsided House vote — and changes made to the money-laundering bill on the floor — erased any lingering controversy that had threatened to keep the provi-

sions out of the anti-terrorism package.

Measures to combat money-laundering usually are aimed at detecting profits from schemes run by drug traffickers and organized crime. In the wake of the Sept. 11 attacks, lawmak-

> *"There are many people who are committed to our destruction. We need to find these people and we need to stop them."*
> —Christopher B. Cannon, R-Utah

ers and the Bush administration have increasingly focused on the ability of terrorist organizations to fund themselves through surreptitious movements of cash throughout the global financial system, including U.S. banks.

To ease a final deal with the Senate, the House dropped a contentious provision of its money-laundering bill that would have banned Internet gambling businesses from accepting payments via credit cards, checks or electronic funds transfers for unlawful gambling.

The House also dropped a provision that would have allowed the Customs Service to search outbound international mail without a warrant and one that would have forced failed businesses to report receipts exceeding $10,000 to the Internal Revenue Service to forfeit property involved in the offense.

Removed, too, was a House provision that would have made it a crime to transport more than $10,000 in illegal proceeds across state lines.

Sources said Oct. 19 that negotiators had ironed out the last differences in the money-laundering language.

Both the House and Senate would ban the undeclared movement of more than $10,000 across U.S. borders. They would give the Treasury Department new tools to track and investigate foreign financial institutions, accounts and transactions deemed to be of "pri-

mary money-laundering concern," or especially prone to money laundering.

U.S. banks maintaining private accounts for foreign individuals would be required to take steps to identify the accounts' owners and the source of the deposited funds, and to report suspicious transactions, although it was not yet clear how large an account would have to be to fall under the new rules.

Securities brokers and dealers also would have to report suspicious transactions to the federal government.

U.S. banks would be prohibited from offering correspondent accounts, which can be used for wire transfers and currency exchanges, to foreign "shell" banks with no physical presence. Banks, however, could offer the accounts to shell banks affiliated with foreign financial institutions that have physical presences.

Moving to Final Passage

The broader anti-terrorism package that negotiators agreed on would give law enforcement agents new tools to eavesdrop on suspects, conduct searches and track Internet communication.

In foreign intelligence cases, investigators would be allowed to use "roving wiretaps," which are linked to suspects rather than individual telephone lines. In nationwide investigations, investigators could get a single warrant or court order for searches and some electronic surveillance that would be good anywhere in the country. They could conduct "sneak-and-peek" searches, done without first notifying suspects.

Leahy and other negotiators said they expected the bill to move quickly to final passage when Congress reconvenes. The Senate could amend the House bill, pass it and then send it to the House for a final vote. But that method would not allow for a conference report detailing the legislative intent behind the final package, which courts examine when laws face constitutional challenges.

For that reason, lawmakers expect to meet formally in a conference committee over the House bill. They already expect legal challenges.

"There will be a full conference," Hatch said.

But Hatch added he expects the conference to be abbreviated, with negotiators likely meeting only once to approve a report on the legislation.

"There's no reason to get in there and blab about this," he said. ◆

Defense Bill Wins Solid House Passage; Side Issues Delay Senate Action

House moves $400 million from missile defense to counterterrorism but leaves base-closing debate for conference

As Congress put aside contentious debates over defense policy in the wake of the Sept. 11 terrorist attacks, the House and Senate moved quickly the week of Sept. 24 toward passage of a $343 billion defense authorization bill that would make hundreds of minor changes in President Bush's fiscal 2002 budget request.

But while the House passed its version (HR 2586) on Sept. 25 by a vote of 398-17, Senate action on its version of the bill (S 1438) was blocked until the week of Oct. 1 because of partisan differences over issues peripheral to the defense budget.

The Senate is slated to vote Oct. 2 on a Democratic cloture petition to prevent Republicans from trying to tack their energy proposals onto the defense bill. Republicans are using that threat to extract from reluctant Democrats a promise of action on the energy bill before the end of the year.

Also blocking Senate action is a battle between Phil Gramm, R-Texas, and Armed Services Committee Chairman Carl Levin, D-Mich., over Levin's effort to end the preferential treatment of federal prison work programs in selling furniture, office supplies and other items to federal agencies.

The prison industries issue may be resolved by the time the Senate returns to the bill, but the chamber may face additional battles over other amendments to the defense bill, including a proposal by Republican Jesse Helms of North Carolina to exempt U.S. military personnel from the jurisdiction of a proposed international criminal court.

Another amendment by Sam Brownback, R-Kan., to waive remaining sanctions on Pakistan also could delay the bill.

The terrorist attacks and subsequent push for bipartisanship significantly tamped down several defense issues that had the potential for triggering bruising battles.

Most significantly, Democrats abandoned, for now, any significant effort to rein in Bush's anti-missile defense pro-

> *"Now more than ever we should hold off further downsizing of our military infrastructure as we analyze how to fight the first war of the 21st century."*
>
> —Jim Bunning, R-Ky.

gram, for which he requested $8.3 billion in fiscal 2002. Days after the terrorist attacks, Senate Democrats dropped their effort to limit program tests that would violate the 1972 Anti-Ballistic Missile (ABM) Treaty.

And on Sept. 21, the Senate adopted by voice vote an amendment by Levin and ranking Armed Services Republican John W. Warner of Virginia that would restore $1.3 billion to the bill. Bush could use the money either to replace the $1.3 billion that Levin's committee cut from the anti-missile request or direct it toward anti-terrorist programs. (*2001 CQ Weekly, p. 2198*)

House Democrats abandoned plans for a $920 million cut in the anti-mis-

sile program, agreeing instead with Republicans on a $265 million reduction.

The mobilization of forces after Sept. 11 also headed off possible fights in both chambers over the Navy's training range on the Puerto Rican island of Vieques. Faced with mass protests against continued use of the range, Bush had announced June 14 that the Navy would pull out in May 2003. (*2001 CQ Weekly, p. 1457*)

The House Armed Services Committee included in its bill a provision that would prevent the Navy from giving up the range until a single substitute was found. The Senate Armed Services panel included no Vieques language in its bill, but a floor fight over the issue had seemed possible in both chambers. The steam went out of the issue, at least for now, when demonstrators on Vieques said they would not interfere with training by ships ordered to the Middle East in response to the attacks.

Base Closing

The most contentious floor fight over a defense issue in either chamber was over Bush's request to close unneeded military bases — something Congress denied President Bill Clinton for years.

The Senate's approval of additional base closures was the most recent skirmish in an ongoing political war.

Earlier this year, Bush and Defense Secretary Donald H. Rumsfeld pushed for more base closings, and the Senate Armed Services Committee included such a provision in its bill. (*2001 CQ Weekly, pp. 1651, 1988, 2079*)

For months, committee member Jim Bunning, R-Ky., had objected that the Pentagon could not document its claim that the earlier closings had saved money. The terrorist attacks buttressed the case against more closures, he told the Senate Sept. 24, because the Pentagon has not decided what new organizations or deployments might be needed in a stepped-up war against terrorism.

"Now more than ever we should hold off further downsizing of our military infrastructure as we analyze how to fight the first war of the 21st century," Bunning said.

Democrat Byron L. Dorgan of North Dakota, whose state is home to two Air Force bases that are among its largest employers, cited the softening economy as an additional argument against confronting localities with the threat of losing a major source of jobs.

"That message . . . to potential investors in literally hundreds of communities across this country [is] that you ought not make investments in those communities now," Dorgan warned. "It is as if you are painting a bull's eye on the front gate of every base."

But Levin and committee member John McCain, R-Ariz., who fought losing battles for base closures in recent years, countered that the terrorist attacks made it imperative that the Pentagon shed unneeded bases to free up money to improve other installations: "We are asking these men and women to live and work in facilities that are, at best, substandard, in some cases, absolutely abysmal because we have too many [bases]," McCain said.

Bunning's amendment was defeated by a vote of 53-47. Democrats supported the tabling motion, 31-19, while Republicans opposed it, 21-28. James M. Jeffords, I-Vt., supported the motion.

On June 7, 2000, the Senate had rejected a proposal for two additional base closing rounds by a vote of 35-63. Fourteen senators who had opposed the earlier proposal supported the current one by voting to table Bunning's amendment. The switchers included eight Republicans — five of whom serve on Armed Services — and six Democrats, conspicuously including Majority Leader Tom Daschle of South Dakota.

Ellsworth Air Force Base is one of the largest employers in Daschle's home state and he had opposed the Clinton administration's calls for additional base closings. However, Ellsworth's future began to look secure in June when the Bush administration announced that it was one of two bases at which B-1 bomber operations would be consolidated.

Base closings may be one of the most highly charged issues in the Senate-House conference on the defense bill, since the House has no language on the subject.

Four Base Realignment and Closure (BRAC) commissions (in 1988, 1991, 1993 and 1995) have closed 97 major domestic bases. Taking account of the up-front expense of moving units to new locations and environmental cleanup at the bases being closed, the net savings by 2001 totaled $14.5 billion and were expected to average $6 billion annually in the future, according to the Defense Department. (*1993 Almanac, p. 465; 1995 Almanac, p. 9-19*)

As the active-duty force continued shrinking to fewer than 1.5 million members — down by nearly 60 percent from its Vietnam War-era peak and about one-third smaller than when the first BRAC round was authorized in 1988 — the Clinton administration repeatedly asked Congress to authorize additional closures. Pentagon officials insisted they were wasting money by trying to maintain facilities that had at least 20 percent more capacity than was needed.

But Congress brushed aside those requests, contending that Clinton had politicized the process in 1995 by trying to preserve thousands of jobs at two huge Air Force maintenance facilities in vote-rich California and Texas.

Prison Manufacturing

The requirement that federal agencies, including the Defense Department, purchase items and services from federal prison work programs, if they are available, has been a perennial issue, with industry, small business and organized labor trying to break what they call an unfair monopoly.

Federal Prison Industries, a government corporation created in 1934, employs about 22,000 inmates in more than 100 prisons, which produce more than 100 types of products, from cleaning supplies to electronic components to commemorative trophies, under the brand name Unicor. In addition to making prisons easier to control by keeping the inmates occupied, the program is touted as a way to teach them marketable skills, generate revenue that offsets some of the cost of incarceration, and give inmates a modest income from which to pay court costs, penalties and restitution.

Barred by law from selling commercially, the system is supported by the requirement that, in effect, gives it the right of first refusal for providing any federal agency with any services or product in the prison industry system's catalogue. In 2000, the system had net sales of $546 million, but spent $411 million to buy raw material, supplies and services from private companies.

Gramm has been the prison industries' leading Senate ally, beating back efforts by Levin to eliminate the system's privileged status in selling to the Pentagon, which buys office furniture from 14 federal prison factories that employ 4,700 inmates in 11 states. Western Michigan is home to several of the country's largest office furniture manufacturers.

In 1999, the last time Levin tried to use the defense authorization bill (S 1059, PL 106-65) to move a provision that would have allowed private firms to compete with prison industries for government sales, Gramm won by the slimmest of margins: A Gramm amendment to strike the provision initially was rejected 49-51, but subsequently was adopted by voice vote after the Senate voted 51-49 to reconsider the issue. (*1999 CQ Almanac, p. 9-11*)

Levin included in the fiscal 2002 bill a similar provision allowing private firms to bid against Federal Prison Industries. Contending that Gramm was stalling Senate action on the bill, Warner, who supports Levin's position, took the unusual step of offering an amendment to eliminate the Levin provision and then moved to table his own amendment, which allowed him to end the delay.

This time, Gramm's position got swamped, with the Senate voting 74-24 to table Warner's amendment. Although Gramm refused to concede, Armed Services Committee sources said he and Levin will probably work out a compromise.

Other Senate Amendments

To clear the way for rebuilding the Pentagon, which was severely damaged by the terrorist attack, the Senate adopted by voice vote a Warner amendment repealing a cap of $1.1 billion on spending to renovate the building, which Congress included in the fiscal 1997 defense authorization bill (PL 104-201).

The limit was intended to control the cost of a reconstruction project slated to run through 2012. The first phase of the work was within days of being completed when a hijacked airliner crashed into the newly renovated section of the building. Some features of the reconstruction, such as the installation of shatterproof windows nearly two inches thick and reinforced walls and floors, are credited with reducing the number of casualties.

Repairs to the building may cost several hundred million dollars, but are not expected to delay the scheduled completion.

The Senate also adopted by voice vote an amendment by Armed Services Committee members Mary L. Landrieu, D-La., and Susan Collins, R-Maine, that would change a provision in the Pentagon's medical insurance program deemed particularly onerous to pregnant women. Under existing law, the wife of a service member can elect health care coverage that allows her to choose her own physician. But once it has been verified that she is pregnant, she may have to be treated by a doctor at a military hospital unless that facility certifies that it cannot accommodate her.

The Landrieu-Collins amendment would eliminate the requirement for a so-called certificate of non-availability, allowing a woman to continue seeing her own doctor through a pregnancy.

The Senate also adopted by voice vote several other non-controversial amendments:

• Pete V. Domenici, R-N.M., to provide $655 million through fiscal 2011 to compensate persons exposed to radiation as a result of nuclear weapons testing or uranium mining.

• Russell D. Feingold, D-Wis., requiring a report to Congress on technical problems with the V-22 Osprey tilt-rotor aircraft, before the currently suspended flight tests are resumed. Flight tests of the aircraft, which the Marines want to use as a troop carrier, were suspended late in 2000 after 23 people were killed in two crashes. (*2001 CQ Weekly, p. 615*)

House Version

The only openly contested issue during House action on the defense bill was the perennially contentious effort, pursued by administrations of both parties, to contract out to private companies some of the work currently performed by federal employees.

On Aug. 1, the House Armed Services Committee adopted by a vote of 34-25 an amendment by Neil Abercrombie, D-Hawaii, that would make it easier for federal employees to compete successfully with private companies for Defense Department work. An amendment that would eliminate the Abercrombie language and give the Pentagon more leeway to "contract out" government jobs was included with several non-controversial provisions in a so-called managers' amendment to the bill, which the House adopted by voice vote Sept. 25.

Immediately before the House voted on passage of the bill, Minority Whip David E. Bonior, D-Mich., offered a procedural motion that, in effect, would have reinstated the Abercrombie provision. Bonior's motion was rejected 197-221 on a vote that broke nearly along party lines.

The most contentious defense policy issue dealt with during House debate, funding for Bush's anti-missile defense program, was handled in a compromise amendment offered by House Armed Services Committee Chairman Bob Stump, R-Ariz. It was adopted by voice vote.

Before the Sept. 11 attacks, Armed Services member John M. Spratt Jr., D-S.C., and senior committee Democrat Ike Skelton of Missouri had planned to offer an amendment that would have cut $920 million from Bush's $8.3 billion anti-missile request, in addition to the $135 million that the Armed Services panel cut when it marked up the bill.

After the attacks, bipartisan negotiators agreed on the Stump amendment that would cut $265 million from missile defense and $135 million from the budget for consultants. That would result in a total reduction of $400 million from Bush's request (including the committee's reduction). The amendment also would add $400 million to the budget to beef up intelligence and anti-terrorism programs.

Reprising what has become an annual battle, the House rejected 199-217 an amendment by Loretta Sanchez, D-Calif., that would have allowed female service members or dependents stationed overseas to obtain privately funded abortions in local U.S. military hospitals.

The House adopted 242-173 an amendment by James A. Traficant Jr., D-Ohio, that would allow military personnel to be assigned to border patrol and customs duties, at the request of the attorney general and Treasury secretary. ◆

Political Participation

This section, presenting a range of articles on key components of electoral and party politics, is divided into two parts: elections, campaigns and voters; and political parties.

Redistricting is the main issue in the first part, which opens with stories on racial representation and party majorities in state legislatures. The first article examines the strategy of "packing"—redrawing district lines to create pockets of minority voters—which once was seen as a way to gain minority representation on Capitol Hill. Now lawmakers disagree over the value of packing and may take their debate to the courts. This article also provides extensive information on the history of redistricting.

The second article covers the struggle between the Democrats and the Republicans over redistricting in Georgia. The Democratic Party has long held a majority in the state and has increased its advantage by drawing new district boundaries. The Republicans are vying for more control, and the outcome will turn on the way new district maps are drawn.

The last article in this part addresses the tone of campaigning following the Sept. 11 terrorist attacks. As part of an attempt to return to normalcy, politicians resumed their campaigning, but seeking public office during a national emergency demanded that they stay sensitive to the public's mood and focus on new issue priorities.

The articles on political parties cover significant elections and retirements and record the progress of the Democratic majority in the Senate. Rep. Nancy Pelosi's election to the position of House Democratic whip—the number two spot behind Minority Leader Richard Gephardt—made her the top-ranking woman in congressional history and put her in an excellent position to contend for a higher national office.

Sen. Jesse Helms's retirement will spark a highly contested election for his seat in the Senate and leave an opening on the Foreign Relations Committee. As soon as Helms announced his retirement, speculation began about the effect his absence would have on the Republican Party in his home state of North Carolina and on Capitol Hill.

The final article in this section gives a detailed overview of Sen. Harry Reid's background and his current role in the Democratic majority as Tom Daschle's second in command. This article also offers insight into the development of Senate leadership.

New Twists
In the Old Debate
On Race and Representation

Democrats, hoping to make white-dominated districts more competitive, are fighting
GOP efforts to further concentrate minority voters. Ultimately, the courts may decide.

After running without major party opposition in 1998 and 2000, Democratic Rep. Robert C. Scott appears a sure bet for re-election next year. Yet Republicans in Virginia insist that Scott, the state's only African-American House member, needs their help.

Virginia GOP leaders — who controlled the state's redistricting this year — made a special point of maintaining a large black population majority in the 3rd District, which Scott has represented since his first election in 1992.

It is a natural outgrowth, they say, of the state's decision 10 years ago to "pack" black residents into the 3rd to give a black candidate such as Scott a strong chance of winning the seat. Before 1992, Virginia had not elected a black congressman for more than 100 years.

This time, however, Scott and Virginia Democrats are crying foul — and are preparing to go to court to block the new map. They insist the Republicans are less concerned with Scott's security than with harming Democrats' chances in the neighboring 4th District, which would lose thousands of black constituents to the 3rd.

"By packing in the 3rd District," Scott complained, "you've essentially eliminated the opportunity of minority voters in the 4th to elect a candidate of their choice."

The political dynamics are changing on the issue of district "packing," the concentrating of minority voters into districts to make them more likely to

elect minority representatives.

Although black and Hispanic activists once supported that approach, Scott and many of his fellow minority incumbents now insist they do not need the extra help.

Of the 56 black and Hispanic members of Congress — all but three of whom represent districts in which minorities make up most of the population — 51 won their seats in 2000 with 60 percent or more of the vote. Only one received less than 55 percent.

Scott, for instance, has made himself popular across racial and party lines with his attention to local interests, including the 3rd District's economically crucial defense industry.

The increasing ability of black and Hispanic incumbents to win with modest majorities or even bare pluralities of minority population has emboldened them to lower their thresholds for what constitutes a minority-influenced district — one in which minorities wield significant political power.

What is more important, they now say, is to spread the wealth by making white-majority districts more racially diverse — giving non-incumbent minority candidates a better chance for victory.

During Virginia's GOP-dominated redistricting process, Scott favored a plan that would reduce the black population of his district from 57 percent to 49 percent, while raising the black portion of the 4th District's population from 39 percent to 53 percent.

Scott speculated that the plan, which the legislature declined to consider, would enable minorities to "elect

a candidate of their choice by 15 to 20 percentage points in both districts."

It is the Republican Party, meanwhile, that has become the primary advocate of beefing up the existing "minority-majority" districts and creating new ones. The roles of the parties have essentially flipped over the years since the Voting Rights Act of 1965 made increased minority political participation a national priority.

"So, there was political pressure within the Republican Party to ensure that minorities could elect representatives of their choice and that the promise of the Voting Rights Act was fulfilled," said Donald McGahn, general counsel of the National Republican Congressional Committee. "Guilty as charged. . . . Should we not do that?"

Tom DeLay of Texas, the House majority whip, testified in April before a redistricting committee in his home state that "GOP members are supporting the Voting Rights Act." DeLay went on to accuse Democrats of "destroying the Voting Rights Act."

Republican Gains

There are 37 African-Americans and 19 Hispanics in the 107th Congress, up from 17 blacks and only five Hispanics prior to 1992 redistricting. Leaders of both major parties say they want to increase those numbers further.

But Republicans and Democrats have different prescriptions for making it happen, raising the likelihood that the redistricting dilemma will end up where it did in the 1990s: the courts.

In that era, federal judges forced

Scott (center left), shown with the Democratic candidate for governor, Mark Warner (center right), opposed a GOP map that retained his district's black majority. He argues the Republicans' map would hurt Democrats' chances in a neighboring district.

alterations in seven states where congressional district maps were drawn following the 1990 census: Florida, Georgia, Louisiana, New York, North Carolina (twice), Texas and Virginia. The courts struck down each state's original redistricting plan as "racial gerrymandering."

As the districts were being drawn, minority activists in several states joined with Republicans in pushing for more minority-majority districts. But minority Democrats now see that these actions also created more conservative-leaning white-majority districts — and helped Republicans gain a House majority in 1994.

For example, in Georgia and North Carolina, where Republicans and minority activists backed plans that created new black-majority districts, the House delegations subsequently went from majority Democratic to majority Republican. Florida, another state where a GOP-black coalition formed, went from 10-9 Republican before the 1992 election to 15-8 Republican today.

Minority activists now denounce the GOP's posture as a scheme to bolster its control of the House.

In Virginia, Democrats note that the new district map written by state GOP leaders this year reduces the black population in 4th District from 39 percent of the total under the current lines to 34 percent.

Democrats argue that Republicans are shrinking the 4th's black population to shore up Rep. Randy Forbes, a white Republican. Forbes defeated an African-American Democrat, L. Louise Lucas, by 52 percent to 48 percent in a June special election to fill the seat of the late Norman Sisisky, a white Democrat.

This kind of demographic change, say critics, violates Section 5 of the Voting Rights Act, which bars certain jurisdictions (mainly in the South) from lessening the political influence of minorities.

And they say it violates Section 2, which applies nationwide and says that the right to vote has been abridged or denied if members of a racial or language minority group "have less opportunity than other members of the electorate to participate in the political process and to elect representatives of their choice."

Another state exhibiting partisan differences over minority redistricting is Texas. A proposal by Republican state Sen. Jeff Wentworth would provide more opportunities for both blacks and members of the state's exploding Hispanic population to win House seats. But it would do so by removing heavily Democratic minority constituencies from the districts of Democratic incumbents, such as Martin Frost in the 24th district and Ken Bentsen in the 25th.

Frost, the House Democratic Caucus chairman who also chairs the Democratic redistricting unit IMPAC

2000, charged that Republicans are "once again working to dilute African-American and Hispanic voting strength in a number of states," adding, "They're not a friend to minorities."

Republicans point to the Voting Rights Act and subsequent court rulings that upheld the concept of packing minorities into single congressional districts so long as that was not the sole criterion used for redistricting.

"Look at Bobby Scott of Virginia," said McGahn of the NRCC. "When was the last time an African-American was elected to the House out of Virginia? Do you want to go back to 1891?"

Moving Into the Suburbs

The partisan impact of redistricting creates a dilemma for blacks, Hispanics and the Democratic Party.

Because a majority of blacks and Hispanics have long backed their party, Democrats once took the lead in calling for districts, mainly in big cities, in which minorities were the dominant constituencies.

But economic gains over the past decade have enabled many blacks and Hispanics to move out of the inner cities and into mixed-race suburbs. The removal of legal and social barriers to political participation made minority voters increasingly vital to many white Democratic House members. These incumbents became loath to lose their minority support bases, even for

Black and Hispanic Members' Districts

The following are the 37 black members and 19 Hispanic members of the House, with their districts ranked from the least non-Hispanic white population to the most, according to the 2000 census. District figures do not add to 100 percent because of the presence of other racial groups; numbers reflect persons identified as being of one race.

State, District	Member (Party)	Ethnic Group	Non-Hispanic White Pop.	Non-Hispanic Black Pop.	Hispanic Population
New York 16	José E. Serrano (D)	Hispanic	2.4%	30.3%	62.9%
California 33	Lucille Roybal-Allard (D)	Hispanic	5.1	3.6	86.0
California 35	Maxine Waters (D)	Black	5.6	33.9	54.2
California 37	Juanita Millender-McDonald (D)	Black	6.1	25.4	57.2
California 31	Hilda L. Solis (D)	Hispanic	9.9	1.1	59.4
Florida 17	Carrie P. Meek (D)	Black	9.9	58.3	27.4
California 30	Xavier Becerra (D)	Hispanic	11.4	2.7	64.3
New York 6	Gregory W. Meeks (D)	Black	11.5	50.7	18.1
New York 15	Charles B. Rangel (D)	Black	12.2	32.4	50.5
Illinois 2	Jesse L. Jackson Jr. (D)	Black	15.2	75.3	7.8
California 34	Grace F. Napolitano (D)	Hispanic	15.4	1.7	72.4
New York 10	Edolphus Towns (D)	Black	15.8	61.0	17.1
Florida 21	Lincoln Diaz-Balart (R)	Hispanic	16.3	3.7	77.5
Michigan 14	John Conyers Jr. (D)	Black	16.4	78.6	1.2
New York 11	Major R. Owens (D)	Black	16.5	65.6	10.8
Texas 16	Silvestre Reyes (D)	Hispanic	17.2	2.7	78.0
New Jersey 10	Donald M. Payne (D)	Black	18.1	59.7	15.8
Maryland 4	Albert R. Wynn (D)	Black	18.3	64.1	10.0
Illinois 4	Luis V. Gutierrez (D)	Hispanic	18.4	7.5	70.1
Texas 15	Rubén Hinojosa (D)	Hispanic	18.4	1.6	78.9
Michigan 15	Carolyn Cheeks Kilpatrick (D)	Black	18.5	69.5	8.2
California 46	Loretta Sanchez (D)	Hispanic	19.0	1.5	62.3
California 32	Diane Watson (D)	Black	19.6	32.3	37.1
Illinois 1	Bobby L. Rush (D)	Black	19.9	69.9	7.5
Maryland 7	Elijah E. Cummings (D)	Black	20.9	74.3	1.3
New York 12	Nydia M. Velázquez (D)	Hispanic	21.1	10.4	48.6
Texas 18	Sheila Jackson-Lee (D)	Black	22.3	40.0	33.4
Texas 30	Eddie Bernice Johnson (D)	Black	22.5	38.9	34.7
Florida 18	Ileana Ros-Lehtinen (R)	Hispanic	23.6	3.8	70.5
Texas 20	Charlie Gonzalez (D)	Hispanic	24.6	5.5	67.0
Texas 28	Ciro D. Rodriguez (D)	Hispanic	25.3	7.9	65.0
Illinois 7	Danny K. Davis (D)	Black	25.7	62.9	5.2
Texas 27	Solomon P. Ortiz (D)	Hispanic	25.8	2.1	70.5
Louisiana 2	William J. Jefferson (D)	Black	26.1	66.4	3.6
Florida 23	Alcee L. Hastings (D)	Black	27.1	54.5	13.1
Arizona 2	Ed Pastor (D)	Hispanic	27.3	4.8	62.5
Alabama 7	Earl F. Hilliard (D)	Black	28.3	69.7	1.0
Pennsylvania 2	Chaka Fattah (D)	Black	28.7	63.9	2.0
Georgia 5	John Lewis (D)	Black	28.9	62.4	5.2
Tennessee 9	Harold E. Ford Jr. (D)	Black	29.1	65.9	2.8
Texas 23	Henry Bonilla (R)	Hispanic	29.2	2.5	66.3
California 42	Joe Baca (D)	Hispanic	30.4	12.0	50.8
Ohio 11	Stephanie Tubbs Jones (D)	Black	31.1	64.2	1.5
New Jersey 13	Robert Menendez (D)	Hispanic	32.2	11.4	47.2
Georgia 4	Cynthia A. McKinney (D)	Black	32.5	49.1	11.0
Mississippi 2	Bennie Thompson (D)	Black	33.0	64.9	1.2
California 9	Barbara Lee (D)	Black	34.8	25.7	17.3
Missouri 1	William Lacy Clay (D)	Black	36.0	59.7	1.2
South Carolina 6	James E. Clyburn (D)	Black	36.7	60.6	1.4
Virginia 3	Robert C. Scott (D)	Black	37.5	56.2	2.7
Florida 3	Corrine Brown (D)	Black	41.5	49.2	5.8
North Carolina 1	Eva Clayton (D)	Black	44.9	50.2	3.0
North Carolina 12	Melvin Watt (D)	Black	45.0	44.2	6.8
Georgia 2	Sanford D. Bishop Jr. (D)	Black	54.8	40.2	3.3
Indiana 10	Julia Carson (D)	Black	57.8	34.1	4.8
Oklahoma 4	J.C. Watts Jr. (R)	Black	77.1	7.4	5.7

White Members, Minority Constituents

The following are the 10 non-Hispanic white House members who represent the largest minority constituencies. While blacks and Hispanics make up most of the minority populations in districts held by black and Hispanic members, people of Asian heritage have significant presence in several districts held by non-Hispanic whites.

State, District	Member (Party)	White Non-Hispanic Population	Black Non-Hispanic Population	Hispanic Population	Asian Population
New York 17	Eliot L. Engel (D)	16.9%	40.3%	35.9%	3.4%
Hawaii 1	Neil Abercrombie (D)	18.5	2.0	5.4	52.8
Texas 29	Gene Green (D)	20.4	15.4	60.9	2.2
California 50	Bob Filner (D)	20.4	10.9	50.8	14.0
California 26	Howard L. Berman (D)	20.6	4.7	65.4	6.4
California 20	Cal Dooley (D)	23.8	5.5	63.7	4.5
California 16	Zoe Lofgren (D)	26.7	3.4	39.8	26.6
Pennsylvania 1	Robert A. Brady (D)	28.0	54.5	11.5	4.2
New York 7	Joseph Crowley (D)	32.8	7.8	39.1	16.7
California 13	Pete Stark (D)	35.1	7.1	22.1	29.9

the good intention of creating more minority-majority districts.

Meanwhile, as blacks and Hispanics have improved their numbers and clout in the House, they have become increasingly confident they can hold their seats with reduced minority support.

Four black House Democrats first elected in 1992 — Corrine Brown of Florida, Sanford D. Bishop Jr. and Cynthia A. McKinney of Georgia and Melvin Watt of North Carolina — continued to win despite court-ordered revisions that turned their districts from majority-black to majority-white.

Yet while those black incumbents were able to win after the black populations of their districts were reduced, it is still rare for minority newcomers to win in mostly white districts.

"The number of African-Americans needed for an African-American candidate to win is directly proportional to the number of white people who live in the district who are willing to vote for an African-American candidate," Watt said. He said the percentage of black voters who are needed in a particular district to elect a candidate of their choice will vary.

Watt said his 12th District has white liberals from Charlotte, Greensboro and Winston-Salem who are amenable to voting for a black candidate. But colleague Eva Clayton in the 1st needs more black voters, Watt said, because many of her white constituents are rural conservatives who are less inclined to vote for a black candidate.

Hispanics: Splitting the Parties

While African-Americans have voted consistently with Democrats, Hispanics have been more willing to give their support to Republican candidates. Still, Democrats are using redistricting to shore up their own Hispanic bases.

Hispanics, their numbers swelled by a huge upturn in immigration from Mexico and Central America, made up 12.5 percent of the U.S. population counted in the 2000 census. Yet just 4.4 percent of House seats are held by Hispanics.

But creating Hispanic-majority districts has proved trickier in some places than building black-majority districts. While African-Americans have tended to reside in large concentrations, Hispanic communities are scattered in a variety of urban and suburban pockets.

In February 1997, a three-judge federal panel ordered changes to New York's Hispanic-majority 12th District on grounds that race was the predominant factor in its drawing — a ruling the Supreme Court upheld in October 1997. The district rambled through the New York City boroughs of Manhattan, Brooklyn and Queens, picking up pockets — some very small — of Hispanic residents.

The most vexing challenge this year for lawmakers in states with large Hispanic populations may be California, where the Hispanic population has boomed to 11 million, or 32 percent of the state's total residents. The state's House 52-member House delegation now includes just six Hispanics, all Democrats: Joe Baca, Xavier Becerra, Grace F. Napolitano, Lucille Roybal-Allard, Loretta Sanchez and Hilda L. Solis.

Democrats control redistricting in California, which is slated to pick up a 53rd District as a result of the 2000 reapportionment. Party officials are trying to accommodate the desires of Hispanics — a major part of their voting coalition — for greater representation.

But party leaders also have to worry about undercutting the security of white Democratic incumbents who currently rely on large Hispanic constituencies.

California's 26th District has a larger Hispanic population (65 percent) than all but two districts in the State. It is represented by "Anglo" Democrat Howard L. Berman.

California's 20th District is 64 percent Hispanic. But it, too, is represented by a non-Hispanic white Democrat: six-term Rep. Cal Dooley. In 2000, Dooley edged Republican Rich Rodriguez, a Hispanic TV newsman, by 52 percent to 46 percent.

The effort to protect non-Hispanic white Democratic incumbents has irked some aspiring Hispanic candidates.

White Democratic Rep. Bob Filner's 50th District is 51 percent Hispanic. In 1992 and 1996, Filner defeated Democratic primary opponent Juan Vargas, a Hispanic who now is a member of the state House committee with jurisdiction over congressional redistricting.

Filner is lobbying the legislature hard to keep his district intact. Vargas

Despite Series of Court Rulings, State Officials Are Left Guessing

Through most of the nation's history, the Supreme Court addressed legislative redistricting with reluctance. Justice Felix Frankfurter wrote in 1946 that redistricting was a "political thicket" that "courts ought not to enter."

Times have changed, and Frankfurter's words have proved prophetic. Redistricting is a thicket, indeed.

The Supreme Court's "one man, one vote" ruling of 1962 and the federal government's enforcement of the Voting Rights Act of 1965 led to a surge in the number of districts designed to increase minority representation.

That, in turn, has led to a wave of lawsuits charging that states have gone too far, or not far enough, to accommodate minorities' political needs — and the judiciary has found itself increasingly involved in redistricting.

The trouble is, nearly a decade of rulings has left states as uncertain as ever about how to draw districts that satisfy the Voting Rights Act by providing opportunities for minorities to get elected, while still passing muster with the courts. Striking that balance seems as problematic as ever.

Over the past decade, federal courts required seven states to revise their district maps: North Carolina, Florida, Georgia, Louisiana, New York, Texas and Virginia. North Carolina had to redraw its map twice.

The plans that the court rejected contained districts, designed to elect black or Hispanic candidates to Congress, that had such contorted shapes they were denounced by critics as "bug splatters" and "Rorschach tests."

The rulings established a pair of broad principles for states to avoid the charge of "racial gerrymandering."

First, race cannot be the predominant consideration in drawing districts, unless a state can show a compelling reason for it. Otherwise, such districts — even those drawn to increase minority representation — violate the 14th Amendment's guarantee of equal protection, according to the courts.

The court has said, however, that if race is only one of many factors considered in drawing a district, then the state need not meet the same constitutional standard as it would if race was predominant.

The problem for state officials now redrawing districts based on the 2000 census is that the court has declined to give a clear definition or a statistical threshold to determine when and how race becomes the "predominant" factor in redistricting. The states want specific instructions, and the courts have not been forthcoming.

The justices' definition of racial gerrymandering seems akin to Justice Potter Stewart's famous 1964 description of pornography: "I know it when I see it."

Officials involved in the current redistricting in states with large minority populations complain that the ambiguity of court rulings has them expecting more lawsuits.

As North Carolina Sen. Brad Miller, a Democrat in charge of his chamber's redistricting efforts, told the Raleigh News and Observer: "If the Lord God Almighty threw down lightning bolts and carved plans into the side of Mount Mitchell, and we adopted them, there would still be challenges to redistricting under every legal theory devised."

Tarheel Sticking Points

Miller's home state produced the most prominent redistricting dispute from the 1990s — a nearly decade-long saga that forced two alterations to the state's district map.

The Supreme Court's first and last words on redistricting over the past decade involved the North Carolina dispute, which ended with a ruling only this April. The protracted legal battle served more to show how convoluted redistricting issues can be than to provide clear guidance to future congressional line-drawers.

When they began redrawing their state's congressional map in 1991, the Democrats who controlled the process in North Carolina were determined to correct a historical condition then common in many Southern states: No black candidate in North Carolina had been elected to Congress since 1901.

The first plan produced by North Carolina's lawmakers linked areas with largely black populations in the rural northeastern part of the state to create a black-majority 1st District.

But North Carolina is one of 16 states, most in the South, whose redistricting plans must be "pre-cleared" by the U.S. Justice Department under the Voting Rights Act because they have histories of racial discrimination. The Justice Department rejected North Carolina's first plan, along with its legislative district maps, saying they failed to provide opportunity for representation to minorities in southern and southeastern North Carolina.

In the 1980s, Justice was not as aggressive in pursuing a major expansion of districts with large minority populations. But the department took a much more activist approach during the round of redistricting that followed the 1990 census, requiring states to create more districts that maximized the voting strength of blacks and Hispanics — even if extraordinary efforts were necessary.

North Carolina's legislators drafted a new congressional map that, while keeping the black-majority 1st District, also created a black-majority 12th District in the Piedmont.

The 12th was artfully constructed. It was dubbed "the I-85 District" for the highway along which it snaked, sometimes narrowing to the width of the road.

The district linked parts of 10 counties, stitching together predomi-

NORTH CAROLINA

North Carolina's 12th District spurred the most protracted redistricting battle of the past decade. As drawn prior to the 1992 election (top map), the 12th snaked narrowly along Interstate 85 to create a black-majority district. A series of court rulings resulted in the redrawing of the district for the 1998 election and again for the 2000 election. The Supreme Court in April finally closed the books on the dispute by upholding the district shown in the bottom map, which follows a less convoluted path than the original. Black Democrat Melvin Watt has held the seat throughout the turmoil.

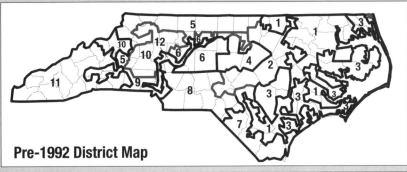

Pre-1992 District Map

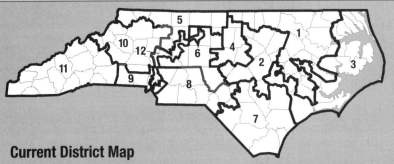

Current District Map

nantly black portions of Charlotte, Greensboro and Durham.

The map had its intended effect in 1992: The state elected two black House members, Democrats Eva Clayton in the 1st District and Melvin Watt in the 12th. But it also drew the wrath of a group of white residents, who sued to overturn the plan.

The plaintiffs argued that North Carolina's 1st and 12th districts virtually guaranteed that black candidates would be elected, and thus were racial gerrymanders that abridged the plaintiffs' 14th Amendment right to equal protection.

Backlash Strikes Twice

A U.S. District Court dismissed the lawsuit against the North Carolina map, but the Supreme Court sided with the plaintiffs in 1993 in a 5-4 ruling. Justice Sandra Day O'Connor wrote for the majority that the 12th District could be viewed only as "an effort to segregate the races for purposes of voting, without regard for

traditional districting principles." The court sent the case back to District Court for further consideration — virtually assuring that the controversy would return to the high court.

After the District Court upheld the two black-majority districts, the plaintiffs again appealed. In 1996, the Supreme Court struck down the North Carolina map, ruling — again 5-4 — that the map violated the 14th Amendment.

As ordered by the court, North Carolina issued a new map in 1997, giving the 12th District a less serpentine shape and reducing the black pluralities in the 1st and 12th districts.

Yet this was not enough to satisfy the plaintiffs. They sued again. And in April 1998, a U.S. District Court sided with them, finding that the new boundaries were not compact and that race was the predominant factor in their creation.

The ruling caused chaos that year by forcing yet another redrawing of the map and delaying the state's con-

gressional primary, scheduled for May 1998, until September.

Meanwhile, even as they prepared a new map and went ahead with the elections, North Carolina officials appealed the earlier lower-court ruling.

In 1999, the Supreme Court ruled that the District Court had not given adequate support for its ruling before the 1998 elections, and the justices sent the case back to the lower court once more for further consideration.

In March 2000, the District Court found again that the legislature was predominately motivated by race in drawing the 1997 lines.

Again, the state appealed, delaying the case until after the 2000 elections — the last before the state was to start the redistricting process all over again.

Still, state officials and others hoped the Supreme Court would use the case to set clear guidelines for what kind of districts it would accept in the next redistricting.

Instead, they got a status-quo ruling based on the same general principles previously stated by the court. On April 18, 2001, the Supreme Court again overturned the District Court's conclusions, saying that the plaintiffs failed to prove that race, rather than politics, was the predominant factor behind the 12th District.

"In a case such as this one," Justice Stephen G. Breyer wrote for the majority, "where majority-minority districts [or the approximate equivalent] are at issue and where racial identification correlates highly with political affiliation, the party attacking the legislatively drawn boundaries must show at the least the legislature could have achieved its legitimate political objectives in alternative ways that are comparably consistent with traditional districting principles."

Through it all, Watt and Clayton proved their political resilience, winning five House elections under different versions of the 1st and 12th districts' lines.

And North Carolina lawmakers are at it again now, drawing new lines based on new census numbers. They hope this time the first plan sticks.

LOUISIANA

Dubbed the "Z with drips," Louisiana's 4th District drawn prior to the 1992 election (left map) zigzagged through 28 parishes (counties); two-thirds of its residents were black, and black Democrat Cleo Fields was elected. Despite a minor revision prior to the 1994 election, a U.S. District Court panel ruled that the 4th was a racial gerrymander. A new map instituted in 1996 (right) completely dismantled the district, distributing its pieces to redesigned districts that had white majorities. Left with no strong base in which to run, Fields did not seek re-election in 1996.

Pre-1992 District Map

Current District Map

told the San Diego Union Tribune in May that Filner "is just one of the most selfish politicians I've ever met."

Hispanic Democratic activists are advancing a plan to increase Hispanic representation. A proposal by the Mexican American Legal Defense Fund and the William C. Velasquez Institute would create a new 53rd District in central California that is 47 percent Hispanic. Also, 38th District GOP Rep. Steve Horn, who won re-election by just 1,800 votes in 2000, would see the Hispanic population in his district rise from 40 percent to 69 percent.

Still, increasing Hispanic representation is complicated by the currently low levels of Hispanic voter registration and political participation. Roybal-Allard's 33rd District, the nation's most heavily Hispanic district (86 percent), cast only 76,762 votes for president in 2000, nearly 30,000 fewer than in the next lowest district in the nation.

Lots of Maps, Few Directions

As they draw new districts with blacks and Hispanics in mind, state officials have an eye on avoiding the battery of lawsuits that caused so much redistricting turmoil in the 1990s.

The court rulings overturning congressional district maps over the past

10 years were results of lawsuits brought by white voters who maintained that certain black- or Hispanic-majority districts violated their political rights to equal protection.

The Supreme Court, in a series of closely divided rulings, often agreed. The one guideline consistently laid out by the court is that states generally cannot use race as the predominant factor in drawing district lines. Doing so, whether to increase minority empowerment or to hinder it, is a violation of the equal protection clause of the Constitution, the court has ruled.

"Most of the decisions of the 1990s led mapmakers to think twice before maximizing minority districts and using race as a major factor," said Jeff Wice, a redistricting attorney who works for Democratic Party interests.

All of the plans that the court nixed over the past decade contained strangely shaped districts that rambled in many directions to incorporate disparate pockets of minority population. The court has upheld the constitutionality of other minority-majority districts.

Yet state officials complain that the courts' rulings otherwise provide them with little guidance on how to approach the minority redistricting issue — making another round of grueling

legal battles a near-certainty.

"The Supreme Court is so good at saying what you can't do rather than what you can do," said Richard K. Scher, a political scientist at the University of Florida.

The court has identified race-neutral criteria including "compactness, contiguity [and] respect for political subdivisions or communities defined by actual shared interests."

That position was reinforced in the court's latest redistricting ruling, which in April finally brought to a close a decade of dispute over the North Carolina district map. A group of plaintiffs, some of whom had participated in suits that overturned two previous versions of the North Carolina map, argued that the 12th District was constructed specifically to elect an African-American member (Democrat Watt).

Lawyers for the state replied that the main intent for the district's design was political rather than racial. In effect, the state argued that most of the Democratic voters who predominate in the district just happened to be African-Americans.

The Supreme Court, by a 5-4 vote, concurred with the state. Justice Stephen G. Breyer, writing in the majority opinion, said race did not pre-

FLORIDA

Florida's redistricting map drawn prior to the 1992 election included a black-majority 3rd District that elected black Democrat Corrine Brown. But a U.S. District Court panel in 1996 found that the wishbone-shaped 3rd (left map) — which rambled about 250 miles from Gainesville in the west to Jacksonville in the northeast then south to Orlando — was an unconstitutional racial gerrymander. Redrawn prior to the 1996 election, the 3rd (right map) — running from the Jacksonville area to Orlando — has a reduced black population; Brown continues to hold the seat.

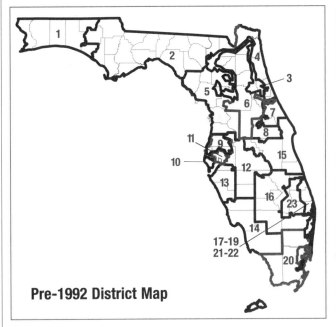

Pre-1992 District Map

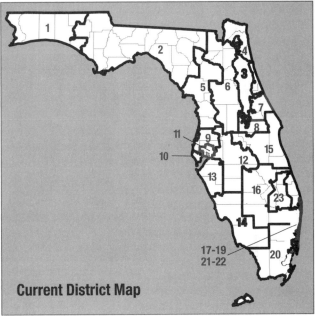

Current District Map

dominate in the redrawing of the 12th District because "race in this case correlates closely with political behavior."

The justices, however, have thus far eschewed laying out statistical thresholds or other specific criteria to define when a state has gone too far, or not far enough, in drawing districts that can be won by minority candidates.

Also clouding the picture for the states is the fact that the Bush administration has not yet established what approach its Justice Department will take on minority redistricting questions.

But the department's position is likely to be clarified soon. Virginia is expected by late August to submit its new map to the Justice Department, which then will have 60 days to evaluate it.

Under Section 5 of the Voting Rights Act, as amended in 1982, 16 states with histories of hindering minority political participation are required to "pre-clear" congressional and state legislative redistricting plans with the Justice Department or United States District Court for the District of Columbia.

The law covers nine whole states — Alabama, Alaska, Arizona, Georgia, Louisiana, Mississippi, South Carolina, Texas and Virginia — and parts of seven others: California, Florida, Michigan, New Hampshire, New York, North Carolina and South Dakota.

When a state submits its plan, Justice Department lawyers compare it to the current map to determine whether minority voting strength is reduced. The department must pre-clear the plan unless it finds it to be retrogressive.

Unfortunately for those state officials responsible for redistricting, the states cannot rely much on the department's actions in the past round of redistricting for direction.

After the 1990 census — during the tenure of President George Bush — Justice officials took the position that states should create any minority-majority district that they could and rejected several states' plans that they believed did not go far enough. But the revised plans enacted by the states contained many of the contorted districts that the Supreme Court ultimately ruled unconstitutional.

New Decision Favors Democrats

The first legal decision of the 2000 redistricting cycle, by a three-judge federal district court panel, appears to side with those who believe minority candidates do not necessarily need minority-majority constituencies to win.

A panel upheld a redistricting plan for the New Jersey Legislature that reduced the black voting-age population in one state legislative district from 53 percent to 27 percent. A group of Republicans had filed the suit on grounds that bloc voting was so prevalent among whites in those districts that blacks would not be able to elect a candidate of their choice.

The decision was a victory for New Jersey Democrats, who favored the plan because it dispersed black voters among several state House districts. The plan appears to give the Democrats an opportunity to win control of the state House, currently 45-35 Republican, in this year's state legislative elections.

"In that case, for the first time, you actually had black Democratic incumbents who were saying, 'We don't need all of these black voters,'" said David T. Canon, a political scientist at the University of Wisconsin at Madison.

Bernard N. Grofman, a political scientist at the University of California at Irvine, said the New Jersey court used what he calls a "functional test standard" that considered factors beyond racial population data, such as crossover voting patterns of white voters, to determine whether there was a realistic possibility that minority voters could elect a candidate of their choice.

"That's a very different analysis than just looking at the overall population proportion or overall registration proportion that is black," Grofman said. ◆

Georgia Remap Merges 2 GOP-Held Districts

Democrats also give selves apparent edge for two new seats

Georgia Democrats have been waiting for years to correct a congressional district map that backfired on them.

They appear to have done everything they can to accomplish that goal with a redistricting plan that was cleared by the Democratic-controlled state legislature Sept. 28 and signed into law by Democratic Gov. Roy Barnes on Oct. 1.

The map gives Democrats the advantage in the two new districts that fast-growing Georgia earned in the 2000 reapportionment. It also creates two other open seats — by merging four Republican incumbents into two districts.

"We are very encouraged by the map," said Kim Rubey, a spokeswoman for the Democratic Congressional Campaign Committee.

The map places Republican Rep. Saxby Chambliss in southeastern Georgia's 1st District, which also is home to Republican Rep. Jack Kingston — leading to speculation that at least one will run for the Senate or governor.

State lawmakers also rearranged the lines of GOP Rep. Bob Barr's district — so much so that Barr has decided to run in the adjacent, redesigned 7th District, where he likely will face a primary showdown with fellow Republican Rep. John Linder.

At the same time, the new map would protect the interests of the state's three African-American House incumbents — Sanford D. Bishop Jr., John Lewis and Cynthia A. McKinney — who were the only Democrats to benefit from the redistricting a decade ago.

Before the 1992 election, Democrats held nine of Georgia's 10 seats and controlled the state's redistricting process. But as party strategists redrew the map to incorporate a one-seat gain, they cut their margins too fine in several districts — in part because of pressure from the U.S. Justice Department, acting under the provisions of the Voting Rights Act, to create two new black-majority districts. The national GOP upswing in 1994 and Rep. Nathan Deal's 1995 switch from the Democratic Party boosted Georgia Republicans to the 8-3 edge they have held since.

The remap could allow Democrats to win as many as seven of the state's 13 districts. "If you look at the past voting behavior, Democrats ought to have seven fairly safe seats," said University of Georgia political scientist

Barr, shown at a 1999 Judiciary subcommittee hearing, has often battled with Democrats and expected a hard time in redistricting.

CQ FILE PHOTO

Charles Bullock.

To accomplish this, Democratic map-makers have given Republicans a virtual lock on the other six districts by packing them with Republican voters. George W. Bush carried each of these districts in the 2000 presidential contest with at least 65 percent of the vote.

Four GOP incumbents — Mac Collins, Deal, Johnny Isakson and Charlie Norwood — appear to have safe seats, while their party seems certain to hold the two districts in which their incumbents are paired.

Domino Effect

Both Barr and Chambliss have raised their political profiles during the current congressional deliberations on national security. Barr, a staunch conservative who voices concerns about the right to privacy, is involved in the debate over how far law enforcement agencies should go in surveillance of individuals. Chambliss chairs the new Select Intelligence Subcommittee on Terrorism and Homeland Security. (*2001 CQ Weekly, p. 2252*)

But their heightened prominence as lawmakers has not insulated them from the grind of politics back home.

A longtime antagonist of state Democrats, Barr so expected to be targeted in redistricting that he sold his home in Atlanta's Cobb County suburbs earlier this year.

Much of Barr's current 7th District is included in the new, Democratic-leaning 11th District. He has decided to run in the new 7th, a heavily Republican crescent north of Atlanta, even though more of the district is currently represented by Linder.

Facing the prospect of an Aug. 20 primary showdown, Barr and Linder will be well funded. Linder had $726,000 cash on hand as of June 30, to $485,000 for Barr.

Some Republicans would like Barr to forgo his plans and instead defend the 11th District. Potential Democratic candidates for that seat include businessman Roger Kahn — who lost by 55 percent to 45 percent as Barr's 2000 challenger — and former Rep. George "Buddy" Darden, who represented much of the district from 1983 until his defeat by Barr in 1994.

There is more uncertainty about whether there will be an incumbent faceoff in the new southeastern 1st District. "I don't think you'll see Jack Kingston and Saxby Chambliss in a primary against each other," said Rob Leebern, Chambliss' chief of staff.

Democrats say they drew the district for Chambliss, who is one of the better known Georgia House members because of his past competitive races and his current position as terrorism subcommittee chairman.

But Chambliss, a mainstream conservative who has drawn support from some Democratic voters in his House contests, is considered by some Republican strategists as a top prospect for one of the nation's key Senate races next year, the challenge to Democratic incumbent Max Cleland.

Chambliss said during the week of Oct. 1 that he is interested in the Senate race and is considering his options. Part of that consideration is the degree to which Cleland is vulnerable in the 2002 race.

Cleland in 1996 won the seat left open by retired Democratic Sen. Sam Nunn (1972-97) by just 49 percent to 48 percent over Republican businessman Guy Millner. He has had a moderate record that Republicans say will provide issues to use against him in conservative-leaning Georgia.

But Cleland, who lost both legs and an arm in combat during the Vietnam War, also will play a role in deliberations over the nation's war on terrorism as a member of the Senate Armed Services Committee.

Kingston, meanwhile, has hinted in the past of interest in running statewide. He, too, is a possible contender against Cleland or a candidate for what appears a long-shot bid to unseat first-term Democratic Gov. Barnes.

Decisions by Chambliss and Kingston may have an impact on Republican colleague Collins. He has long flirted with running for governor or senator, though he has ultimately chosen each time to seek re-election to the House.

Republicans concede they will lose House seats in Georgia but are not prepared to accept Democratic predictions of a 7-6 majority. While two of the four open seats (the 12th and the 13th) appear to be strongly Democratic, two others (the 3rd and the 11th) appear more competitive.

"To automatically assume that we're going to go down to six I think would be incorrect," said Carl Forti, spokesman for the National Republican Congressional Committee.

Republicans also point out that Georgia is but one piece of the redistricting puzzle. A ruling by a state judge in Texas could result in big Republican gains there, and Forti notes that new maps have not yet been proposed in Pennsylvania, Florida and Ohio, where Republicans control the redistricting process.

Republicans may pursue legal challenges to the Georgia plan. Georgia also is one of 16 states wholly or partially covered by Section 5 of the Voting Rights Act, which requires jurisdictions with a history of voter discrimination to get their redistricting plans "pre-cleared" by the Justice Department.

But it will be hard for opponents to argue that the plan weakens representation for Georgia's black residents, who make up 28 percent of the population. Along with preserving the seats held by the three black Democratic incumbents, the map creates two open districts, the 12th and 13th, in which blacks make up more than 40 percent of the population.

The 13th District, which has several spindly appendages and touches parts of 11 counties, includes some areas now represented by veteran Democrat Lewis. He volunteered to give up some of his loyally Democratic black voters to help his party win the 13th. ◆

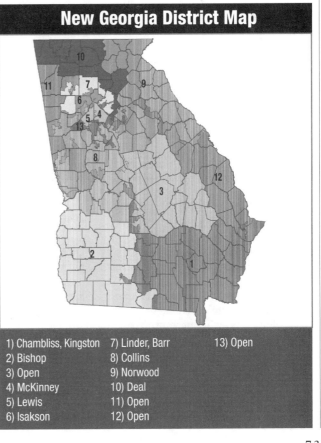

Current Georgia District Map

1) Jack Kingston (R)	7) Bob Barr (R)
2) Sanford D. Bishop Jr. (D)	8) Saxby Chambliss (R)
3) Mac Collins (R)	9) Nathan Deal (R)
4) Cynthia A. McKinney (D)	10) Charlie Norwood (R)
5) John Lewis (D)	11) John Linder (R)
6) Johnny Isakson (R)	

New Georgia District Map

1) Chambliss, Kingston	7) Linder, Barr	13) Open
2) Bishop	8) Collins	
3) Open	9) Norwood	
4) McKinney	10) Deal	
5) Lewis	11) Open	
6) Isakson	12) Open	

Candidates Gradually Resume Campaigning, With Partisanship Muted

Ads and rhetoric are softened; national party committees also suspend major fundraising and political activity

A subtle television ad, first run Sept. 18, heralded Mark Earley's return to campaigning for governor of Virginia, a state that experienced terrorist horrors one week earlier.

The ad interspersed images of Earley and other Virginia Republicans — Gov. James S. Gilmore III, who chairs the Republican National Committee (RNC), and Sens. John W. Warner and George F. Allen — with scenes of two of Earley's children installing an American flag on a front porch. A narrator hailed Earley, a former state attorney general, for his efforts to protect the security of schoolchildren.

The gentle message contrasted efforts by Earley and his GOP allies, prior to Sept. 11, to portray Democratic nominee Mark Warner as too liberal for conservative-leaning Virginia.

Earley faces a dilemma shared by candidates across the nation: When, in the wake of terrorist attacks that killed more than 6,000 people on U.S. soil, will voters tolerate a return to full-throated partisanship?

"There's no model here," said political scientist Mark Rozell of Catholic University in Washington. "There's no previous example that comes close to this from which we can draw any conclusions about what candidates should be doing at a time like this."

Those most immediately affected by the nation's drastically changed political atmosphere are running in contests being held in this "off year."

They include candidates for governor (Warner and Earley in Virginia, Democrat Jim McGreevey and Republican Bret Schundler in New Jersey); hopefuls in special elections for House seats in Arkansas, Florida, Massachusetts and South Carolina; and candidates for mayor of New York, where the primary — underway Sept. 11 when hijacked jets destroyed the World Trade Center — was rescheduled for Sept. 25.

"We took a hiatus from our door-to-door campaign, and the television sta-

> *"There's no model here. There's no previous example that comes close to this from which we can draw any conclusions about what candidates should be doing at a time like this."*
>
> —Mark Rozell, Department of Political Science, Catholic University

tions have pre-empted all ads," said Philip Schoettlin, campaign manager for Republican John Boozman, a candidate in the Sept. 25 primary to succeed former Republican Rep. Asa Hutchinson (1997-2001) in Arkansas' 3rd District. Hutchinson now heads the federal Drug Enforcement Administration.

"We're trying to stay focused," Schoettlin continued. "We just don't want to intrude."

The prospect of campaigning in a time of national uncertainty also challenges those preparing for the 2002 elections, including battles for control of the narrowly divided Senate and House.

All of the national party committees have suspended major fundraising and political activities. "It's just not an appropriate time for politics," said RNC spokesman Trent Duffy on Sept. 20.

Numerous candidates put off cam-

paign-related events. Among them was former cabinet secretary Elizabeth Dole, who had been expected on Sept. 11 to announce a bid for the GOP nomination to succeed retiring North Carolina Republican Sen. Jesse Helms.

Slowly Off the Sidelines

There is no better example of the suspension of politics as usual, and the public's desire for political unity, than what has transpired in New York City in the wake of the terrorist outrages.

There has been discussion about whether it would be legally possible to extend the tenure of Republican Mayor Rudolph Giuliani, who is nearing the end of his second term and cannot run again. Before Sept. 11, public opinion was divided over Giuliani's manner and stormy personal life. But his leadership of the city through its greatest crisis has given him nearly mythic stature.

Few political analysts think the city will suspend its regular election cycle. Still, the four major Democratic candidates — city Public Advocate Mark Green, Bronx Borough President Fernando Ferrer, city Comptroller Alan Hevesi and city Council Speaker Peter Vallone — and two Republican hopefuls, media magnate Michael Bloomberg and former Democratic Rep. Herman Badillo (1971-77), forswore most visible campaign activity.

The attacks also had personal ramifications for this fall's campaigns for governor. The Pentagon is located in Virginia. Many New Jerseyites live within view of Manhattan, and state residents were among the victims of the attack on the World Trade Center. The hijacked flight that crashed in rural Pennsylvania originated in Newark.

The Virginia candidates are edging back on to the trail, if gingerly. In tandem with the ad's release, Earley said he would resume his campaign. Not doing so, Earley said, would be tantamount to allowing the terrorists to subvert the nation's election process.

"I hope you agree with me that we must all resolve to never give terrorists

California Democrats' Remap
Puts Two of Their Own in Tough Spots

Most election-related politics was on hold during the period of national shock and mourning that followed the Sept. 11 terrorist attacks.

A prominent exception was the effort by the legislature in California, the nation's most populous state, to complete congressional redistricting.

California's Democratic-controlled legislature faced a Sept. 14 deadline for completing all measures in this year's session. On Sept. 13, lawmakers cleared a redistricting bill that benefits most incumbents of both parties; Democratic Gov. Gray Davis is expected to sign the remap.

The only current members put at political risk by the plan are Democrats Gary A. Condit and Bob Filner. But the threat they face is not primarily from Republicans — it is from challengers within their own party.

California will have 53 seats, a one-seat gain. Democrats are widely expected to win 33, one more than they currently hold.

Yet Condit — already facing problems because of his relationship with intern Chandra Levy, who has been missing since May — has been given new district lines that will make it harder for him to win re-election. (*2001 CQ Weekly, p. 2018*)

Condit's record as a conservative Democrat has enabled him to win the 18th District, a Central Valley constituency that leans Republican.

But the new 18th drawn by the legislature includes nearly 140,000 residents of Democratic-leaning Stockton, whose presence may favor a more liberal-to-moderate Democratic candidate in the March 5 primary.

Filner's difficulty stems from the desire of Hispanics, who make up about a third of California's population, to expand beyond the six seats they hold in the state's House delegation.

Filner could face a competitive challenge from state Rep. Juan Vargas, whom he defeated in primaries in 1992 and 1996 in a San Diego-based district, the 50th.

The remap plan issued by state Democrats included a Hispanic-majority district in the Los Angeles area — created in part by dismantling the 38th District held by GOP Rep. Steve Horn, who announced Sept. 4 that he will not run for re-election next year. (*2001 CQ Weekly, p. 2060*)

But that was not enough to satisfy many Hispanic activists, including Vargas, a member of the state Assembly redistricting committee.

Under the plan passed by the legislature, Filner would have to run in a new 51st District that reaches from San Diego along the state's border with Mexico, taking in all of heavily Hispanic Imperial County. But the overall Hispanic population of the district, 53.3 percent of the total, is only slightly higher than the 50.8 percent in Filner's current district.

On the other hand, the remap adds Democratic voters to the districts of seven Democrats — Lois Capps, Susan A. Davis, Cal Dooley, Jane Harman, Michael M. Honda, Adam B. Schiff and Ellen O. Tauscher — who in 2000 took 54 percent of the vote or less.

The plan appears to protect 19 of the 20 GOP members. It also appears likely that a newly drawn 21st District in the Central Valley — made up of parts of districts represented by Republicans Bill Thomas and George P. Radanovich and Democrat Cal Dooley — will go Republican, offsetting the party's loss of Horn's seat.

the satisfaction of suspending the process of democracy. To do so would reward their heinous acts and devalue the devastating loss of American lives," Earley said in a written statement.

Democrat Warner resumed TV advertising Sept. 20. His campaign manager, Steve Jarding, said a day earlier that the time was nearing for the candidates to resume discussing their differences on everyday issues such as education, transportation and public safety.

"They may have been blotted out by the constant news coverage of the past week, but at some level all of those issues that resonated and mattered on Monday a week ago obviously still matter, and I suspect they will matter on the 6th of November," Jarding said.

University of Virginia political scientist Larry J. Sabato said voters will not punish candidates for debating domestic issues. "These are state races," he said. "I don't think anyone's going to hold it against a candidate because he discussed education or transportation outside the context of Sept. 11," he said.

It is possible, Rozell said, that the public's overwhelming focus on attacks and the nation's response could make prospects more difficult for underdog candidates such as Earley, who trailed Warner by 6 percentage points in a Mason-Dixon poll released Sept. 20.

But Sabato said the new political environment also could make the race a "tabula rasa," or blank slate.

There appeared to be a slower return to normalcy in New Jersey's contest to replace Republican Donald T. DiFrancesco, who became acting governor in January after GOP Gov. Christine Todd Whitman became Environmental Protection Agency administrator.

This looms as a big problem for Republican nominee Schundler, who is trying to buck a strong Democratic trend in recent New Jersey elections. Polls show him trailing McGreevey by nearly 20 percentage points.

Schundler, who from 1992 until this June was mayor of Jersey City, held a news conference Sept. 17 to discuss the resumption of his campaign. He said it would have a new focus on rebuilding the regional economy and protecting the state from terrorist attacks.

McGreevey did not campaign the week of Sept. 17. "The enormity of the tragedy has compleingly overwhelmed politics as usual," said McGreevey spokesman Richard McGrath. ◆

Pelosi's Vote-Counting Prowess Earns Her the House Democrats' No. 2 Spot

New minority whip says her election will help strengthen her party's support among women, promises to reach out to all factions

Lobster sandwiches and other lavish menus for strategy lunches were among the early indications that Nancy Pelosi had the organizing prowess to win. But when the ballots were tallied, there was even clearer evidence of why House Democrats had picked her as their top vote-counter: Pelosi proved she could count votes.

Going into election day, San Francisco's eight-term congresswoman predicted that she would win the office of House Democratic whip with 120 votes. She won 118.

Her opponent, Steny H. Hoyer of Maryland, said before the election Oct. 10 that he had the commitments of 106 of his colleagues. Only 95 cast their secret ballots for him.

David E. Bonior of Michigan has been the party whip for a decade, longer than any other person, and while the Democrats are in the minority, the post is second in the party hierarchy behind Minority Leader Richard A. Gephardt of Missouri. That means when Bonior steps down in January to concentrate on his gubernatorial campaign, Pelosi will become the highest-ranking woman in congressional history — eclipsing Maine's Margaret Chase Smith, who chaired the Senate Republican Conference from 1967-72.

The attainment, she suggested, will help her party enhance its standing with women voters, a key constituency as Democrats seek to win control of the House next year.

"My victory is a big opening for the Democratic Party. What it says is the Democratic Caucus was willing to make history and make progress," Pelosi said the afternoon of her victory. "This is energizing for our base . . . for people who aren't proactive."

In addition to cracking the congressional glass ceiling, Pelosi's election also establishes a place in the top tier of the Capitol Hill leadership for California, which has one out of every eight House seats — 32 of which are now

Pelosi, left, celebrated her Oct. 10 election over a breakfast buffet in the Cannon Building with supporters including, from her left, Patrick J. Kennedy of Rhode Island, Nita M. Lowey of New York, Sam Farr and Lynn Woolsey of California and Jan Schakowsky of Illinois.

held by Democrats. The combination is sure to place her on the short list of women mentioned as possible candidates for national office.

A Fresh Face

In the near term, Pelosi's victory ended a three-year campaign in which the loyalties of House Democrats were tugged at by two vigorous and veteran politicians. Both are Appropriations Committee members with deep — and often intersecting — veins of support in the caucus. They even share the same formative Capitol Hill experience, having interned together 38 years ago for Sen. Daniel B. Brewster, D-Md. (1963-69).

Hoyer presented himself as the more moderate of the two, someone who as whip would help put swing districts in the Democratic column. Pelosi, a solid liberal, stressed her prolific fundraising ability and her years as a party organizer as well as her potential to be a "fresh face" for the party. (*CQ Weekly, p. 2321*)

While Pelosi promised to reach out

to all factions in the party, some moderates expressed concern that having such a vocal liberal as second-in-command could hurt House Democrats' chances of winning back the House next November.

"In a war, you want people who are strong on defense, and when the economy is in trouble, you want somebody who is strong on fiscal matters," said James P. Moran of Virginia, a member of the moderate New Democrats and a Hoyer backer. "The fact that we have a woman in line is good, but I don't think gender is the most important consideration."

Added David E. Price of North Carolina: "Nancy will need, early in her tenure, to reach out very deliberately to all the elements of the party. . . . And she will be aware of the dangers of being typecast. She'll need to send some very strong signals."

Others who favored Hoyer conceded that Pelosi had won — she took 55 percent of the vote — by assembling backers across the Democratic ideological spectrum. "Blacks supporting both candidates, women supporting both candidates, liberals, moderates," noted John M. Spratt Jr. of South Carolina. "By winning, Nancy proved to a lot of people she will lead from the middle."

Pelosi shrugged off concerns that her liberalism would hurt the party. "I'm a non-menacing progressive Democrat," she said. "I think I'm non-menacing in how I go out to the public."

Her post-election public debut came Oct. 12, when she headed to New Jersey to host a fundraiser for second-term member Rush D. Holt. She is set to raise money for other Democratic colleagues this month in Indiana and California, where she has concentrated most of her career's money-raising enterprises.

Pelosi said she would not, as Bonior did, relinquish her committee assignments. She is top Democrat on the Intelligence Committee, which has gained new prominence since the Sept. 11 terrorist attacks. (*2001 CQ Weekly*, p. 2304)

Republicans declined to predict whether they would gain any political advantage from Pelosi's victory. "It depends on how she conducts herself as whip," said Thomas M. Davis III of Virginia, chairman of the National Republican Congressional Committee.

Likely Rivals

Within minutes of her victory, speculation began on when Pelosi would seek to move up the leadership ladder — and who her rivals would be. Gephardt seems likely to resign as floor leader when the 108th Congress begins, either to become Speaker if the Democrats have won the House or to leave the leadership altogether if they have failed to in four straight elections.

At the same time, Democratic Caucus Chairman Martin Frost of Texas and Vice Chairman Robert Menendez of New Jersey will have reached their term limits in those jobs, and each has expressed interest in being floor leader. Frost would be seen as a candidate of the party's more moderate members.

"First we have to win the House back," Pelosi said when asked if she would run for leader next fall. "My colleagues will make judgments about that in the future."

Having lost his second whip's race — he was bested by Bonior in 1991 — Hoyer declined to comment on his future plans in the House. But some suggested that he could be elected whip next year by positioning himself as a moderate to

Re-Energizing the Money Chase

By electing Nancy Pelosi their House whip, Democrats are elevating a prodigious fundraiser who could crank up a money-raising machine that recently lost two top stars: former President Bill Clinton and Patrick J. Kennedy of Rhode Island, who previously ran House members' fundraising arm.

Pelosi excels at arranging the type of large events — with marquee names that attract wealthy donors — that propelled record growth in Democratic Party coffers during the late 1990s. Her San Francisco district is home to some of the party's most reliable individual donors, and California has long been a bastion for Democrats seeking money. This year it has ranked second to New York for contributions to the Democratic Congressional Campaign Committee (DCCC), according to the Center for Responsive Politics.

Kennedy, who headed the DCCC for the 2000 elections, backed Pelosi. "She's the best fundraiser outside [Minority Leader Richard A.] Gephardt in the Democratic Caucus," he said. "Nancy is better than I am."

Steny H. Hoyer of Maryland, whom Pelosi defeated, is no minor-leaguer in the money chase. His AmeriPAC, which has consistently ranked among the best-financed of the Democratic leadership political action committees, raised $680,000 in the 2000 election cycle. But when Pelosi decided to start a similar committee, it quickly eclipsed those of Hoyer and Gephardt. Pelosi's PAC to the Future raised $1.2 million and handed out $875,000 to Democratic candidates and committees for the 2000 election. It also has raised unrestricted "soft money" contributions.

Pelosi's reliably Democratic district means she has not had to raise enormous sums for herself — just $410,000 for her 2000 race, of which 68 percent came from PACs, the most generous of which were labor unions'. But 94 percent of the money PAC to the Future brought in during the past two years came from individuals, including $955,000 from 400 Californians.

Brushing aside concerns that Pelosi's liberalism could turn off some donors, especially those from the business community that Kennedy and others worked hard to cultivate, Kennedy said, "What they're going to see is excitement, renewed energy and an appeal that is incredibly powerful. The business community will go where the momentum is."

New York's Nita M. Lowey, the new DCCC head, said Pelosi is wasting no time: "Five minutes after the election, she said, 'When are we sitting down?'"

balance a Majority Leader Pelosi.

Both camps worked tirelessly until the last minute. On the surface, Pelosi's efforts were more robust.

Her aides ordered outsized campaign buttons in red and blue; Hoyer's camp relied on peel-off stickers. Climaxing a strategy of having expensive catering at campaign strategy sessions — to bolster attendance among the lawmakers — Pelosi invited colleagues to snack from a breakfast buffet down the hall from where the election was held. Hoyer's team offered no snacks. Pelosi's aides telephoned to wake up her backers at 7:30 a.m. — more than two hours before the balloting. Private planes had been reserved in case any of Pelosi's backers had failed to return to Washington by other means. (None had).

And while four of Hoyer's aides

stood outside the Cannon Caucus Room checking off the names of lawmakers as they entered for the election, they were no match for the dozen Pelosi aides clogging the doorway — who used walkie-talkies to send out still more aides in search of supporters who had not yet entered the room.

In the end, 213 votes were cast for Hoyer and Pelosi, one ballot was turned in blank and only one member of the Democratic Caucus did not show up. James A. Traficant Jr. of Ohio, ostracized since he supported Republican J. Dennis Hastert for Speaker this year, said he was never told when the election would occur and only learned of it as it was happening. He dispatched an aide with a note announcing his vote — for Hoyer — after Pelosi had already been declared the winner. ◆

Sen. Helms' Retirement Will Leave Void for GOP Foreign Policy Conservatives, Set Up Tough Partisan Fight for His Seat

When North Carolina Republican Jesse Helms retires from the Senate in January 2003, foreign policy conservatives will be without a powerful champion on Capitol Hill for the first time in decades.

"There will be a very significant national vacuum on foreign policy," said Nebraska Republican Chuck Hagel, a member of the Foreign Relations Committee on which Helms is ranking Republican.

Helms, 79, who announced Aug. 22 he would not seek a sixth term, has been a political lightning rod because of his controversial stands on domestic issues — from his criticisms of homosexuals and opposition to abortion, to accusations that he exploited racial tensions in his election campaigns.

But his weightiest influence may well have been on foreign policy. As the senior Republican on Foreign Relations for nearly a decade and its chairman from 1995 until the Democrats' Senate takeover in June, Helms has advanced his brand of populist conservatism.

He has combined vigorous anticommunism with a suspicion of international organizations and a skepticism about arms control accords.

He followed conservatives such as Sen. Barry Goldwater, R-Ariz. (1953-65, 1969-87), the 1964 GOP presidential nominee and former chairman of the Armed Services Committee. Helms, fueled by his religious beliefs, added an emphasis on moral considerations.

He will leave no obvious successor in the ranks of senior Republicans. His top GOP spot on Foreign Relations, by seniority, would go to Richard G. Lugar of Indiana. The top Republican on the Senate Armed Services Committee is John W. Warner of Virginia. Both are veteran members of the pro-business foreign policy establishment whose free-trade philosophy Helms has frequently challenged with his advocacy of sanctions on trade and aid to affect other countries' behavior.

By Miles A. Pomper

Helms, shown during a 1999 hearing while serving as chairman of the Foreign Relations Committee, helped set the tone for the nation's foreign policy debates for nearly 30 years.

Foreign policy analysts say Helms does have ideological heirs on foreign policy, such as Republican Sens. Jon Kyl of Arizona, James M. Inhofe of Oklahoma and Robert C. Smith of New Hampshire, and House Majority Whip Tom DeLay, R-Texas.

Other Republicans have echoed Helms' emphasis on conservative moral and religious positions, including Reps. Frank R. Wolf of Virginia and Christopher H. Smith of New Jersey and Sen. Sam Brownback of Kansas.

But former House Foreign Affairs Chairman Lee H. Hamilton, D-Ind. (1965-99), said none of those members would be able to match Helms' institutional power and national profile. "It will be a while for another conservative spokesman on foreign policy to emerge," Hamilton said.

Helms pioneered the use of direct mail political fundraising, creating an unmatched national conservative constituency that he used to advance foreign policy planks in the 1976 and 1980 Republican Party platforms.

Helms softened on some issues in recent years, most notably advancing legislation with Foreign Relations Chairman Joseph R. Biden Jr., D-Del., to pay off a significant chunk of U.S. debts to the United Nations. He has supported efforts to combat HIV/AIDS in sub-Saharan Africa and ease the debt burden of some of the world's poorest nations.

His trademark tactic, which earned him the sobriquet "Senator No," was to block action on nominations or legislation he opposed. Helms challenged a number of nominations made by his ally, President Ronald Reagan, and killed President Bill Clinton's selection of Massachusetts GOP Gov. William F. Weld as ambassador to Mexico in 1997.

He led opposition to the Panama Canal Treaty in 1978, and he opposed such arms control accords as SALT II in 1979, the Intermediate-range Nuclear Forces Treaty in 1988 and the Comprehensive Test Ban Treaty in 1999. (*1978 CQ Almanac, p. 379; 1979 CQ Almanac, p. 411; 1988 CQ Almanac, p. 379; 1999 CQ Almanac, p. 9-40*)

But Helms negotiated a series of understandings that helped frequent adversary Clinton win the two-thirds majority he needed to pass the Chemical Weapons convention in 1997. (*1997 CQ Almanac, p. 8-13*)

In a 1998 speech, Helms outlined his philosophy on the Foreign Relations Committee as "the Senate's brake" on foreign policy: "It is our job to say to presidents and secretaries of state, when they come demanding quick action on 'urgent' treaties and legislation, 'slow down, let's think on this a little'. . . . And sometimes our job is to say 'no'."

Turning on Their Heels

Despite Helms' place in recent political history, his retirement announcement had to share media attention with the jockeying for the race to succeed him.

Grabbing the most attention was North Carolina native Elizabeth Dole, a former secretary of Labor and Transportation and the wife of former Kansas Republican Sen. Bob Dole (1969-96), the 1996 GOP presidential nominee.

Dole, who made a brief bid for the GOP presidential nomination in 2000, recently registered to vote in Salisbury, N.C., using her mother's address.

Some GOP strategists view Dole as the high-profile candidate they need to hold Helms' seat, something they likely must do if they hope to regain Senate control in the 2002 elections.

Another Republican says he is in the race: former Charlotte Mayor Richard Vinroot, who lost to Democrat Michael F. Easley as the 2000 GOP nominee for governor. Other Republicans considering the race include former Sen. Lauch Faircloth (1993-99), who lost in 1998 to Democrat John Edwards, and Rep. Richard M. Burr.

North Carolina Secretary of State Elaine Marshall has announced her intentions to run for the Democratic nomination. Other possible Democratic candidates include former state House Speaker Dan Blue, state Superior Court Judge Ray Warren and businessman Mark Erwin, a former ambassador to the African island nations of Mauritius, the Seychelles and the Comoros.

But several prominent Democrats have stated they are not interested, including James B. Hunt Jr., who served a record tenure as North Carolina governor (1977-85, 1993-2001) and was Helms' challenger in an epic 1984 Senate race. ◆

Sen. Reid: The Great Facilitator Of the New Democratic Majority

Nevada's senior senator becomes Daschle's unobtrusive, facile right-hand man

Quick Contents

Two months ago, Harry Reid was the back-channel guy who quietly surrendered a committee chairmanship to lure James Jeffords out of the GOP. Now he is front and center as Majority Leader Tom Daschle's trusted second-in-command of an ever-fragile Senate majority.

Here's the line on Harry Reid, the Senate's No. 2 Democrat: Mild-mannered Mormon. Nonstop presence on the floor. Loyal partisan who nonetheless works well with each of his colleagues.

Reid, a third-term Nevadan, is by all accounts a major asset to the Democrats' fragile Senate majority, performing the hour-by-hour, day-to-day grunt work that makes his colleagues' lives easier. Majority Leader Tom Daschle, D-S.D., trusts him completely — and relies on him heavily. And when Reid gives his word to his Republican rivals, they bank on it.

All of that is true. But there is another thing: Reid knows how to fight. Especially when it involves his home state.

The former middleweight, 61, takes on the task of running the Senate floor with a boxer's tenacity. Reid is on the floor more than virtually any other senator, trying to organize the flow of debate, minimizing down time and constantly prodding things along. No job appears too small.

But while he has a boxer's instincts, Reid also knows that in the notoriously difficult-to-manage Senate, the carrot is often a far more effective tool than the stick.

"I've tried to establish the fact that I try to be fair," Reid said in a July 17 interview. "I've

CQ Weekly July 21, 2001

always tried to treat somebody like I would like to be treated."

If Democrats make the Senate trains run on time, much of the credit will accumulate to Reid. Democrats won victories in passing a campaign finance overhaul bill (S 27) when they were still in the minority, and they passed their first big test as the majority party in muscling through a patients' rights bill (S 1052) that has attracted a veto threat from President Bush.

Now, the focus is on appropriations, which Democrats will make their top priority in the weeks leading up to the August recess. Reid is a member of the powerful Appropriations Committee, and he will be a very busy man as the Senate tries to reach Daschle's goal of passing nine of the 13 spending bills through the Senate by Aug. 3.

Reid has been the Democratic whip since 1999. To a far greater degree than his predecessor, Wendell H. Ford, D-Ky. (1974-99), Reid is a traffic cop on the floor. "I felt that if there was a continuous presence on the floor, so someone knew what was going on at all times, things would work better," Reid said. "And that has proven to be so."

Those who offer a more tempered view of Reid say his single-minded attention to the floor has its limits. He is a tactician but no big-picture visionary.

"He does not have the kind of strategic vision that Daschle has at all," said a former Democratic leadership aide.

And Reid is by no means the ideal politician. He does not relish the retail side of politics. He is not good at honing or delivering sound bites. He prefers reading books to attending fundraising dinners.

"I'm not really much of a social guy," admits Reid, who is married with five children. "I don't like parades. I don't like banquets. I don't like public gatherings."

Car Bombs and Attempted Bribes

Reid's nice-guy demeanor makes it easy to forget how tough he can be. He grew up poor in the tiny mining town of Searchlight, Nev., which Reid feted in a 1998 book called "The Camp That Didn't Fail." His father, a hard-drinking miner, killed himself.

Reid's political mentor was former Nevada Democratic Gov. Mike O'Callaghan (1971-

Reid, far left, has made focusing on floor action the hallmark of his tenure as the Democratic whip, which colleagues say allows Daschle, center, to pursue strategy.

79), who first got to know Reid as Reid's high school civics teacher and boxing coach in Henderson. At the age of 30, Reid was elected lieutenant governor on the same ticket as O'-Callaghan. In 1974, Reid lost a close race for the Senate to Republican Paul Laxalt (1974-87).

O'Callaghan subsequently named Reid chairman of the Nevada Gaming Commission to oversee the state's top industry at a time when it was under the influence of organized crime. It was an eye-opening experience, during which he feared for his life and had to fight for his reputation.

"They put bombs on my car, there were threatening phone calls at night, people tried to bribe me and went to jail," Reid told the Las Vegas Review-Journal in 1999.

"People sometimes forget that he grew up in a very rough-and-tumble political world in Nevada, and you don't go through all the experiences that he's had without understanding how politics works," said an admiring Daschle staff aide.

Reid won a House seat in 1982 and claimed Laxalt's Senate seat in 1986.

In the Senate, Reid has fought hard for Nevada, directing federal dollars to the state from his perch on Appropriations.

And when it comes to Nevada, Reid can play bare-knuckle politics. Take, for example, a 1996 incident in which Reid killed a plan by fellow Nevada Democrat Richard H. Bryan (1989-2000) to sell federal land in the state. The proceeds were to be used for education, water projects and the purchase of environmentally sensitive land elsewhere. Former Bryan aides say Reid nixed the measure — very popular in Nevada — to blunt the political fortunes of one of the bill's top backers, then-Rep. John Ensign, a freshman Republican from Nevada who gave Reid a huge re-election scare two years later.

"The reason why he killed it was that Ensign was the sponsor on the House side . . . and he didn't want Ensign to do well," said a former Bryan staff aide. "He killed this public lands bill that everyone in Nevada loved so Ensign wouldn't get any credit, even though Bryan had been working on it for something like four years."

When the bill finally passed in 1998 (PL 105-263), in the midst of his big battle with Ensign, Reid shared credit

'Welcome to the Majority'

After six weeks in the majority, Senate Democrats got their first taste of stalling tactics by minority Republicans the week of July 16. And Harry Reid, D-Nev., took the brunt of the lesson.

In short, Republicans slowed action on must-pass spending bills to force votes on President Bush's judicial and agency nominations.

Both parties are still finding their way in their new roles, and, as expected, tempers have flared in the process.

For Reid, the soft-spoken majority whip, who also was floor manager of the held-hostage energy and water appropriations bill (HR 2311), frustration with the GOP tactics prompted a rare outburst. As Democratic whip, Reid has been an emissary in talks about exchanging completion of his bill for action on Bush nominees, and he issued a thinly veiled salvo at another senator — something he is typically loath to do.

"I don't understand who's running the show on the Republican side," a frustrated Reid said at a July 19 news conference, noting that various GOP representatives were floating proposals. "One of the senators . . . brought me this deal yesterday," Reid said, referring to Jon Kyl, R-Ariz., who was threatening to clog the Senate. "I said, 'Who do you represent?' He said, 'I represent the Republican Senate and the president of the United States.'"

Added Reid: "Well, he certainly didn't represent . . . Sen. [Minority Leader Trent] Lott [R-Miss.], and he certainly doesn't represent the administration."

Kyl privately told fellow Republicans that he had not said it that way, and he was not at all pleased. The hard feelings intensified, which then exacerbated the slowdown on Reid's appropriations bill.

"All I say to Democrats is, 'Welcome to the majority,'" said Lott.

for the very legislation he had undermined two years before.

Reid beat Ensign by only 428 votes after a sometimes brutal campaign that Reid admits was poorly run on his end. He ended up firing his longtime chief of staff and campaign manager and subsequently shook up his Senate staff as well, installing an unusually large press shop that now numbers five people.

"It was just awful. Everything was horrible," Reid said of the 1998 debacle. "It'll never happen again." He is already raising money for the 2004 campaign.

Ensign easily won Bryan's Senate seat last year and now the pair, perhaps surprisingly, get along famously, Reid says. They jointly greet constituents on most Thursday mornings over coffee and bagels, for example, and they are tightly united in a longstanding battle to block storage of nuclear waste at Nevada's Yucca Mountain.

"With Ensign and I," Reid now says, "just everything has jelled."

Ensign agreed. He said the 1996 incident over the lands bill was "tough at the time, but you know what? You put things behind you. You have to."

He added that the two met with their staffs after he won his Senate seat to assure that their offices work together. "Since then, it's developed into a friendship. I really like Harry now."

With Bryan, the two Democrats were always friendly, but competitive tensions flared. One public split between the two opened after Bryan voted against the Democrats' tax-heavy 1993 budget plan. Reid issued a statement blasting Bryan, though not by name. "Naysayers who oppose the budget lack the courage to do the right thing," the statement said. A big rift developed, but the two reportedly patched things up, said a longtime Nevada reporter.

Daschle's Trust, Daschle's Authority

For Reid, it is the Senate floor where he is most comfortable. He says he has the best job in politics; at least it is one to which he seems well-suited.

"Harry Reid has become indispensible," Daschle said in an interview. "It is remarkable the degree to which he is willing to dedicate his energies on a daily basis to helping our caucus, and really helping the Senate manage the many challenges we face on the floor each day."

Said friend Orrin G. Hatch, R-Utah: "He's one of the people you can work with. He's pleasant, unassuming, but tough. . . . I have a lot of respect for him. Harry's a straight shooter."

Reid's power also flows from his close relationship with Daschle. Members know that when Reid is working the floor, he speaks on Daschle's behalf.

"He has full authority to make decisions on my behalf, but when he doesn't believe he is in a position to make a decision, he comes to me," Daschle said.

Reid and Daschle served in the House together and were elected to the Senate in the class of 1986. Reid was a top lieutenant in the operation that engineered Daschle's one-vote win in 1994 to be Democratic leader. (*1994 Almanac, p. 17*)

Whittling it Down

Reid's willingness to do the back-room labor on the floor is the key to his growing power and influence. Simply put, Reid makes it easier for his colleagues to do their jobs. They appreciate it, and in return, try to help him do his. Steadily, the chits accumulate.

If you want to give a floor speech or offer an amendment but have to cut out to attend a meeting or a fundraiser, Reid will help you out.

"His greatest joy is when he has 300 amendments that have to be dealt with on the floor and he'll whittle it down and get it all done in a day and make everybody happy," said Charles E. Schumer, D-N.Y.

For example, one of Reid's primary tasks is to help arrange the flow of debate, lining up members to speak and offer their amendments at set times so senators do not waste a lot of time waiting their turn. He tries to minimize the length of quorum calls — except, of course, when that time can be used to negotiate the unanimous consent agreements that are so crucial to keeping the Senate from bogging down.

"You always see people coming up to Harry Reid on the floor, and they're usually saying, 'Harry, I can't be here after 5 o'clock,' or, 'Harry, I've got something at 4, but I can be here at 6,'" said Tom Harkin, D-Iowa. "And he has to somehow keep everybody in line. And it is a tough job."

In the Senate, it is difficult to find anyone willing to admit ill feelings toward him. Even his GOP counterpart, Whip Don Nickles of Oklahoma, with whom Reid sparred for weeks over precious office space during the transition to Democratic control, praised him.

"His word's good," Nickles said. "To me, that's one of the most important things you can say about any senator."

Said Wisconsin Democrat Russell D. Feingold: "He's a huge favorite in the caucus. So he's an ideal guy to have to do some of the dirty work. We also recognize that he's putting in an unbelievable amount of time on the floor working for the caucus. He has a right to try to hunker down on us every once in a while."

While Reid is often smooth and solicitous to his fellow senators, he also does not suffer fools gladly. He is known to bring the hammer down on an uncooperative colleague.

"I have seen him get very tough with some of our colleagues when the occasion requires," Daschle said, "in fact, probably much more aggressively verbally than I have been. But that's the exception, and I think he uses those exceptions very effectively."

Reid tries to balance the interests of his party colleagues, which often conflict with one another, to advance the agenda of the caucus as a whole. He tries to get everyone to give a little.

"It works for the whole caucus because he accommodates everybody," said Joseph R. Biden Jr., D-Del. "He's able to jump in and say, 'Now look, so-and-so did this and you ought to do that.'"

When it comes to sacrificing, Reid has sometimes lead by example.

His most recent, and perhaps most noteworthy, act of selflessness took place in the spring when Democrats were courting potential party-switching Republican James M. Jeffords of Vermont. As a Republican, Jeffords was chairman of the Health, Education, Labor and Pensions Committee. For becoming an Independent who caucused with Democrats, he was named chairman of the Environment and Public Works Committee. The senior Democrat who relinquished his chairmanship? Harry Reid.

Reid denies any quid pro quo, but virtually everyone takes it on faith that Jeffords was promised the chairmanship before he announced his switch.

"The best example of how he is a team player . . . is giving up his chairmanship for Jeffords to come over," said Biden. "That's a big deal. How many other guys would have walked up and said, 'If we get him, I'll give up my chairmanship.'"

But that does not make him a pushover, colleagues insist. "He's tough, but I've found that when he says no to me I know it's not arbitrary," Harkin said. "He's weighed everything, and this is the best he can come up with and he tells you that."

Added a senior Democratic staff aide: "He is a very shrewd politician who understands what motivates people, and he uses that knowledge to great effect."

'OK, Harry'

Among Reid's most ardent fans remains Daschle, who because of Reid is relieved from constantly having to tend to the floor. With Democrats now controlling the Senate and with a Republican replacing Bill Clinton in the White House, Daschle has assumed the mantle of a national Democrat. Daschle has not ruled out the possibility of running for president in 2004.

"Reid seems like he's the chief of operations, where Daschle is freed to roam a little bit . . . to do the vision thing," said the chief of staff to a senior Democrat. "That's incredibly freeing."

Minority Leader Trent Lott, R-Miss., has no such luxury, and more to the point had no such luxury when he was majority leader. Nickles is a once and possibly future aspirant to be the Senate's No. 1 Republican. The two have had their share of clashes in Lott's five-year tenure as Republican leader.

"Lott is forever looking over his shoulder at Nickles," said a senior Democratic aide. "Daschle . . . never has to look over his shoulder."

Lott also does not have colleagues willing to spell him from the hours and days that must be spent on the floor. "I don't know that we have anybody on our side who is willing to do the sheer grunt work that Harry Reid's willing to do," said Phil Gramm, R-Texas.

But with Reid, it is the sense that he is not angling to move up, which is why colleagues say he is so effective at keeping people in line and now keeping the Senate moving.

"If some other senator came up and asked, 'Could you take one for the team,' you'd say, 'When did you ever take one for anybody? Give me a break,'" Biden said. "But you look at Harry and say, 'OK, Harry.'" ◆

Politics and Public Policy

The term *public policy making* refers to action taken by the government to address issues on the public agenda; it also refers to the method by which a decision to act on policy is reached. The work of the president, Congress, the judiciary and the bureaucracy is to make, implement and rule on policy decisions. Articles in this section discuss major policy issues that came before the federal government in the latter half of 2001.

The first four articles in this section address matters related to domestic security and personal freedom. New proposals to strengthen law enforcement's surveillance capabilities have prompted questions about the effect of increased security on citizens' rights to privacy. An article on the Office of Homeland Security explores in detail the new cabinet-level agency and the goals of its director, former Pennsylvania governor Tom Ridge. Other articles cover the federal role in securing America's infrastructure and its airspace.

Congress's tactics to stimulate the economy and address the adverse financial repercussions of the Sept. 11 attacks are detailed in the next article. This story defines the lines of debate and compromise as each party proposes different means to reach the same end—economic stimulus.

The debate over the use of stem cells in research has been highly controversial and hotly contested on Capitol Hill. Lawmakers have struggled to understand the science and cover all angles of the issue. This debate marked a turning point not only for medical research but potentially for the abortion controversy as well. The article on stem cell research provides an overview of the issue and offers insight on pending legislation.

Rounding out the section are discussions of other significant public policy topics: a new energy conservation plan that would allow drilling in protected areas, provide funding for research, increase emissions standards and deregulate utilities; Speaker Dennis J. Hastert's continued efforts to produce a Republican win on managed care; and an in-depth examination of competing education bills.

These significant issues are clearly explained in the articles that follow. Because many of the topics discussed here will remain at the top of Congress's agenda in the months ahead, the articles are valuable contributions to issue studies, predictors of legislative outcomes and primers on the policy-making process.

Surveillance: Playing Catchup

Suspects' technological sophistication challenges the law's ability to adapt

Back in J. Edgar Hoover's day, you tracked the bad guys from the back of an unmarked Chevy and tapped their phones with a pair of alligator clips. Now the bad guys use multiple digital cell phones and encryption software on their laptop computers, leaving local and federal agencies scrambling to keep up.

Surveillance these days can mean eavesdropping satellites, facial-recognition scanners and souped-up computers with "packet sniffing" software to survey electronic mail.

The problem for Congress is how to adjust laws to help the FBI and other intelligence agencies track suspected terrorists through the thickets of modern technology without violating the privacy of millions of innocent people.

Privacy, particularly electronic privacy, is already a big worry for most Americans. (*2001 CQ Weekly, p. 412*)

Already, many employers monitor their workers with cameras and soft-

CQ Weekly Oct. 6, 2001

ware. Retailers large and small go to great lengths to learn the habits of consumers. Internet retailers' practice of attaching "cookies," or specialized software that tracks Web browsing, has sparked a debate over whether new protection is needed for personal information in cyberspace.

But in a time of national emergency, the question now is whether law enforcement has enough power to locate and follow the country's enemies.

"We're in a situation now where the good of society has to take some precedence over what's good for individuals," said Frank W. Connolly, an authority on computer science and information systems at American University in Washington, D.C. "But there still needs to be some counterbalancing to avoid having another McCarthy era."

Tracking communications in cyberspace has received particular attention since Attorney General John Ashcroft submitted draft anti-terrorism legisla-

tion to Congress on Sept. 19. The Department of Justice is seeking expanded power to monitor e-mail and Web use. Evidence already has shown that terrorists involved in the Sept. 11 attacks on New York and Washington bought plane tickets and conducted other business online. (*2001 CQ Weekly, p. 2210*)

Congress frequently has updated laws to give law enforcement the ability to keep up with new technologies. The 1994 Communications Assistance for Law Enforcement Act, or CALEA, (PL 103-414), for example, expanded federal wiretapping to keep pace with new telephone technology. But the advent of new technologies and services, such as Internet instant messaging, has left the FBI complaining that it needs even more authority to head off cybercrime. (*1994 Almanac, p. 215*)

The House Judiciary Committee sought to address some of the lag between laws and technology Oct. 3 by approving legislation (HR 2975) that

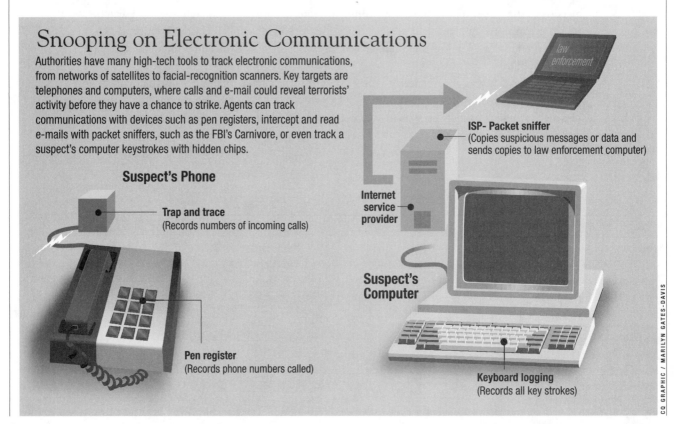

Snooping on Electronic Communications

Authorities have many high-tech tools to track electronic communications, from networks of satellites to facial-recognition scanners. Key targets are telephones and computers, where calls and e-mail could reveal terrorists' activity before they have a chance to strike. Agents can track communications with devices such as pen registers, intercept and read e-mails with packet sniffers, such as the FBI's Carnivore, or even track a suspect's computer keystrokes with hidden chips.

law enforcement

Suspect's Phone

Trap and trace
(Records numbers of incoming calls)

Pen register
(Records phone numbers called)

ISP- Packet sniffer
(Copies suspicious messages or data and sends copies to law enforcement computer)

Internet service provider

Suspect's Computer

Keyboard logging
(Records all key strokes)

CQ GRAPHIC / MARILYN GATES-DAVIS

would, among other things, increase law enforcement authority to conduct surveillance of phone and Internet communications. It would expand the definitions of two devices now used to track telephone calls: pen registers, which record the numbers dialed on a phone, and "trap-and-trace" devices, which identify the originating number of a phone call, similar to Caller ID.

Setting Traps

Pen registers are an old standby in the surveillance game. The devices originally were attached to phone lines and made ink marks on paper, which corresponded to the numbers dialed on a rotary phone. If going to a suspect's house was too risky, agents could track calls from the phone company's local switching office. Some older phone company offices still have dust-covered desks and chairs near switchboards that were reserved for the FBI.

Experts warn that applying pen register and trap-and-trace surveillance to the computer world could be legally and technically difficult.

Electronic information — whether it is e-mail from a suspected terrorist or an online shopping order from a busy parent — is fragmented into seemingly indistinguishable packets of digital data consisting of a series of ones and zeroes arranged in codes that travel at blinding speed on the Internet's multiple networks. A single message that might be text, a photograph or the recording of a popular song is divided into perhaps millions of packets, all traveling independently to a common coded address, where they are reassembled and displayed.

The process is preferable to communicating by sound or radio waves, both of which can be subject to interference or becoming degraded over distances. But to intercept the digital information, authorities have to decide where to set their trap, then break into the packets to see whether they contain any relevant information.

"It's kind of a moving target," said Seth Schoen, staff technologist at the Electronic Frontier Foundation, a San Francisco civil liberties group that opposes much expanded electronic surveillance. "This isn't like a phone system, where you have just one kind of service provided a single way."

To conduct a trap-and-trace investigation, authorities only need a court order and do not have to show "proba-

High-tech companies want to help the government, Seiffert says, but they are worried about the complex issues involved.

ble cause" that a crime is being committed. Privacy and civil liberties groups worry that breaking into the packets could constitute monitoring the content of the conversation. They argue that law enforcement should be held to the higher legal standard used to justify wiretapping — that is, to produce for a judge compelling evidence that a suspect is involved in a crime.

The best-known Internet trap-and-trace system is the FBI's Carnivore software, which can monitor specific e-mail and Web activity in real time. It first attracted congressional attention and concern during the 2000 debate over online privacy legislation. *(2000 Almanac, p. 19-15)*

Carnivore, which would be allowed by the legislation that the House Judiciary Committee approved, is proprietary government software loaded on a personal computer that runs on the Windows operating system. The computer then is attached to an Internet service provider's routers and servers — the point where the service collects traffic from its customers and sends it over high-speed lines to its destination. Carnivore is known as a packet sniffer for the way it investigates or sniffs each packet of information that travels on the network. Most computers only look at the address code on a packet.

Carnivore's network interface operates in what is known as "promiscuous

mode" — it sweeps up the Internet service's electronic information as it passes by, filters out target data, makes copies of the relevant packets and stores the copies on its hard drive. This allows authorities to track what Web sites a suspect visited, what the suspect looked at on each site, who the suspect sent e-mail to and even who visited his Web site, if he had one.

Agents set the filtering levels, telling the computer what information to keep and copy and what to ignore.

The situation troubles civil liberties groups, which believe the surveillance should be subjected to stricter judicial review, like a wiretapping permit. Another concern is that Carnivore can be adapted to track all of the sites visited from a particular computer, which could pose privacy concerns if a suspect uses a public computer in a library or a cybercafe.

Privacy advocates say policymakers have to take into account the many kinds of intrusions that strong surveillance technology can create when drafting laws.

"As technology develops, so too should the government's ability to carry out its law enforcement and counterterrorism functions," Jerry Berman, executive director of the Center for Democracy and Technology, a Washington cyberliberties group, told the Senate Judiciary Subcommittee on Constitution, Federalism and Property Rights during an Oct. 3 hearing. "Injudicious changes . . . threaten basic freedoms guaranteed by the Constitution."

Criminals might evade devices such as Carnivore with encryption software that uses mathematical formulas to disguise and scramble files and e-mails so that no one except the intended recipient can read them. The message is unscrambled using a private key that is accessible only with a password.

In such cases, authorities can turn to a controversial device known as a keystroke logger — a computer chip placed between the keyboard and processor of a suspect's computer to record each keystroke. The device enables law enforcement officers to decipher the password and break the encryption code, as well as obtain any documents the suspect may have written.

But to decipher the information, authorities must physically install the chip. Agents may be able to gain access using a search warrant. But the legal standards are murky — the lawyer for a suspected New Jersey mobster has challenged evidence the FBI collected against his client using the device, arguing that his client's constitutional rights were violated because authorities should have obtained a wiretapping order, which requires judicial review.

Ports of Entry

Telecommunications and technology companies are wary of the push for expanded surveillance tools, fearing that Congress may force them to add features to their equipment to make it easier for authorities to eavesdrop. That could drive up costs and hurt competitiveness.

Debate has raged since the passage of CALEA, for example, over how many ports wireless phone companies should reserve for law enforcement equipment that can connect to their networks.

Lawmakers such as Sen. Judd Gregg, R-N.H., have tried to include language in anti-terrorism legislation that would require software makers to give law enforcement agencies keys to commercially available encryption technology, allowing agents to decode secret messages with ease.

"We're strongly committed to helping the government on national security, but also are very concerned about the complexity of new issues that are being thrown at the industry and what is technically feasible," said Grant E. Seiffert, vice president of external affairs and global policy for the Telecommunications Industry Association, a Washington high-tech trade group.

New consumer features on wireless phones already may be helping authorities track suspects. As of Oct. 1, the Federal Communications Commission began requiring new wireless phone handsets to include global positioning chips that communicate with satellites — similar to the GPS feature in portable navigation systems — as part of an enhanced 911 system. The technology could help agents pinpoint a suspect's location, though the 911 feature can be turned off if the user is not making an emergency call.

The government's surveillance powers reach far beyond domestic telecommunications systems, however. A network of communications satellites known as Echelon and dating from the 1970s allows the super-secret National Security Agency to siphon phone conversations from anywhere in the world. The system has triggered widespread concern in Europe that it might be used for industrial espionage. However, a 1999 European Parliament report found little proof the system was being used to aid American companies, adding that European police themselves were collaborating on projects to increase telephone and Internet surveillance.

While e-mails, passwords and other electronic signals help identify suspects, other technologies are being developed that use mathematical formulas to recognize such personal aspects as a person's face, gait or fingerprints.

Face-recognition technology, part of a larger field known as biometrics, has existed in various forms since the 1970s and already has found applications in automated teller machines, casino surveillance systems and airport security.

The technology breaks down facial characteristics into a set of 20 to 100 numbers known as an eigenface, from the German prefix "eigen," meaning "own" or "individual." Each number has some component of the overall picture — a mustache, say, or the angle at which the person is looking at the camera. Authorities can use software to compare their stored images of suspects with those captured on video surveillance monitors.

The technology first became widely known to the public when it was used to scan the crowd at the Super Bowl in Tampa in January and match the images against mug shots of criminals. Visionics Corp., a Jersey City, N.J. maker of biometrics scanners suggested in the wake of the terrorist bombings that the devices should be installed in airport check-in locations and baggage handling areas and at border crossings.

Simon Baker, a research scientist at Carnegie Mellon University in Pittsburgh who works on face-recognition projects sponsored by the Department of Defense, said government interest in the technology increased after the 1998 bombings of U.S. embassies in Kenya and Tanzania.

"Research is trying to expand the technology to the point where the numbers more directly correspond to the shape of the face, skin tone, how they walk or even how fast they blink," Baker said. "From that, you could conceivably try to understand people's actions and behavior and see something, like if someone in an airport lounge looks tense."

In the longer run, researchers hope to combine face-recognition with other biometrics, such as the unique pattern of a person's fingerprint or the iris in his eye. Fingerprint verification already is widely used to ensure that only authorized individuals log on to certain police computers or to authenticate a letter of credit to transfer money.

Beyond 'Brute Force'

Researchers acknowledge that such devices may conjure images of an Orwellian society, but they stress harm only comes when the technology is used the wrong way.

"The brute force method is to hire more guards everywhere," said Naeem Zafar, president of Veridicom Inc., a Santa Clara, Calif., company that makes fingerprint verification systems. "They ask more questions, but they don't really know who you are. With the technology, you get a very high degree of accuracy."

Closed-circuit television cameras in England led to declining crime rates in a number of cities, according to British government reports.

Courts ultimately will determine the scope with which new surveillance technologies can be applied. The Supreme Court in June ruled that federal agents violated a suspect's constitutional rights when they used a thermal imaging scanner during an investigation of marijuana growers who were using federal land. The camera-like heat scanner was aimed at the suspect's house and showed the location of heat lamps that helped grow plants in the suspect's attic. Justice Antonin Scalia, writing for the 5-4 majority, said the use of a device not available to the general public to explore details of a home that would otherwise be unknown without physical intrusion constituted an unreasonable search without a warrant.

Civil libertarians say such legal decisions should give lawmakers pause before enacting sweeping laws in response to the Sept. 11 attacks.

"Just as President Bush and his military advisers are taking their time in planning their response [to the terrorist attacks], to ensure that they hit the terrorist targets with a minimum of collateral damage, so it is incumbent upon this Congress to avoid collateral damage to the Constitution," said the Center for Democracy and Technology's Berman. ◆

Defining Homeland Security

Lawmakers move to give Ridge clear authority and control of counterterrorism budget

Republicans and Democrats are willing to give President Bush his homeland security chief as part of the short-term response to the terrorist attacks, but they remain unyielding on their prerogative to set the parameters for the new post.

If it takes months to produce legislation that lays out the authority of the new Homeland Security Council, so be it, say lawmakers. Their intent is to ensure that Pennsylvania Republican Gov. Tom Ridge, Bush's pick for the job, has all the tools to succeed.

"In the strongest terms, we have to explain his authority as well as responsibility," which must be "bestowed by an act of Congress," said John McCain, R-Ariz., a member of the Senate Armed Services Committee.

Congress' aim is to pass legislation that would make the new job subject to Senate confirmation and give the office, which is to centralize and coordinate more than 40 agencies and departments, control over the $11 billion the government spends each year on counterterrorism — an amount that is likely to climb considerably.

The White House envisions Ridge's job as similar to that of national security adviser, an Eisenhower-era post that owes its creation to congressional passage of the National Security Act of 1947 but does not require Senate approval. In administrations since the 1950s, the role of national security adviser has evolved based on presidential expectations and the force of the personality in the job, with some advisers often eclipsing members of the Cabinet.

Ridge met Sept. 25 with Bush and other administration officials to work out the details of the new job, which he will start Oct. 8. The White House sees the Homeland Security Council as including the attorney general, the secretaries of Defense, Treasury, Agriculture, and Health and Human Services, the directors of the FBI and Federal Emergency Management Agency (FEMA) and the new chief.

Bush administration officials have said Ridge's job can be created by executive order and does not require congressional action. But some lawmakers disagree, reflecting what has become a tussle for power between the two branches of government since the Sept. 11 terrorist attacks in New York and Washington.

The urgency of counterterrorism legislation gave way to a more cautious approach on Capitol Hill as lawmakers asserted their authority and put bills addressing the law enforcement investigation at the top of the priority list.

"Those [bills] that meet those tests, we ought to take up on a fast-track basis," Senate Intelligence Committee Chairman Bob Graham, D-Fla., said in a Sept. 25 interview. "Those that don't ought to be considered in a traditional hearing process."

Aid to Intelligence

Consistent with the regular order, the House Select Committee on Intelligence took the first steps Sept. 24 to come to the aid of the CIA and other spy agencies that have been criticized for failing to foresee the attacks. The committee approved, by voice vote, a fiscal 2002 intelligence authorization bill (HR 2883 — H Rept 107-219) that Chairman Porter J. Goss, R-Fla., said would add significantly to the Bush administration's request before the attacks.

Spending is classified, but recent intelligence budgets are thought to have been in the range of $30 billion. Congressional sources said the committee increased intelligence spending by nearly 9 percent over the current level, excluding funds in the supplemental spending bill. (*2001 CQ Weekly, p. 2126*)

Goss said the House bill adds "a significant amount" over the Senate committee's bill (S 1428) for such critical areas as human intelligence and electronic eavesdropping.

The intelligence authorization bill is guaranteed to win widespread support when it reaches the House floor the week of Oct. 1. But a provision that would rescind CIA guidelines governing the recruitment of foreign intelligence agents with questionable backgrounds is expected to raise concerns among lawmakers troubled about using spies with suspect human rights records.

"Nobody wants to be soft on terrorism. But we do have people saying they don't want us to get out of bounds," Goss said Sept. 25.

The bill also would establish a commission to examine why the intelligence agencies failed to warn of the attacks. The committee report on the authorization bill said it "has been concerned for some time that intelligence agencies were not well-positioned to respond to the national security challenges of the 21st century, including terrorism."

The 10-member bipartisan commission would be appointed by the president along with House and Senate leaders, and would devote six months to examining the failure of intelligence agencies to anticipate the attacks. The committee, however, cautioned against singling out the agencies.

"If blame must be assigned, the blame lies with a government, as a whole, that did not fully understand nor wanted to appreciate the significance of the new threats to our national security, despite the warnings offered by the intelligence community," the committee's report said.

In the Senate, Robert G. Torricelli, D-N.J., promised to introduce legislation to create a board of inquiry to carry out a similar role.

Working Out the Details

Bush announced in his Sept. 20 speech to a joint session of Congress that Ridge would head the Office of Homeland Security. Since then, there have been more questions than answers about the job.

Graham met Sept. 25 with Bush's national security adviser, Condoleezza Rice, about his bill (S 1449) that would make Ridge's position subject to Senate confirmation and give it control of all counterterrorism spending. Although the meeting failed to produce a consensus, aides said Graham and Rice agreed to continue talking.

Graham also worked with Attorney General John Ashcroft and other lawmakers on separate legislation (S 1448) that would give intelligence agencies more tools to fight terrorism. Elements of the bill may be incorporated into an anti-terrorism package proposed by Ashcroft that is the subject of negotiations between the Justice Department and leaders of the House and Senate Judiciary committees.

For years, several expert panels and many lawmakers have called for a single federal official or office to set policy and direction for the many agencies fighting terrorism. The Senate Governmental Affairs and House Government Reform committees are expected to hold hearings this month on legislative proposals to create a new homeland security agency.

Bush said in a Sept. 27 speech that Ridge's job will be "to coordinate activities to make sure that anybody who wants to harm America will have a hard time doing so, to make sure that we're as strong at home as we are abroad, to make sure our resources are deployed effectively."

President Bill Clinton tried a similar but less sweeping approach to reorganizing the White House to fight terrorism. In 1998, Clinton created a coordinating office within the National Security Council and appointed Richard A. Clarke to oversee both counterterrorism efforts and a related initiative to combat attacks on computer-based telecommunications systems and other networks.

Many lawmakers have praised Clarke's efforts but complained that he lacks the authority to be effective. The New York Times reported Sept. 28 that Clarke would be put in charge of a new Office of Cyber-Security under Ridge that would work to prevent and respond to hacker attacks.

"If he [Ridge] doesn't have to be confirmed, my worry is that he would be advisory," said Charles E. Schumer, D-N.Y., a member of the Senate Judiciary Committee. "While his power would be enormous in the first six months, it would eventually fade. And as the president correctly said, this is going to be a long-term fight."

But some lawmakers said that in the wake of the worst terrorist attacks on U.S. soil, Ridge has the political fire-

Tom Ridge

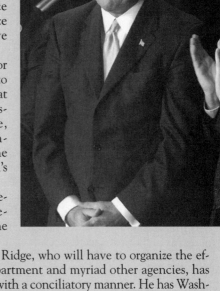

Few politicians have stepped into the nation's political arena as boldly as Tom Ridge, President Bush's choice to head the new Cabinet-level Office of Homeland Security. Fewer have done so with so much at stake.

The popular Republican governor of Pennsylvania was little known to most Americans until Sept. 20. That was when Bush, before a joint session of Congress, named Ridge, right, to coordinate the government's response to terrorism — the most present danger to the nation's security.

Bush chose Ridge, 56, in part because he is a trusted ally who received serious consideration for the 2000 vice presidential nomination.

Ridge also brings relevant skills. Ridge, who will have to organize the efforts of the CIA, FBI, Defense Department and myriad other agencies, has succeeded politically as a moderate with a conciliatory manner. He has Washington experience, as a six-term House member (1983-95). And Ridge knows the military, having enlisted in the Army and earned the Bronze Star in Vietnam after graduating from Harvard.

Ridge is expected to resign as governor Oct. 5 and take his new post three days later.

power to do almost anything he wants.

"In the short run, he has all the authority he could ever have," said Judd Gregg of New Hampshire, ranking Republican on the Senate Appropriations subcommittee that funds the departments of Commerce, Justice and State. "The president is standing right beside him, and whatever he wants right now, he's going to get out of the administration."

Former Rep. Lee H. Hamilton, D-Ind. (1965-99), urged lawmakers to pass legislation that would clearly define Ridge's duties. Hamilton served as a member of a terrorism panel headed by former Sens. Warren B. Rudman, R-N.H. (1980-93), and Gary Hart, D-Colo. (1975-87), that earlier this year recommended creating an executive office that would combine the functions of several existing agencies, including the Coast Guard and Border Patrol.

"I am suspicious of interagency cooperation," Hamilton, director of the Woodrow Wilson International Center for Scholars, told the newly created House Intelligence Subcommittee on

Terrorism and Homeland Security on Sept. 26. "When you have a challenge of this urgency, you have to have authority in the [new] agency to act."

Lawmakers in both parties predicted that without budget authority, Ridge would be stuck in a position similar to the director of the Office of National Drug Control Policy — a post that has been less effective than hoped because it has limited control of spending.

Other lawmakers stressed the importance of Ridge's interaction with high-ranking officials such as FBI Director Robert Mueller and CIA Director George J. Tenet, as well as the Defense Department bureaucracy. Some experts said he also should develop good relations with Congress. Former deputy defense secretary John J. Hamre urged lawmakers not to go behind Ridge's back.

"Don't go scheduling meetings [on terrorism] without coordinating with him first — make him your focal point," Hamre, who is now president of the Center for Strategic and International Studies, told the House Intelligence subcommittee.

Even if Ridge can foster good relations within the administration and on Capitol Hill, he still faces several other immediate challenges. One of the most difficult, Goss said, will be to define what constitutes terrorism.

Although the World Trade Center and Pentagon attacks were clearly terrorist acts, Goss said other cases can be far less clear-cut. For example, he noted that in the United Kingdom there remains considerable disagreement over whether members of the Irish Republican Army should be considered terrorists. "That's one of Tom Ridge's jobs — getting a handle on what terrorism is," Goss said. "It's a good question, and it's going to be very controversial."

Graham said his legislation to create a new homeland security office would not be acted on without congressional hearings.

Graham's second bill (S1448), cosponsored by Dianne Feinstein, D-Calif., would change several laws, including the Foreign Intelligence Surveillance Act of 1978, to enhance the ability of the CIA and FBI to infiltrate terrorist "cells" and collect information.

The White House has not yet decided whether to support the measure, and Senate Republicans were reserving judgment, awaiting word from the administration.

Easing Restrictions on Sources

Graham's bill also is aimed at making it easier for the CIA to recruit foreign agents. It would allow intelligence officials to "establish and maintain an intelligence relationship with any person for purposes of acquiring information" on a variety of terrorist targets.

During the mid-1990s, former Director of Central Intelligence John M. Deutch ordered the CIA to review all its contacts and operations to determine if any involved links to human rights abuses. The agency subsequently developed guidelines that require field officers to obtain approval from CIA headquarters before establishing a relationship with an individual who had engaged in disreputable activity.

Many lawmakers and terrorism experts said those guidelines must be eased or abolished to develop better sources, although agency officials have insisted they have not presented a barrier to recruiting.

Former State Department counter-terrorism ambassador L. Paul Bremer III said he has been contacted by intelligence officials since the Sept. 11 attacks saying the guidelines have had a "chilling effect" on recruiting agents. His commission recommended in its report that the guidelines be rescinded.

> *"One of Tom Ridge's jobs [is] getting a handle on what terrorism is. It's a good question, and it's going to be very controversial."*
>
> —Porter J. Goss, R-Fla.

"I'm astounded that 15 months after our finding, nothing has been done," Bremer told the House Intelligence terrorism panel Sept. 26. "It was the central recommendation of our report."

Republicans won approval Sept. 13 for an amendment to the fiscal 2002 spending bill for the departments of Commerce, Justice and State that would rescind the guidelines. (*2001 CQ Weekly, p. 2155*)

Members of the House subcommittee said they also saw a need for change. They said their committee's fiscal 2002 authorization bill would order the CIA to come up with more flexible guidelines on recruitment.

"While we would like the CIA to handle this internally, it's a critical issue, and it needs to be addressed and will be addressed in our bill," said Saxby Chambliss, R-Ga., the subcommittee's chairman. "It's for them to decide what those guidelines ought to say."

Chambliss predicted that Congress would still have a role in determining the extent of the new guidelines. "I feel certain that they [CIA] would come to us and say, 'Here's what we're thinking about doing,' and there would be a discussion in the Intelligence Committee," he said.

Chambliss and other committee members, however, said the provision was the subject of considerable debate in the panel's closed-door markup. Nancy Pelosi of California, the committee's ranking Democrat, has said she agrees with CIA officials that the guidelines have not been a hindrance to obtaining information and she remains concerned about the agency's closer association with individuals guilty of human rights abuses.

"Some people feel very strongly that we need very careful guidelines," said Jane Harman of California, the terrorism subcommittee's ranking Democrat. "But it's all a question of balance."

Recruitment Drive

The House's intelligence authorization bill contains a number of provisions to reflect the needs of the intelligence agencies since the attacks.

The bill would increase language training across intelligence agencies and promote a more focused analytical effort against terrorist targets. In the days after the attack, Mueller made an appeal on the FBI Web site for translators with backgrounds in Farsi, Pashto and Arabic, with the promise of an hourly payment of $27 to $38. The agency was flooded with calls.

Over the long term, the legislation would encourage recruitment of a broad ethnic and cultural mix of workers, increase investment in new technologies and encourage changes in how the intelligence community is structured.

Some lawmakers have said the inability to predict the attacks represented a massive intelligence failure. The Senate Intelligence Committee's ranking Republican, Richard C. Shelby of Alabama, criticized Tenet, a former Democratic committee staff director and holdover from the Clinton administration.

"I personally like George Tenet, and he has done some good things, but I believe the job is getting away from him," Shelby said Sept. 26 on NBC's "Today" show.

Many other lawmakers, however, said they believe such criticism is either premature or unwarranted. In a vote of confidence for Tenet and his CIA employees, Bush made a personal appearance at CIA headquarters in Langley, Va., on Sept. 26.

"I've got a lot of confidence in [Tenet], and I've got a lot of confidence in the CIA," Bush said. "And so should America." ◆

America's Infrastructure at Risk: What Is the Federal Role?

Cyber-terrorism leads list of threats as lawmakers seek new level of coordination

Quick Contents

Congress is acutely aware of how vulnerable the nation's vital infrastructure is but has no clear plan for protecting computer and communications networks and the thousands of miles of pipeline, rivers, roads and rails.

Officials in Albermarle County in central Virginia are accustomed to receiving guidance from the Federal Emergency Management Agency or the state capitol in Richmond in times of crisis, such as a hurricane or flood. But as they watched in horror as the Sept. 11 terrorist attacks unfolded on television, they were unable to reach beleaguered federal and state offices for advice.

So the county officials turned to their own disaster plan and went into a self-declared crisis mode, convening a meeting and then fanning out to protect a list of places they had previously identified as potential terrorist targets, such as a small nuclear reactor at the University of Virginia, the Defense Department's National Ground Intelligence Center, and even cultural sites such as the rotunda Thomas Jefferson designed at the University of Virginia and his home at Monticello.

"We had to transition from being stunned observers to the realization we had to do something," said county spokeswoman Lee Catlin. "There's wasn't much guidance early on because the federal and state officials were concerned with their own needs."

Albermarle County may have been better prepared than most places to deal with the

CQ Weekly Sept. 29, 2001

possibility of a terrorist strike. But in towns, counties and states across the country, as well as in Congress, the events of Sept. 11 made painfully clear how vast and vulnerable is the nation's vital infrastructure.

Thousands of miles of pipeline, tens of thousands of miles of power lines, switching stations, reservoirs, rivers, bridges, roads and rails often lie unguarded. Power plants, refineries, substations and chemical works are largely attended by private security companies.

Lawmakers fear that an assault on a key infrastructure system — telephones, pipelines, computers — could leave society stranded without basic needs. Numerous doomsday scenarios exist, such as terrorists unleashing computer viruses that gridlock the air traffic control system or spreading toxic chemicals or germs in water supplies.

Despite widespread concern, however, few lawmakers have a firm idea about what Congress could or should do. Since the attacks, key lawmakers have received detailed briefings about infrastructure weaknesses, particularly in the area of energy. But several said they are weeks away from finalizing potential legislative solutions that could help coordinate the patchwork of local, state, federal and private agencies responsible.

"It's a terrible problem. Everything's vulnerable," said John D. Dingell, D-Mich., the dean of the House and ranking Democrat on the Energy and Commerce Committee. "I'm ready to do something, but what? Show me the framework and let's go."

Searching for a Response

Some members of Congress see the proposed Office of Homeland Security as a means to focus the government's response, beginning with coordinating the efforts of federal agencies and establishing interim goals. The office will include a component devoted to cyber-security.

Others, such as Dingell and House Energy and Commerce Committee Chairman Billy Tauzin, R-La., are asking federal agencies themselves whether they think changes in the law are needed.

And lawmakers are turning to recommendations in a 1997 report by the President's Commission on Critical Infrastructure Pro-

A police officer blocks the entrance to Quabbin Reservoir in Belchertown, Mass., more than a week after the attacks. The reservoir supplies water to the Boston area.

AP PHOTO / NANCY PALMIERI

tection, chaired by Robert T. Marsh. Those recommendations included better coordination on security matters between competing companies and between industry and government.

The Marsh Commission proposed waiving some antitrust restrictions that limit communications between companies. The panel also suggested concealing some sensitive information from the public through exemptions to the Freedom of Information Act (PL 90-23).

Key lawmakers who have been briefed about the security risks say that in the next few weeks Congress may vote on legislation aimed at protecting energy infrastructure.

Tauzin said he was shocked in his Sept. 25 briefing with Energy Department Deputy Secretary Frank Blake to learn of "two or three [energy system weaknesses] that I didn't know about." He said more briefings are expected the week of Oct. 1 that may determine which changes require legislative action. Tauzin assumes that some legislation will be needed, and that action will come quickly.

"I've learned enough about the potential of these [terrorists] in this country that I believe we need to move very rapidly," he said.

Modern Threats

Public officials have long known that the nation's infrastructure is vulnerable: 200,000 miles of oil pipelines, 103 nuclear plants and approximately 2,500 hydropower dams are all potential targets.

But the dangers no longer come solely from explosives or armed assault. Telecommunications networks, power grids, pipelines, nuclear plants and refineries now are largely automated, making them vulnerable to computer hackers, viruses, worms and other devastating forms of electronic intrusion. Experts say major facilities could be manipulated by a few savvy keystrokes.

Cyber-terrorism is a new threat that government officials have not fully analyzed. Experts say the Y2K computer problem raised awareness about shortcomings but that vulnerabilities remain.

"A cyber-attack could potentially impact our national economy, infrastructures, businesses and our citizens in very harmful ways," Republican Gov. James S. Gilmore III of Virginia, chairman of a domestic terrorism task force, told the House Intelligence Committee

On the Drawing Board

Congress has not developed a general legislative approach to protecting the nation's vital infrastructure. One energy bill even leaves a blank space for provisions the Bush administration may supply later. Several options are on the table for computer security, including:

• **S 803** by Joseph I. Lieberman, D-Conn., and Fred Thompson, R-Tenn., which would create a new position of federal chief information officer within the Office of Management and Budget to oversee federal cyber-security efforts. It also would authorize a National Academy of Sciences study of computer crisis management, assess federal agencies' information technology needs and provide expanded training.

• **S 1456, HR 2435** by Robert F. Bennett, R-Utah, and Jon Kyl, R-Ariz., in the Senate and Thomas M. Davis III, R-Va., in the House, which would encourage information sharing between the private sector and government about computer attacks. The bills would encourage companies in telecommunications, energy, financial services, information technology, health care and other sectors to share information about computer security threats confidentially by exempting their reports from disclosure under the Freedom of Information Act. The companies would receive exemptions from antitrust laws to work together to combat security weaknesses. The government would analyze the reports, issue warnings and devise remedies for security lapses.

in a hearing Sept. 26. Such an attack, alone or as part of a coordinated assault, "could be substantial and devastating," Gilmore said.

A study released in June by the National Petroleum Council, a government advisory panel, explained the risks.

"In the past, most oil and natural gas vulnerabilities and threats could be negated by physical means," said the report by the panel, which was initially led by Dick Cheney before he left oil services corporation Halliburton Co. to run for vice president. "Today, however, the physical fortress can be rapidly bypassed by the electronic key."

With the Internet now connecting more than 109 million computers, officials worry about malicious acts that could shut down critical government applications and business transactions.

And the scattershot nature of disaster preparedness is perhaps nowhere more apparent than in the safeguards for defending government and private computer systems. Increasingly sophisticated attack technology can, at any point in time, cripple hundreds of thousands of connected computers, jeopardizing everything from 911 and emergency services phone exchanges to the sensors and remote controls

that measure water levels in reservoirs.

Even subtle attacks could be devastating. A series of computer intrusions by unknown parties, first detected in March 1998 and dubbed Moonlight Maze by security experts, included an incident in which a Hewlett-Packard Co. printer at the Navy's Space and Naval Warfare Systems Command Center in San Diego was programmed to print out additional copies of all documents on a printer in Russia.

Experts have long warned that the government lacks a plan for dealing with such attacks and that local, state and national agencies do not share enough information. In 1998, President Bill Clinton issued a directive to coordinate the federal government's effort to deal with damage to the nation's infrastructure, including electronic attacks.

Among other things, it set up a mechanism through which federal agencies could collaborate to identify weaknesses in their own systems and take remedial steps to correct them. But, government auditors say many of the goals of the Clinton directive have not been achieved.

For instance, the FBI's National Infrastructure Protection Center (NIPC), which expanded with the 1998 directive, has not been able to fully exchange information about security breaches and computer crime with agencies such as the Defense Department and the Secret Service, according to General Accounting Office (GAO) studies.

Tangled bureaucracies are part of the problem. The studies found that some agencies do not routinely report security problems to NIPC because many federal agency information technology officers send the data to the General Services Administration.

Limited resources also hamper federal efforts, according to experts. The Critical Infrastructure Assurance Office, which is part of the Department of Commerce's Bureau of Export Administration, studies the relationships between key computer systems across more than a dozen federal agencies that could be vulnerable to terrorist attacks. Its annual budget is $5 million.

"It's only when senior management of companies or a federal agency really care about security that things will be done adequately," said Michael A. Vatis, the first director of NIPC (1998-2000) and now director of Dartmouth College's Institute for Security Technology Studies. "Otherwise, the resources and prioritization won't be there."

NIPC gets generally high marks for investigating and responding to attacks on computers. But to date, it has developed only limited capabilities to warn of future assaults. The GAO reported this month that the office has been operating with only 13 of the 24 analysts it estimates are needed to develop long-term analytical capabilities.

The absence of a central security clearinghouse has meant that the responsibility for protecting the nation's vital infrastructure has been spread among some 20 federal agencies.

Among the programs is the Department of Energy's Argonne National Laboratory in Illinois, which operates a center that identifies weaknesses in private and public telecommunications, energy, water, and banking and finance systems and assesses the damage that disruptions would cause.

The Federal Emergency Management Agency's U.S. Fire Administration directs efforts to boost the security of computer systems operated by local fire and emergency service providers.

The Department of Commerce's National Institute of Standards and Technology operates a computer security resource center that develops new encryption standards for scrambling sensitive information and tests network security.

But many warn that a much more coordinated response will be necessary to head off threats if the United States attacks terrorist groups or their havens overseas. Experts believe that hackers sympathetic to the Afghan government or suspected terrorist Osama bin Laden could launch a wave of cyber-attacks. Many government and private systems are unprepared to take precautions, such as plugging security holes on computer servers or encrypting databases.

"For the past 13 years, we have relied heavily on the ability of the Internet community as a whole to react quickly enough to security attacks to ensure that damage is minimized and attacks are quickly defeated," said Richard D. Pethia, director of the CERT Centers at Carnegie-Mellon University in Pittsburgh, a leading cyber-security think tank. "Today, it is clear that we are reaching the limits of effectiveness of our reactive solutions."

Protective Measures

Congress' earlier efforts in this area have been to encourage cooperation between industry and government agencies.

Sens. Fred Thompson, R-Tenn., and Joseph I. Lieberman, D-Conn., inserted language in the fiscal 2001 defense authorization bill (PL 106-398) requiring federal agencies to develop information security programs and submit them to annual audits. It also directed the Office of Management and Budget (OMB) to establish government-wide policies to safeguard federal information systems. (*2000 Almanac, p. 8-23*)

Legislation (S 1456) introduced by Republicans Robert F. Bennett of Utah and Jon Kyl of Arizona is designed to encourage companies in the telecommunications, electric power, oil and gas, banking and finance, and transportation sectors to share security information by guaranteeing them confidentiality.

The bill would exempt reports on computer attacks from the Freedom of Information Act and provide an antitrust law exemption for companies that worked together to fight hacking, viruses, worms and other types of computer infiltration.

Republican Rep. Thomas M. Davis III, whose Northern Virginia district includes many Internet companies, is sponsoring a similar bill (HR 2435). The bills have been well received by high-tech groups, which have been reluctant to share security information because it could reveal proprietary information and subject them to antitrust lawsuits.

During the Sept. 26 hearing, Gilmore's task force recommended establishing a special federal court to handle cyber crimes, creating a government-funded consortium of nonprofit groups to implement a plan to enhance cyber-security and reviving Y2K task forces among government and private sector entities with a new focus on computer-based security.

Lawmakers in both parties also are looking at ways to protect the nation's energy supply, such as buying more crude oil for the Strategic Petroleum Reserve. However, lawmakers acknowledge that if the oil were needed, the process of refining and delivering it could take time.

Senate Energy and Natural Resources Committee Chairman Jeff Bingaman, D-N.M., who chaired a three-hour closed-door briefing Sept. 26 with Department of Energy and industry officials, applauded all of the proposals.

Bingaman said the panel was "trying to decide what needs to be done legislatively and then decide whether to move it through as part of other legislation or separately."

Frank H. Murkowski of Alaska, ranking Republican on the Senate energy panel, is preparing to shop around a new version of energy legislation (S 389) that leaves space for provisions to "protect critical energy infrastructure." The provision is likely to be based on administration recommendations.

The newly developed House subcommittee on terrorism will probably figure prominently in the debate as well.

A key Senate Democratic aide said that lawmakers are unsure about how broad any legislative response would need to be.

"Everyone's trying to wrap their minds around the question of: What does Congress need to do?" said the staffer. "We don't have a definitive answer to that yet, but we're working on it." ◆

Bush Wants Joint Federal-Private Effort To Increase Airport Security

In-flight protections would include technology to land hijacked planes by remote control, transponders that cannot be turned off and on-board security cameras

Congress is expected to debate and may clear aviation security legislation the week of Oct. 1 that would expand the number of air marshals aboard domestic flights, help airlines protect flight crews and put the government firmly in control of airport security.

The largest issue still not settled is whether all security personnel should be federal employees, as most Democrats want, or contract workers under federal supervision, as President Bush and most Republicans favor.

Neither the administration nor congressional leaders have decided exactly what kind of aviation security agency to create or which federal department it should operate under.

As a temporary measure, Bush has authorized state governors to call up National Guard members and, after they are trained by the Federal Aviation Administration (FAA), station them at airport security checkpoints at federal expense. The administration hopes that will give travelers more confidence in airline safety.

"Get on board," Bush told a crowd at Chicago's O'Hare International Airport. "Do your business around the country. Fly and enjoy America's great destination spots."

Though Bush's proposals enjoy broad support, Democrats have begun complaining that the administration is giving short shrift to labor.

Democrats may try to attach separate legislation that would provide extended unemployment and other benefits for aviation workers laid off since the Sept. 11 terrorist attacks in New York and Washington. Labor benefits were kept out of a $15 billion aid package (PL 107-42) enacted Sept. 22 to help the nation's airlines recover some of the losses they suffered as a result of the attacks. (*2001 CQ Weekly, p. 2215*)

While many Democrats and some Republicans favor completely federalizing the thousands of jobs of workers

President Bush shakes hands with an airline pilot Sept. 27 at Chicago's O'Hare International Airport, where the president outlined his plan to improve aviation security.

who screen baggage and passengers at the nation's airports, the administration has opposed the idea.

Bush wants the government to be responsible for security, but he wants the responsible agency to be able to out-source the personnel.

A senior administration official who briefed reporters on Bush's plan was blunt about why the White House does not want thousands of new civil service security personnel: "When you have private contractors, the federal government has much more flexibility in terms of hiring and firing. And I think that a lot of people will come to see that that actually contributes to safety because the federal government will have much more latitude to take employment actions when they think that safety standards aren't being met."

The legislation, coming on the heels of new restrictions imposed by the FAA, would be the most comprehensive aviation security campaign in decades.

Many of the proposals Bush outlined Sept. 27 were already under consideration in Congress. He wants them in place within four to six months.

Sweeping Changes

The proposals include $500 million in grants and matching funds to help airlines pay for more secure cockpits, adding cameras that would alert flight crews to suspicious activity in their cabins, and new radar transponders that pilots could not turn off to make their planes less visible to air traffic controllers.

The administration also pledged to work with airlines and pilots to develop and install new aviation technology, including remote controls that could be used from the ground to land hijacked aircraft.

Bush wants to permanently expand the air marshal program, which was created in the 1970s and reorganized in 1985 (PL 99-83) after a TWA flight was hijacked to Lebanon. Since the Sept. 11 attacks, a number of law enforcement agencies have lent personnel to the FAA to ride planes. (*1985 Almanac, p. 41*)

"We will make our standards tougher and better, and more consistent all around the country," Bush said.

Bush's most sweeping and most controversial proposal would create a federal agency to assume management and control of airport screening and security at the nation's 420 commercial airports.

Some members of both parties who opposed significantly expanding the federal work force applauded the Bush proposal.

"This is a major step forward in restoring consumer confidence in our nation's airlines," Senate Minority Leader Trent Lott, R-Miss., said Sept. 27.

Rep. Juanita Millender-McDonald, a Democrat from California, asked: "Why would you put another bureaucracy in place when you already have a bloated government?"

Airport security should be a joint project of federal and local governments, she said. "This has to be a shared responsibility."

Robin Hayes, R-N.C., a member of the House Transportation and Infrastructure Committee, said putting an airport checkpoint worker in a federal uniform "while doubling his salary and calling him an FAA employee doesn't solve the problem."

Some Democrats such as Ernest F. Hollings of South Carolina, chairman of the Senate Commerce, Science and Transportation Committee, have tried for years to federalize security workers, believing they belong under national control and standards.

"No one would think of a private corporation running the FBI," Hollings said Sept. 27. "We're going to insist on progress in airline and airport security through federalization."

Question of Jurisdiction

Congress also has not decided which federal department should be responsible for security. Some lawmakers want the Transportation Department in charge working through the FAA; others have more confidence in the Justice Department.

Millender-McDonald said some lawmakers are wary of the FAA, which has been criticized as being too slow to modernize the air traffic control system and ease flight congestion. (*2001 CQ Weekly, p. 1488*)

The Bush administration appears to favor a new agency, but one that could work under the powers of an existing department without the need for much new legislation.

"There's not anything wrong with the FAA," an administration official said Sept. 27. "We're moving to a new type of security arrangement in the United States, one that hadn't been contemplated before and is not contemplated by the current organizational structure of the FAA, or of its current capacity."

William O. Lipinski of Illinois, ranking Democrat on the House Transportation Subcommittee on Aviation, said in a Sept. 25 interview that he thought security would be run by a newly created organization within the Transportation Department.

"I think the screeners will wind up in a not-for-profit corporation, which means they will be given very good wages and very good benefits," he said.

But James L. Oberstar of Minnesota, ranking Democrat on the Transportation Committee, was cool to that proposal. "I'm troubled by reports of proposals to create a nonprofit organization that would conduct the screening," he said. "That would not be a step forward; at best it would be a step sideways."

Another issue Congress must decide is whether security would be funded through annual appropriations, passenger ticket fees or from other sources. "I'm not sure how we're going to fund this," Speaker J. Dennis Hastert, R-Ill., told "Meet the Press" Sept. 23. "It might be the government's responsibility to do that."

Debate Ahead

House Transportation and Infrastructure Chairman Don Young, R-Alaska, said Sept. 27 he hoped an aviation security measure would be ready for House floor action early the week of Oct. 1.

In an earlier interview, Young, a supporter of organized labor, said he did not want the aviation security bill to go to the floor without including aid for airline employees that he and other members failed to get into the airline bailout package.

"We're trying to do this simultaneously," Young said.

In the Senate, Majority Leader Tom Daschle, D-S.D., said he wants to add labor provisions from a bill (S 1454)

introduced by Jean Carnahan, D-Mo., to the aviation security package.

Bush's security proposal follows new initiatives imposed by the FAA following the attacks, which included a ban on knives and requirements for airports to conduct daily security checks of facilities and airliners, greater vehicle surveillance, the elimination of curbside and off-site baggage check-ins and the restriction of gate areas to ticketed passengers. (*2001 CQ Weekly, p. 2150*)

It is also similar to a bipartisan aviation security bill (S 1447) introduced in the Senate Sept. 21. Senate and House leaders from both parties negotiated the proposals with the White House the week of Sept. 24. Hollings said congressional leaders would work with the administration through the weekend, with Senate action coming as early as Oct. 1.

The House Transportation Committee intended to use testimony from aviation security hearings held Sept. 21 and 25 as a guide in writing its bill, although Aviation Subcommittee Chairman John L. Mica, R-Fla., said he was sure the legislation would not include federal employment for airport security employees.

"We're going to federalize the process, but not have 22,000 federal workers," he said in a Sept. 25 interview. Transportation Secretary Norman Y. Mineta told lawmakers Sept. 21 that making airport screeners federal employees would cost an estimated $1.8 billion a year.

Several of the suggestions made at the Sept. 25 hearing were incorporated into the security packages, including fortified cockpits, a federal takeover of passenger and baggage security checks at airports, an additional law enforcement presence throughout the aviation system and splitting the cost of such security between the federal government and private sector.

Bush and Congress omitted a proposal by Duane Woerth, executive director of the Air Line Pilots Association, that pilots be allowed to carry weapons. Woerth asked the Aviation Subcommittee to reverse an FAA ban on pilots carrying firearms to allow their use in defense of the cockpit. "Allowing specially trained and screened pilots to carry weapons in the cockpit is a priority," Woerth said.

"There may be better ways to do it than that, but I'm open for any suggestion," Bush said Sept. 26. ◆

Backers of Aid for Aviation Workers Have Limited Legislative Options

Democrats and a small number of Republicans who want to enact extra benefits for airline and aviation workers laid off since the Sept. 11 terrorist attacks may have lost their leverage when Congress cleared an airline bailout bill Sept. 21 without addressing labor issues.

President Bush has been cool to the idea of added financial aid for the more than 110,000 people left jobless by the airline crisis. The White House said Bush was willing to negotiate a general economic stimulus plan that would help such workers.

Republican leaders in the House and Senate, who kept the labor provisions off the bailout bill (PL 107-42), say the best thing Congress can do for workers is help revive the airline industry and convince the public through tough security legislation that it is safe to fly.

Some Democrats were bitter that the benefits were not included in the airline legislation. "Why in this chamber do the big dogs always eat first?" complained Jay Inslee, D-Wash., during the House debate.

House Minority Leader Richard A. Gephardt, D-Mo., was adamant that the House take up a labor bill, and he wrung from Speaker J. Dennis Hastert, R-Ill., a pledge to at least debate such a measure.

"We need to pass this bill, and we need to do it as soon as possible, and we're deadly serious about this," Gephardt said Sept. 25. "I'm not hung up on how it gets done, I'm hung up on that it gets done."

Senate Majority Leader Tom Daschle, D-S.D., warned the administration that Democrats might not support an aviation security bill (S 1447) unless it includes labor provisions.

"We've got to be a compassionate country in times like this," Daschle said. "We have to find ways to strengthen working families, and that's all we're trying to do here."

But Democrats would run a sub-stantial political risk in blocking legislation that would authorize more sky marshals on planes and stricter standards for security checkpoints on the ground.

Organized labor is backing a $3 billion package (S 1454) introduced by Daschle and Democrat Jean Carnahan of Missouri, which relies heavily on the airline industry in St. Louis, and a similar bill in the House (HR 2946) introduced by Alcee L. Hastings, D-Fla., whose district relies on tourism and travel generated by the Miami, Fort Lauderdale and West Palm Beach airports. The House bill is cosponsored by Melissa A. Hart, R-Pa., whose district is adjacent to Pittsburgh International Airport and its US Airways hub.

Added Benefits

Both measures would provide financial assistance, health care coverage and retraining to airline industry employees who have lost their jobs as a result of the terrorist attacks. Benefits would be distributed by the Labor Department through provisions of a 1974 trade law (PL 93-618) designed to help workers who lost their jobs as a result of increased imports. The bills would give some displaced airline workers up to 52 weeks of additional unemployment insurance and cover their health insurance for up to 18 months.

"I want us to be sure that while we are protecting planes, we are also protecting people," Hastings said Sept. 25. "It's one thing for us to protect planes, as we did last week, but it's just as important for us to protect the people who service them."

Daschle wants to add the labor provisions in Carnahan's bill to the airline security package (S 1447) introduced Sept. 21 by Commerce Committee Chairman Ernest F. Hollings, D-S.C.

"Just as we took care of the companies' bottom line, we need to take care of the workers as they come off the assembly line," said Rep. Rick Larsen, D-Wash., whose Seattle-area district has been shaken twice this year — by the loss of Boeing's corporate headquarters and the layoff of some 30,000 manufacturing workers.

In the House, a largely Democratic group that also includes Transportation and Infrastructure Chairman Don Young, R-Alaska, wants to merge Hastings' bill with the airline security bill the committee is expected to consider the week of Oct. 1.

Although Hastert is reviewing the labor provisions, other Republicans are opposed.

"The model of thought that says we need to go out and extend unemployment benefits and health insurance benefits and so forth is not, I think, one that is commensurate with the American spirit," said House Majority Leader Dick Armey, R-Texas. He said there was a better chance for a general economic stimulus package.

Senate Minority Leader Trent Lott, R-Miss., who does not want the aviation security and labor packages combined, nevertheless held out the possibility of extending some assistance to workers.

Labor leaders stepped up pressure for such legislation. "Now that airlines have received a multibillion-dollar relief package, it is time to finish the job by providing basic protections to airline workers who brace for severe economic hardship in the wake of the terrorist attacks," said Sonny Hall, president of the Transportation Trades Department of the AFL-CIO.

Senate Health, Education, Labor and Pensions Committee Chairman Edward M. Kennedy, D-Mass., is seeking support for a proposal that would provide up to $31 billion for workers affected by the attacks. He is hoping to include it in an economic stimulus package to counterbalance tax cuts being sought by Republicans.

Sharply Divergent Stimulus Proposals Taking Shape in House and Senate

GOP leaders emphasize tax cuts and Democrats push for spending programs, but both sides recognize compromise will be essential to enactment

Although they are moving down two very different policy paths for stimulating the economy, House and Senate leaders are employing remarkably similar tactics: Ask for more than you really need. Compromise later.

House GOP leaders are focusing almost exclusively on an unrealistically large set of tax cuts as they push ahead; Senate Democrats are responding in kind with equally implausible short-term spending proposals.

Any stimulus bill that becomes law is going to have to win votes from both sides. That means that in the resulting stew of tax relief proposals and spending plans, only one outcome is certain: Neither side will be entirely satisfied.

"It's going to have to be fair. It's going to have to have some things in it that Republicans and Democrats feel strongly about," said Senate Minority Leader Trent Lott, R-Miss. "We'll get to conference and work it out."

Mindful that the Democratic-controlled Senate will demand a more restrained approach on tax cuts than they prefer, House GOP leaders are prepared the week of Oct. 22 to push through a stimulus package (HR 3090) that satisfies their conservative base by providing hefty tax reductions, many of them permanent. The bill contains tax cuts totaling $99.5 billion in 2002, and $12 billion in unemployment assistance.

For their part, minority House Democrats are hoping to offer a roughly $100 billion alternative that would be split into three parts: temporary tax relief; assistance for unemployed workers; and transportation, building and water projects.

The White House has repeatedly taken a tough public posture against additional spending beyond a $40 billion emergency appropriations bill (PL 107-38) and a $15 billion airline bailout package (PL 107-42) that passed last month. At the same time, however, the White House has repeatedly said it wants a bipartisan bill. That means ac-

Thomas, center, has pleased the GOP base with his tax cut-heavy stimulus bill. Baucus, left, has fellow Democrats pressing for spending. They will iron it out in conference.

cepting some spending sought by Senate Democrats. The White House's GOP allies in Congress are wary.

"There's a lot of worry about the Democrats loading this up with social spending that has zero stimulative effect," Orrin G. Hatch, R-Utah, said Oct. 16 on his way out of a meeting with Treasury Secretary Paul H. O'Neill and GOP senators. At the same time, Hatch added, "Almost everyone understands that we're going to have to pay some tribute to Democrats. . . . Nothing's going to get through here without bipartisan support."

'Show Business'

The same cannot be said of the House, where Ways and Means Committee Chairman Bill Thomas, R-Calif., at the urging of GOP leaders, is moving a one-sided stimulus bill that drew no Democratic support at an Oct. 12 markup, and is expected to fare similarly on the House floor.

"It was an ugly markup. The chairman walked away from a bipartisan, bicameral process," Democrat Earl Pomeroy of North Dakota said Oct. 17. "I hope it was an aberrant afternoon."

Senate Republicans and Democrats

alike joined the chorus of criticism, saying the measure was too bloated and eventually will be scaled back.

"It doesn't pass the laugh test," Senate Budget Committee Chairman Kent Conrad, D-N.D., said. "That's not a stimulus package . . . it's a political agenda."

Perhaps most unexpectedly, O'Neill made the same point on Oct. 15, speaking to FedEx Corp. workers in Memphis. "Part of what you saw . . . was show business," O'Neill said, referring to the Ways and Means markup. O'Neill said members moved the bill so they could tell their constituents, " 'I voted for the things you want.' "

O'Neill hastened to clarify the comments in the face of Republican ire. At the Oct. 16 meeting, said a top Senate GOP aide, the message from Republican senators was, "If you don't have anything nice to say, don't say anything at all."

After the session, O'Neill obliged, calling the Ways and Means vote "useful and important" and saying the administration was "gratified that there's movement in the House."

"We're going to end up with something that's within reach of what the president has asked for."

Tax Break for Multinationals Decried, But Probably Destined to Pass

Many House Democrats angrily cited a hefty tax break that would benefit the financial services and manufacturing industries as the clearest example of all that is wrong with the GOP-backed economic stimulus bill. But the provision will nonetheless probably make it into whatever finally passes — with plenty of help from Democrats.

The House bill (HR 3090) would make permanent an expiring provision in the tax code that allows U.S. financial services companies and manufacturers with operations abroad to defer taxes on the income they earn overseas. Unless it is extended, the provision will lapse at the end of the year; making it permanent would cost $21 billion over 10 years.

"We are selling out to some rich lobbyists who want some $21 billion loophole that has no place in a stimulus bill," Pete Stark, D-Calif., complained at an Oct. 12 Ways and Means Committee markup. "That's unpatriotic and it's despicable." (*2001 CQ Weekly, p. 2390*)

Other Democrats joined in the chorus against the provision that day, but some Democrats — Senate Finance Committee Chairman Max Baucus of Montana prominent among them — are staunch supporters of legislation (HR 1357, S 676) to make it permanent. Insurance companies stand to reap a windfall. One cosponsor is Ways and Means Democrat Earl Pomeroy of North Dakota, a former state insurance commissioner who received the most insurance in-dustry campaign donations of any House candidate in the 2000 cycle, according to the Center for Responsive Politics.

Pomeroy's brother, Glenn, lobbies on other issues for the reinsurance arm of General Electric, one of the provision's main advocates.

A spokesman for House Ways and Means Democrats said they will include a one-year extension of the provision in the alternative they plan to offer to the stimulus bill during floor debate the week of Oct. 22. And senior Finance Committee Democrat Kent Conrad of North Dakota said the Senate is likely to support a "multiple-year" extension of the provision, because U.S. firms "have serious competitiveness problems" with foreign rivals.

Supporters in both parties and on K Street — a powerful coalition including GE and Citigroup, as well as manufacturing giants such as Caterpillar — say the provision is crucial to protect U.S. companies from double taxation at home and abroad.

"Allowing this to expire would be the absolute antithesis of economic stimulus," said Kimberly J. Pinter, an international tax analyst at the National Association of Manufacturers.

The measure is one of a series of "extenders" included in the House bill — which also contains temporary extensions of other expiring provisions, such as employment tax credits — and is almost certain to be a part of the Senate bill, aides say.

The provision in question, is designed to allow multinational finan-cial services firms to enjoy the same tax treatment as do other U.S. companies with operations abroad. The tax code allows most such companies to postpone U.S. taxes on their foreign income until it comes back to the U.S. parent through a dividend, interest payment or other means.

In a bid to prevent companies from exploiting deferral by leaving income in offshore tax havens, a 1962 tax law (PL 87-834) established a provision known as subpart F that excluded "passive income" — investment that is primarily financial and does not involve active management of a business — thereby making it subject to U.S. taxation. The 1986 tax law (PL 99-514) first subjected financial services companies' income to subpart F, making their foreign income taxable in the United States. The firms chafed under it for more than a decade until they won an exemption in 1997 (PL 105-34).

That relief has been extended on a temporary basis ever since, and for the industries' lobbyists and champions in Congress, the economic stimulus package is their last opportunity of the year to make it permanent, or at least to extend it again.

"The way we're looking at it is, 'What will enhance the ability of companies to enter now into long-term arrangements that will help to stimulate the economy?'" said Lisa Tate, a tax lobbyist for the Coalition of Services Industries. "The financial services industry is one of the main engines that make this economy go."

Business lobbyists with a stake in the measure know that victories won in the House may prove to be temporary. Alan Kranowitz, a lobbyist for the National Wholesaler-Distributors, said the Senate bill will be dictated partly by "whatever can garner 60 votes" — the number needed to break a filibuster or overcome points of order on the floor. Kranowitz said the real stage for action will be a House-Senate conference "with a smaller group of friends."

Nuts and Bolts

Although there are numerous obstacles in the way of a deal among Republicans, Democrats and the White House, most everyone remains optimistic that final agreement will ultimately be reached. In fact, despite healthy philo-sophical differences between the parties on taxes, that portion of the final bill may be the easiest to foresee.

Anybody following the process closely know that several widely-backed tax provisions will be part of whatever becomes law.

There is broad consensus behind the biggest chunk of the House measure, at least in 2002 costs — speeding up the rate at which businesses can write off capital purchases. Under the House bill, the accelerated depreciation would last three years, at an estimated cost of $40 billion in 2002. That alone is more than Democrats want to spend on tax relief, so they likely will propose shortening the term and keeping its cost closer to $20 billion, staff aides and lobbyists said.

There is also widespread support for a provision that would lengthen from two years to five years the period of time companies have to apply current losses to reduce their tax liability from past years. Although this "carryback" change would cost an estimated $4.7 billion in 2002, it is appealing to lawmakers because it almost makes up for itself over the decade, with 10-year costs of only $450 million.

Both parties appear willing to include a package of "extenders" in the final bill, including one that would allow financial services firms to continue to defer taxes on income earned abroad.

Another element of the House bill almost certain to be included in the final package is a tax rebate for low- and middle-income individuals who did not receive one this year under Bush's $1.35 trillion tax cut (PL 107-16) because they do not pay income taxes. GOP conservatives hold their noses when they mention the provision but concede it is the political price they must pay to get the tax relief measures they want enacted into law. The White House backs the rebate.

"We had to pay some debts in this bill," Rep. Jennifer Dunn, R-Wash., told a group of conservative economists at an Oct. 16 forum held by the Institute for Policy Innovation, referring to the rebate. But she warned that the political reality is that "this bill's probably not going to get better," expressing frustration that the Senate's continued bipartisan negotiations had eroded opportunities for more generous tax breaks.

"It's difficult because you have to sit there and watch them all being friends," Dunn said. "I think we're going to be battling to keep the good things in this bill that we have."

One such provision Republicans are fighting to preserve is a permanent repeal of the corporate alternative minimum tax (AMT) — a parallel tax system that limits the amount of deductions and credits companies can claim — and a refund of the additional taxes that they

paid because of the AMT since 1986, at a total cost of $25 billion in 2002. (*2001 CQ Weekly, p. 2390*)

While some Democrats might support repeal of the corporate AMT, which by itself is estimated to cost only $6.3 billion in its first year, they also are considering changing but not eliminating the system, for instance by allowing AMT payers to take advantage of the more generous depreciation schedule regularly taxed firms enjoy.

An immediate refund of accumulated AMT credits, most concede, is unlikely to survive.

"If you wanted to get the corporate AMT repealed, might you not go further than you intended?" Kranowitz said, referring to the House bill. "I suspect that there are other things in there that are bargaining chips as well."

Fork in the Road

In the Senate, however, things are still one step removed from the bargaining stage. Slowed but not completely stalled by anthrax-related building closures on Capitol Hill the week of Oct. 15, negotiations between Senate Finance Committee Chairman Max Baucus, D-Mont., ranking Republican Charles E. Grassley of Iowa and O'Neill continued, focusing mostly on unemployment and health care provisions.

"We're all on the same track, the same page — not on the specifics, but certainly on the general substance," Baucus said, speaking of the entire stimulus package.

Congressional and administration aides say the two top Senate tax writers are indeed close together, but the crucial decision — whether to move forward with a bipartisan package or part ways at the behest of their party leaders — has not been made.

"Grassley and Baucus are in pretty strong agreement, but their caucuses are not," said a Grassley spokeswoman.

An administration official said beyond some general agreement about the size of the economic stimulus that is needed and the general components, the principals are "not there on strategy. . . . There's two schools of thought: One, let's just do it totally bipartisan, and the other is, let's do our own bill, come in a little high and go from there," the official said. "When they can each answer that, you'll start to see some movement."

Both are proceeding on two tracks simultaneously, negotiating with each

other to find a bipartisan compromise while talking internally with their caucuses to put together a more partisan package.

The two tracks have to cross sometime, most acknowledge.

Battle Grounds

Grassley, Baucus and O'Neill made little progress, for example, the week of Oct. 15 on the unemployment and health provisions. Grassley says they would not stimulate the economy, but Democrats insist they must be part of any deal.

House Democrats are expected to include a $30 billion package for displaced workers in their stimulus alternative, based largely on two proposals they offered — and saw resoundingly rejected — at the Ways and Means markup. Their plan would expand unemployment benefits and provide government subsidies to help laid-off workers purchase health care from their former employers under a program known as COBRA.

Baucus and Edward M. Kennedy, D-Mass., the chairman of the Senate Labor, Health Education and Pensions Committee, are working together to craft a similar plan for the Senate stimulus bill.

Democrats also are following up on a request from Majority Leader Tom Daschle of South Dakota for a package of infrastructure spending projects.

"We can't do it all with tax cuts," said Democratic Whip Harry Reid of Nevada. "It's clear to me that we must have as part of an economic stimulus package a job-creating mechanism."

In testimony before the Joint Economic Committee on Oct. 17, Federal Reserve Chairman Alan Greenspan was skeptical of the stimulative nature of infrastructure spending, saying its ability to help the economy is limited by its parochial nature.

"There is a thing called politics," Greenspan said. "The propensity to create projects has not always been directly related to enhancing private productivity."

Even Democrats acknowledge the feeding frenzy surrounding the stimulus package is not limited to tax cuts.

"It's not just on the tax side, it's on the spending side," Conrad said. "People have had these proposals in their desk drawers for years, and all of a sudden they're crucial to our response to Sept. 11." ◆

Senate Awaits First Legislative Shot In Battle Over Stem Cell Research

If Democrats push to overturn Bush policy, GOP would likely seek to ban human cloning

The debate over human embryonic stem cell research is turning into a political test of nerves in the Senate, with Democrats and Republicans seemingly daring each other to draft new rules for groundbreaking biomedical studies.

Senate Democrats would like to overturn President Bush's decision of Aug. 9 to restrict federal funding for stem cell research to those cell lines already extracted from embryos. Although they lack the votes to override a Bush veto, forcing the issue could allow Democrats to portray Republican defenders of the Bush policy as obstructing critical biomedical research.

Republicans would likely respond with an amendment to ban human cloning. Many Democrats and Republicans who support stem cell research also oppose cloning human embryos, even if it would help develop new treatments. Opponents of cloning particularly fear the prospect of laboratories cloning embryos for the sole purpose of extracting their stem cells and creating high-tech tissue factories.

"We expect that during the stem cell debate, we will debate the cloning issue also," said Sen. Rick Santorum, R-Pa.

Democrats returned from the August recess openly skeptical of Bush's policy, which he announced after weeks of deliberation. (*2001 CQ Weekly, p. 1983*)

Sen. Edward M. Kennedy, D-Mass., chairman of the Health, Education, Labor and Pensions Committee, has not decided whether to mark up a stem cell bill in committee, according to a spokesman. Patient advocacy groups and the biotechnology industry are pressing for expanded rules on research, although they concede that Bush's policy is highly unlikely to be amended with Republicans in control of the House.

Democrats also could take up legislation (S 723) by Sen. Arlen Specter, R-Pa., that would allow federal funding of stem cell research without restrictions.

Specter, the Republican who is most critical of Bush's funding policy, has hinted he may offer his bill as an amendment to the fiscal 2002 Labor-HHS-Education spending bill once it begins to move.

Christopher J. Dodd, D-Conn., has sug-gested that one way to modify Bush's policy would be to enact a series of "sunset provisions" that would allow periodic agency reviews of whether scientists have access to a sufficient number of stem cells. Such a move could allow derivation of more stem cell lines.

"We're not going to resolve this issue with a piece of legislation or a speech [such as the president made in announcing his policy] on Aug. 9," Dodd said. He complained that Bush's cutoff date for defining cell lines available for research was inflexible.

Master Cells

Stem cells are primordial "master" cells that can evolve into virtually any kind of human tissue. Extracted from surplus, days-old embryos that are developed through in-vitro fertilization and that otherwise would eventually be discarded, the stem cell colonies, or lines, can multiply endlessly under the right conditions.

Scientists do not yet know precisely how the cells differentiate into individual tissues, but they have achieved limited success coaxing the cells into becoming certain components, such as blood cells. Research on stem cells is controversial because abortion opponents equate such embryos with a person.

The National Institutes of Health has identified 64 existing lines developed by 10

Quick Contents

Senate Democrats would like to overturn President Bush's policy of only paying for research on stem cells that have already been extracted from human embryos. But they lack the votes to override a veto. If a stem cell bill comes to the floor, Republicans plan to counter with legislation that would ban cloning. Many supporters of stem cell research oppose cloning.

Thompson testified Sept. 5 that researchers have access to adequate lines of stem cells to do necessary research. Bush's policy, he said, would spur such research.

research institutions, companies and universities located in the United States, Sweden, India, Australia and Israel.

Democrats and some Republicans said the White House position limiting research to stem cell lines derived before Bush's speech on Aug. 9 would limit the ability of scientists to study the ways that the so-called "master" cells may provide cures for Alzheimer's disease, juvenile diabetes and a host of other afflictions.

"Imagine if we had imposed a similar restriction on the use of fetal tissue in 1954, a year before Jonas Salk announced that he had used fetal tissue in developing the polio vaccine that saved countless lives," Kennedy said at a Sept. 5 hearing on stem cell research.

Democrats' misgivings about the Bush policy dominated the hearing. Their concerns appeared to be bolstered by Health and Human Services Secretary Tommy G. Thompson, who conceded that only 24 or 25 of the 64 stem cell lines approved for federal funding were fully developed and ready to be used for studies. The remaining colonies may not be sufficiently developed to be used in experiments.

However, Thompson said that because stem cells can divide endlessly, there are enough viable lines available to supply every researcher who receives government funding. He predicted more stem cell lines would become available before the first federal grants for embryonic stem cell research are awarded, in about nine months.

Specter, who appeared as a witness at the hearing, questioned whether Health and Human Services officials misled the president by neglecting to state that some of the 64 eligible stem cell lines were not fully evolved. Thompson responded that his department consistently had stated the cell lines were at different stages of development.

In two hours of testimony before the committee, Thompson repeatedly characterized the Bush decision as a necessary step to spur basic stem cell research by academic scientists. He said further questions about the quality of the available stem cells, their suitability for use in treatments and the possible merits of finding new sources would be left to private industry and, possibly, future administrations.

"The beauty of this thing is the basic research can be done," Thompson told reporters afterward. "Don't you think we should take however many lines we have, start the research, then two years from now, review the work and see where we are?"

Thompson did say the White House would under no circumstances alter its position and allow funding for research on stem cells derived from embryos after Aug. 9. Privately funded research institutions and corporations are not restricted and may derive new cell lines.

Thompson, a former four-term Wisconsin governor, tried to alleviate concerns about researcher access to the cell lines by announcing what he termed a "breakthrough agreement" reached the evening before the hearing that will allow government scientists access to five embryonic stem cell lines that have been fully derived by researchers at the University of Wisconsin.

A foundation affiliated with the university owns patents on the stem cells and said it will offer the same terms to university scientists around the country. None of the foreign entities that have derived stem cells have entered into such agreements.

Debating Details

Democrats weighing whether to challenge Bush's decision must decide whether to spend political capital embracing a position that involves destroying more embryos and forcing a vote on an issue that the public and some lawmakers are still straining to understand.

The Senate hearing at times illustrated how the issue can quickly turn into a highly technical debate over how many stem cells are needed to conduct meaningful research. Thompson and lawmakers, for example, tried to parse whether stem cells that were multiplying but had not yet firmly established a colony should be counted in a registry of available cells the government is compiling.

Democrats also might question whether Bush's restrictions on research might somehow compromise safety.

Practically all of the stem cells derived so far were developed in the presence of a layer of "feeder" cells from mice that provide the primitive human cells with nourishment. At the Senate hearing, Hillary Rodham Clinton, D-N.Y., questioned whether such mixing of human and animal cells could transmit viruses and other contamination to the human cells. Clinton suggested that a policy encouraging derivation of more stem cells could accommodate better ways of developing cell lines that may not have to involve animal cells.

Thompson said the process should not be an impediment to stem cell research, adding that he had no reason to believe any of the cell lines are contaminated. Thompson produced a Food and Drug Administration letter stating that a number of human clinical trials had been approved for drugs developed with mice feeder layers.

Cloning Arguments

Many Republicans are all but certain that Democrats will bring a stem cell bill to the Senate floor and hope to use a human cloning ban as a kind of trump card.

Sam Brownback, R-Kan., said that in that case, he will press for a floor debate on a comprehensive cloning ban (S 790) he authored. Brownback is even reaching out to left-leaning human rights and environmental groups, who have misgivings about human genetic manipulation and who could pressure liberal Democrats to join a bipartisan coalition against cloning.

"For too long, the abortion debate divided people on crucial issues of human dignity we all feel strongly about," said Andrew Kimbrell, executive director of the International Center for Technology Assessment, a Washington group active on food safety and environmental issues.

The House passed an anti-cloning measure (HR 2505) by Dave Weldon, R-Fla., that was virtually identical to Brownback's language, 265-162, on July 31. (*2001 CQ Weekly, p. 1920*)

Biomedical research advocates believe the Senate would be reluctant to act on legislation that effectively would criminalize some laboratory procedures. Many predict the session will end in an impasse.

"There will be a lot of posturing and jostling on the issues," said Daniel Perry, executive director of the Alliance for Aging Research, a Washington-based group in favor of stem cell research. "We're talking about legislators who are not entirely at home in the language of cellular biology. It may take more time and thoughtfulness to decide how to appropriately regulate the unknown powers of these cells." ◆

GOP Tempers Energy Plan With Eye to a Wary Public

Eager for solid results to take home, House leaders bypass bitter fights for now

Cheney answers questions on the GOP energy plan at a July 16 town meeting in Monroeville, Pa.

When President Bush started talking about a national energy strategy, the major industries involved, including oil, coal and nuclear power, agreed not to fight among themselves.

The only way to get such a plan through Congress, they decided, was to join forces and convince lawmakers and the public that the nation's growing appetite for energy requires as many different sources as possible.

"I'm not in the position of saying we need more nuclear, but not coal," said Joe F. Colvin, president and chief operating officer of the Nuclear Energy Institute, the nuclear industry's Washington lobbying arm. "It's not a matter of choices; we need all the energy we can get."

The omnibus energy legislation the House is scheduled to consider the week of July 30 is a product of this cooperation, distilled by a White House task force led by Vice President Dick Cheney. The package of bills now consolidated into one measure (HR 4) has something for almost everyone — from coal and nuclear reactors to natural gas, hydroelectric and renewables.

But a plan designed for maximum appeal hits Congress at a time of minimum cooperation. Chafed by summer heat and sweltering politics, the parties are fighting about everything from patients' rights to campaign finance. While the energy package appeals to many Democrats, its size and scope will touch off brush fires over environmental protection, federal lands, industrial subsidies and automobile efficiency.

In the Senate, Energy and Natural Resources Committee Chairman Jeff Bingaman, D-N.M., is waiting with a broad bill guaranteed to spark further conflict: It would authorize billions of dollars in new spending on energy efficiency, renewable energy and research on global warming.

The battle in the House will focus on a plan to open Alaska's Arctic National Wildlife Refuge (ANWR) to oil and gas exploration. Environmentalists call it the Holy Grail, and Republicans know they will probably lose — if not on the House floor, then almost certainly in the Senate. (*2001 CQ Weekly, p. 428*)

Their disappointment is tempered by the knowledge that Congress does not have the final word on much of the nation's energy policy. Administration officials are busy writing federal regulations for energy production, public lands, mining and the environment that are more friendly to industry than the Clinton White House would have allowed.

Republicans have tried to reduce friction in their energy bill. The whole issue of electricity, for instance, has been put off until fall because it is complex and divisive. Liability protection for nuclear power plants also has been deferred. But Democrats find plenty to worry over.

"There are a lot of very important and somewhat controversial issues in an energy bill," House Minority Leader Richard A. Gephardt, D-Mo., told reporters July 26. "Whether we're going to drill in the Arctic Wildlife in Alaska is one question. CAFE [vehicle fuel economy] standards is another question. I think, again, how we pay for needed tax incentives for renewables, solar energy, wind energy . . . are also concerns."

The legislation that goes before the House ranges from $33.5 billion in tax incentives for energy producers and consumers to a requirement that the government consider producing more energy on federal lands from the wind, the sun and underground heat.

Mindful that the public is suspicious of their motives, Republicans included a requirement for a modest increase in Corporate Average Fuel Economy (CAFE) standards for sport-utility vehicles (SUVs) and other light trucks, and mandatory energy efficiency for federal buildings.

Such a range of initiatives, Republicans say, could help protect the legislation when it reaches a more hostile Senate in the months ahead. (*2001 CQ Weekly*, p. *1768*)

"I anticipate going into the recess with a lot of momentum," said Kyle McSlarrow, the chief of staff for Energy Secretary Spencer Abraham.

Crisis Management

A crisis is usually necessary to push new energy policies through Congress, though it does not guarantee success. Despite the Arab oil embargo of the 1970s, for instance, President Jimmy Carter could not persuade Congress to pass laws forcing Americans to conserve. (*1979 Almanac*, p. *12*)

A decade later, conflict in the Persian Gulf and rising oil prices helped President George Bush and Congress enact broad energy legislation in late 1992 (PL 102-486). (*1992 Almanac*, p. *231*)

The law was designed to promote nuclear power and natural gas and create greater competition and efficiency in the electric utility industry. Many lawmakers said it did not do enough to reduce U.S. reliance on imported oil, however.

During the past decade, the strength of the U.S. economy and President Bill Clinton's focus on social policy returned energy to the back burner. The political climate began to change with last year's high gasoline prices, cold weather in the East, South and Midwest, and California's electricity shortages. (*2000 CQ Weekly*, p. *2548*)

The lawmaker perhaps most interested was House Majority Whip Tom DeLay of Texas, the point man on energy for congressional Republicans. He has led a Republican task force that developed the legislative package, and like other conservatives, he has sought to portray the issue in national security as well as economic terms.

"When the proportion of oil we import from a volatile region rises, average Americans grow more vulnerable to supply interruptions and international conflicts," DeLay said in a June 21 floor speech. "When we have an opportunity to reverse this trend, we need to seize upon it."

Bush and Cheney, who have both worked in the oil industry, declared that they wanted to emphasize domestic oil and gas production to deal with a developing "crisis" in energy. Cheney riled some lawmakers when he said April 30 that conservation was a "personal virtue" but had no part in a sound energy policy.

Polls have shown that the public is concerned about the environment as well as energy, and as gasoline prices and

Bush Energy Task Force

The Republican energy bill (HR 4) the House is scheduled to debate the week of July 30 consolidates four measures approved by committees. Here are the major elements and areas of potential conflict.

PRODUCTION HR 2436
• Drilling for oil and gas in Alaska refuge (ANWR)
• Incentives for deep-water drilling in Gulf of Mexico
• Fewer restrictions on energy production on federal lands
Problems: Congress is unlikely to approve ANWR drilling. Environmental groups are geared up to fight opening federal lands to energy exploration.

RESEARCH HR 2460
• Funding for nuclear energy research, including fuel-reprocessing
• Research on cleaner burning coal with a reduction of some pollutants
• Funding for oil and gas research
Problems: Environmentalists and some scientists oppose any moves to reprocess spent nuclear fuel.

TAXES HR 2511
• Tax credits for energy-efficient products, including cars
• Credits for new coal technology
Problems: Environmentalists criticize subsidies for the coal industry. Democrats say the bill would cost too much and force Congress to use Social Security and Medicare trust funds.

CONSERVATION HR 2587
• Higher CAFE standards for SUVs
• Subsidies for new coal technology
• Energy and efficiency programs
Problems: Some lawmakers will push for much higher CAFE standards. Critics say the plan would provide too many subsidies for coal and utility industries.

ELECTRICITY No administration bill
A Senate GOP plan proposes a major deregulation of utility companies, but no moves are likely until September.
Problems: The power industry is complicated. Some worry that utilities will use their market power to stifle competition. Congress and the states disagree over jurisdiction.

Democrats Ramp Up 'Green' Legislation In Displeasure Over Bush's Kyoto Stand

Senate Democrats, calling President Bush's refusal to endorse modifications to the 1997 Kyoto Protocol on global warming "deplorable and arrogant," are planning a steady drumbeat of initiatives on climate change leading up to the 2002 elections.

Democrats said the administration should have worked with the 178 countries that agreed July 24 in Germany to revise the pact, which aims to cut emissions of the "greenhouse gases" believed to be a main contributor to rising temperatures worldwide.

"I'm very disappointed with what has happened in the Kyoto treaty," said Senate Majority Leader Tom Daschle, D-S.D. "When it comes to environmental issues, we are minimizing ourselves. That's a dangerous position for the United States to be in."

Republican Policy Chairman Larry E. Craig of Idaho said the Kyoto pact was the "product of politics, not science." He and other GOP lawmakers are working with the White House on their own initiatives to combat global warming.

Bush's approach to the talks is the latest in a string of White House moves that could cost Republicans voter support on environmental and energy issues.

Environmentalists and several moderate Republicans have criticized Bush for his retreat in March from a pledge to regulate carbon dioxide as a pollutant. The administration has faced opposition to its proposal to drill in Alaska's Arctic National Wildlife Refuge. And Democrats say Bush's energy plan focuses more on increased production than it does on steps that could reduce the use of fossil fuels that produce greenhouse gases.

Senate Minority Leader Trent Lott, R-Miss., said he does not consider Bush's rejection of the Kyoto Protocol to be a political liability for the GOP. "They may try to make an issue out of it, but I may try to give

Jeffords said at a July 26 hearing on power plant emissions that he will continue pressing the White House to regulate carbon dioxide.

[Democrats] an opportunity to vote on the Kyoto treaty. How would they vote on that?" he said.

Lott said many senators from both parties oppose the treaty. He cited a 95-0 vote in 1997 — before the pact was finalized — on a non-binding resolution by Robert C. Byrd, D-W.Va., and Chuck Hagel, R-Neb., that called on the Clinton administration to support the protocol only if it imposed emissions restrictions on developing nations. (*1997 Almanac, p. 4-13*)

Senate Democrats, meanwhile, are poised to mark up a number of bills or riders dealing with climate change. They include:

• Legislation to rival GOP energy proposals. The Democratic plan, expected to be marked up by the Energy and Natural Resources Committee Aug. 1, would, among other things, create a Department of Energy office and a data analysis center for climate change policy; modify greenhouse gas emission reporting; and authorize billions of dollars for research to reduce greenhouse gases.

• A bill (S 1008) by Byrd and Ted Stevens, R-Alaska, that would create an office to oversee policy on climate change and authorize $4.8 billion over 10 years for increased research. (*2001 CQ Weekly, p. 1378*)

• A bill (S 556) by Environment and Public Works Committee Chairman James M. Jeffords, I-Vt., who caucuses with Democrats, that would regulate four major pollutants that contribute to climate change — carbon dioxide, sulfur dioxide, nitrogen oxides and mercury.

• Riders to a variety of bills that would address environmental policy and seek increased funding for programs related to climate change.

For example, John Kerry, D-Mass., wants to add language during the Foreign Relations Committee's scheduled Aug. 1 markup of the State Department authorization bill (HR 1646) that would require the administration to inform Congress how it is dealing with global warming.

Kerry also plans to introduce a non-binding amendment to the

State Department bill calling on the United States to participate in negotiations that could lead to ratification of the Kyoto treaty.

Bipartisan Proposals

Several Senate Republicans — concerned that environmental issues are taking on a higher political profile — are cooperating with Democrats on measures both sides could support.

For example, GOP lawmakers are working with Ron Wyden, D-Ore., chairman of the Energy and Natural Resources Subcommittee on Forests and Public Land Management, on bills that would encourage better conservation practices by farmers and other landowners.

Wyden and Sam Brownback, R-Kan., introduced conservation legislation (S 1255) on July 26 that includes incentives for ranchers, farmers and other landowners who plant trees and participate in soil conservation.

And John McCain of Arizona, ranking Republican on the Commerce, Science and Transportation Committee, is working with panel Democrats to fashion legislation that would, among other things, redirect funding, as well as authorize additional money, for environmental research at several federal agencies. Climate change is something "you can't help but pay attention to," said McCain.

Senate leaders say a number of the measures could face floor votes.

"I don't know that you'll see one big package that will sweep across the floor being called 'climate change,'" Craig said. "But my guess is that in the end, you'll see six or eight pieces [making] a package that will probably work."

In May, the House adopted a sense of Congress amendment by Robert Menendez, D-N.J., in the State Department authorization bill (HR 1646) that calls on the administration to "demonstrate international leadership and responsibility in mitigating the health, environmental and economic threats posed by global warming." (2001 CQ Weekly, p. 1026)

House appropriators also stripped from several spending bills language that would have banned the use of funds to implement the Kyoto treaty.

Democrats' Criticism

Despite several bipartisan proposals, deep philosophical and political differences remain between the most conservative Republicans and many Democrats on the best way to reduce greenhouse gases.

Those divisions were apparent during a Senate Energy and Natural Resources Committee hearing July 24 on climate change issues to be considered in the upcoming Senate energy debate.

Dianne Feinstein, D-Calif., called the U.S. absence from the Kyoto Protocol "deplorable and arrogant," adding, "When it comes to taking the actions that are necessary, I find [the United States] really backwards."

The Kyoto Protocol commits industrialized nations to reduce greenhouse gases to 1990 levels over several years. Revisions approved in Bonn, Germany, would give countries with large areas of farmland and forest — which absorb carbon dioxide — more leeway in meeting deadlines for reducing emissions.

To take effect, the protocol must be ratified by the 55 countries believed to be responsible for a majority of the world's greenhouse gas emissions. So far, 30 nations have ratified the treaty, none of them with large industrial bases.

When Bush announced in March his decision to withdraw from the treaty, he said it was a flawed agreement that would harm the U.S. economy. Former President Bill Clinton signed the treaty but never sent it to the Senate because of opposition by conservatives.

At the July 24 hearing, Wyden challenged Deputy Energy Secretary Francis Blake to offer suggestions for "finding common ground and actually making progress" on cutting emissions.

When Blake said the administration preferred to research new technology to reduce emissions instead of pursuing an international treaty Bush considers dead, Wyden scoffed.

"I don't want to doubt your sincerity here, but I think the proposition that out of this research you're going to get 180 nations to [admit] they're wrong and you're right is a very dubious proposition," he said.

And Byrd said he was disappointed the talks "lacked the type of leadership that only the United States can provide."

Republicans defended Bush's decision not to participate, saying the treaty is flawed and that the underlying science on global warming is still unclear. Lawmakers "still want to maul this issue to death for the politics of it because [they] think it will somehow bring votes," Craig said.

Looking Ahead

The White House has announced initiatives to help support scientific studies about climate change and to spur research into pollution-reducing technology. But Bush also is pursuing an ambitious energy plan that has been criticized by environmentalists.

At the July 26 Environment Committee hearing, Jeffords told EPA Administrator Christine Todd Whitman that his first priority is to get support for his four-pollutant bill.

Whitman responded that Congress should pursue a three-pollutant bill because there is broad consensus on regulating sulfur dioxide, nitrogen oxides and mercury. She also suggested that if the standards are high enough in a three-pollutant bill, some existing regulations may become unnecessary.

"We believe there could be significant regulatory relief for the utilities," Whitman said. Among the regulations she said could be eliminated "if the standards are high enough" are "new source review" pollution equipment requirements for upgraded power plants; air quality standards near national parks; and two Clinton administration policies aimed at preventing smog-forming pollution that crosses state lines.

Jeffords said he will keep pushing for carbon dioxide regulation and other measures to protect air quality.

"We can sit here and bemoan the fact that the United States has been left out of an important international treaty," he said. "Or we can take action now to improve air quality and protect the environment."

public outrage receded this summer, the administration has softened its rhetoric and begun emphasizing conservation and renewable energy sources.

Cheney has been less visible on energy issues since Democrats began investigating the process his task force used to develop the administration's energy plan. Their presumption is that he was more solicitous of the executives from the energy industry than he was of environmentalists and conservationists. The task force has refused to turn over records to the General Accounting Office (GAO).

House Democrats Henry A. Waxman of California and John D. Dingell of Michigan asked for the GAO probe. They said the energy task force's closed-door approach mirrored former first lady Hillary Rodham Clinton's White House health care task force in 1993, which was the subject of widespread Republican complaints over its secretiveness. (*2001 CQ Weekly, p. 1669*)

Big-Time Production

The debate over issues in the GOP energy package is in many ways the same as in 1992 and earlier years, with lawmakers struggling to bridge the gap between energy production and environmental protection, between the public's appetites and its attitudes.

Congress has debated the fate of ANWR for decades. It was an effort to open the refuge to drilling in 1989, in fact, that led Democrats to call for a national energy strategy to put such decisions in context.

Then-Sen. Al Gore, D-Tenn. (1985-1993), called the 1992 legislation "the last of the big production bills" and "a well-intentioned anachronism."

House Science Committee Chairman Sherwood Boehlert, R-N.Y., an influential moderate on energy and environmental issues, has much the same thing to say about the current legislation. "It still is too focused on energy production," he said.

House members have until the evening of July 30 to submit proposed amendments to HR 4 to the Rules Committee, and Boehlert hopes to add one that would require higher fuel-efficiency standards for SUVs. He has introduced legislation (HR 1815) that would phase in stricter standards until they average 27.5 miles per gallon for both cars and light trucks by 2007. Current passenger car fleets must meet

that level, but light trucks are required to meet only a 20.7 mpg mandate.

Boehlert appeared at a July 25 news conference with a new grass-roots organization called Republicans For a Responsible Energy Plan. The group called for a greater emphasis on energy efficiency and renewable sources and said they opposed drilling in ANWR.

Gephardt and Democratic Caucus Chairman Martin Frost of Texas have urged House Speaker J. Dennis Hastert, R-Ill., to allow for separate up-or-down votes on as many as seven contentious issues, including CAFE, ANWR, price controls for wholesale electricity on the West Coast, and a waiver for states such as California to quit using cleaner-burning but pricier gasoline as long as they meet clean-air regulations. (*2001 CQ Weekly, p. 1061*)

Though Boehlert stands a chance of prevailing on CAFE standards, any other major changes are more likely to occur in the Senate.

The Senate Energy and Natural Resources Committee is expected to start work on its own comprehensive bill Aug. 1, but it will take up only energy research and development, issues on which there is general agreement.

The legislation that Bingaman will introduce is far less focused on traditional sources than on greatly enhancing research into developing new sources. It contains a series of provisions that would increase research and development into energy efficiency, renewable energy and fossil energy programs.

Energy efficiency would receive the biggest increase, from $625 million in fiscal 2002 to $983 million in fiscal 2006. Renewable research funding would increase from $450 million to $733 million over the same period, according to a summary developed by Bingaman's staff.

By comparison, research into fossil energy sources, such as oil and natural gas, would receive a significantly smaller increase, from $460 million to $558 million.

The legislation also would deal with vehicle fuel efficiency, increased use of alternative fuels and mechanisms to integrate future energy policy and global climate change policy.

Power Lobbying

Having come this far, the energy industry has put considerable influence and money into backing the House legislation.

Republican lobbyist and former Rep. Vin Weber, R-Minn. (1981-93), and GOP advertising consultant Alex Castellanos have formed a group called Citizens for Real Energy Solutions that will portray the Republican plan as a balanced approach.

The Nuclear Energy Institute joined several other industry groups in mid-May to form the Alliance for Energy & Economic Growth, a coalition of more than 400 chambers of commerce, trade associations, energy companies and other groups.

The alliance has spent a reported $1 million on advertisements with waving American flags and children and a warning that national security and the American lifestyle could be at risk without an energy policy.

In addition to the Nuclear Energy Institute, the alliance's founders include the American Gas Association, National Mining Association and U.S. Chamber of Commerce. According to the Center for Responsive Politics, the four groups, plus the Edison Electric Institute, contributed a combined total of nearly $3 million in soft money, PAC and individual contributions during the 1999-2000 election cycle, the bulk of it to Republicans.

Alliance spokesman Bruce Josten, the U.S. Chamber's executive vice president, said in a July 20 statement that the package of House bills "provide a framework for the sort of comprehensive approach — from energy research to infrastructure and supply — that is urgently needed to safeguard the nation's future prosperity."

Republican political strategist Ed Gillespie leads a coalition of conservative groups called the 21st Century Energy Project. The coalition spent a reported $500,000 on an ad campaign to promote the administration's energy plan. (*2001 CQ Weekly, p. 1317*)

Environmentalists have responded with a campaign that is less costly but even more aggressive. After months of lobbying to save ANWR from oil explorations, they have broadened their attack to most of the House Republican plan.

A recent fact sheet by the Natural Resources Defense Council referred to the "top 10 problems with the House polluter payday energy bills."

Bush administration officials have stepped up their own public relations effort. In a July 25 National Press Club speech, Abraham challenged critics of

Frustrated GOP Leaders Struggle With Defections Over Rules

As the House prepares to take up comprehensive energy legislation the week of July 30, Republican leaders face yet another threat by members to defeat the rule governing floor debate.

This one comes from Democrats, who generally oppose rules written by the GOP majority. It seems unlikely Democrats will draw the Republican support necessary to defeat the energy rule, but the challenge caps a tumultuous month for Republican leaders who have faced a succession of rebellions within their ranks against procedural motions.

Such motions are considered congressional "inside baseball" and are little followed by the general public. But they are of extreme importance in the House not only because they provide a manageable framework for legislative debate, but also because they symbolize party unity.

When 19 Republicans voted against the rule for debate on campaign finance legislation (HR 2356) on July 12, it was seen as a daring slap against the leadership and particularly against Speaker J. Dennis Hastert, R-Ill. *(2001 CQ Weekly, p. 1672)*

The Rules Committee, which writes the guidelines for debate and submits them like legislation for consideration on the floor, is an arm of the leadership. All Republican panel members are appointed by the Speaker. Democratic members are appointed by Minority Leader Richard A. Gephardt, D-Mo.

Action taken by the Rules Committee is carefully overseen — if not orchestrated — by the leadership. But the job of the Rules Committee has grown increasingly difficult in recent years as the Republican majority has slowly shrunk to just a six-member voting margin. And as House Republicans rush to bring a slew of legislative priorities to the floor in the final days before the August recess, the committee has become even more

critical to leaders who want rules that make it easy to pass favored legislation quickly.

The most dramatic blow for GOP leaders came during debate on the campaign finance bill, when Hastert was handed his first defeat on a rule since becoming Speaker in 1999.

Exactly one week later, a group of moderate Republicans threatened to vote against the leadership on another procedural matter — a motion to recommit that would have replaced a GOP bill with the Democratic alternative — after the Rules Committee refused to allow a floor amendment on President Bush's faith-based initiative (HR 7). *(2001 CQ Weekly, p. 1744)*

After two days of frenzied negotiations, GOP leaders won over most of the rebels, and only four Republicans ultimately defected.

Trouble for VA-HUD

Then on July 26, party leaders saw 26 mostly conservative Republicans vote against the rule on the fiscal 2002 VA-HUD appropriations bill (HR 2620). The conservatives opposed $1.3 billion in emergency funding for disaster relief from June's Tropical Storm Allison. Such emergency designations allow Congress to ignore self-imposed budget caps, and conservatives wanted the rule to define emergency spending in an effort to prevent future attempts to circumvent the caps.

"We've got to draw the line now or we never will," said Jeff Flake, R-Ariz. "That would be the real disaster, if we ignore the spirit of our own rules."

Problems with the rule had delayed consideration of the spending bill, but in the end conservative opposition was not enough to defeat it. Thirty-eight Democrats voted in favor of the rule, which as adopted 228-195.

Democrats are invoking the earlier GOP rebellions in the effort to de-

feat the rule on energy legislation (HR 4) expected the week of July 30.

"We would like to work with you to avoid the fiasco of the campaign finance rule so that we can actually debate, in a fair and democratic fashion," Gephardt and Martin Frost of Texas, the ranking Democrat on the Rules Committee, wrote Hastert on July 20.

Democratic opposition alone is not enough to defeat a rule, but when Republicans join in, the leadership can lose.

Rules Committee member Porter J. Goss, R-Fla., said the pre-recess legislative crunch — and the desire to move bills — adds to the difficulty in winning unified GOP support.

"In these closing benchmark days, there may be a greater tendency to move something out of the oven before it's completely baked," he said. "It's like a seven-month pregnancy. We'd like to have the nine months."

Goss and others say intraparty skirmishes over procedural motions are not only common, but expected.

"Because of the narrow majority, we have a small band of people that can cause problems on a rule," said panel member John Linder, R-Ga. "We actually have these all the time."

Panel members usually are very close to the leadership, and often come from safe districts that give them the freedom to cast "tough" votes that conform to the party line even when they do not play well with hometown constituencies.

Linder said that, despite the panel's reputation for doing only what the leadership wants, it has become more independent under the chairmanship of Republican David Dreier of California, who took control of the panel in 1999.

"He's been very generous in allowing us to have input," Linder said. "David makes sure our staffs are involved in discussions on the rules."

the administration's plan to "stop hiding behind energy myths," and he emphasized the administration's desire for a multifaceted solution.

"We need to increase the role of renewables — and we will — but we also need to maintain the role of traditional sources, like hydropower and nuclear," Abraham said.

Abraham, a former senator, also is lobbying behind the scenes. After the Press Club speech, he met privately with Senate Minority Leader Tom Daschle, D-S.D. Daschle told reporters that the conversation focused on "the mutual interests that Republicans and Democrats have in moving energy policy reform."

Off the Books

Beneath the cordial rhetoric, Daschle and other Democrats worry that the administration will try to implement some of its more controversial energy proposals through regulation rather than legislation.

Of the 105 recommendations in the Cheney energy task force's report, only 20 would require congressional action. Administration officials say their authority to make administrative changes has been largely overshadowed by the ANWR debate in assessing the relative success of the administration's approach to energy.

On July 26, for example, the Energy Department proposed efficiency regulations for central air conditioning systems and heat pumps that were below what the Clinton administration had planned. The proposal, which had been expected for weeks, would require manufacturers to increase air conditioner and heat pump efficiency by 20 percent, instead of the 30 percent ordered by former Energy Secretary Bill Richardson. The new plan pleased industry officials but infuriated environmentalists. (*2001 CQ Weekly, p. 990*)

One of the most contentious of upcoming policy reviews is the administration's commitment to re-examine "new source review" regulations, which require industries to obtain federal air pollution permits when they make major modifications to production facilities resulting in increased emissions.

Utilities with coal-fired power plants have a big stake in the outcome, since they are a principal pollution source.

Another potential flash point is an administration promise to reconsider a two-decade-old ban on reprocessing

Gephardt and Rep. Jay Inslee, D-Wash., left, at a May 15 news conference on energy.

spent nuclear fuel. Reprocessing would reduce the amount of nuclear waste that must be buried in underground repositories, but critics warn that lifting the ban could lead to the proliferation of nuclear weapons.

"It's too early to know where they're going to come down on some of these things," Bingaman said. "But some of them could become very controversial."

Fixing the Grid

Of all the energy issues Congress and the White House will tackle in the months ahead, none is more controversial than proposals to deregulate the $220 billion electricity market, which is sometimes called the last great government monopoly.

Earlier this year, as California officials groped for a way out of their electricity crisis, there appeared to be little sentiment in Congress for rapidly moving ahead on a comprehensive bill to restructure the industry. But lawmakers have come to realize that any energy policy must include electricity language. (*2001 CQ Weekly, p. 226*)

In the House, DeLay convened a series of closed-door meetings among electricity lobbyists and congressional aides to try to add deregulation language to the energy package. But the talks fell apart over two issues that have stalled action in recent years: whether states or the federal government should be responsible for supervising electricity networks, and how the federal government should address

"market power," the clout that established utilities can wield to control markets and forestall competition. (*2001 CQ Weekly, p. 1650*)

Since then, Bingaman has outlined his ideas for how to proceed in September. His proposal would expand the jurisdiction of the Federal Energy Regulatory Commission (FERC) to public and cooperative utilities as well as private ones and set up "regional regulatory compacts" that would handle transmission planning, expansion and location.

The proposal would repeal the Public Utility Holding Company Act (PUHCA), enacted in 1935 to halt abuses by electricity and gas holding companies. Utilities want the law repealed so they can diversify and do business outside their franchise areas. But in a nod to consumer groups and municipal utilities, Bingaman's proposal would endorse repeal only if FERC was given more power to address market power problems.

Energy lobbyists say Bingaman's proposal is similar to the approach discussed in the meetings in DeLay's office and also is in line with an energy restructuring plan the Bush administration is expected to issue this summer.

"The prospect of legislation is very real," said Joe Nipper, chief lobbyist for the American Public Power Association, which represents municipal utilities.

However, some Republicans remain skeptical. Frank H. Murkowski of Alaska, the Senate Energy Committee's ranking Republican, said he is reluctant to give FERC more power at the expense of the states. Passing electricity legislation "is going to be awfully tough," Murkowski said. "I'm not sure that we can legislate a solution."

The issue of how much jurisdiction FERC should have "remains a very fundamental issue," agreed longtime Washington utility lobbyist Randy Davis. "If you can't do that, what does that do to the rest of the package?"

Most lawmakers remain optimistic that they can reach agreement on a broad energy package this fall. Among other things, they say, energy has become too important to both parties to fall victim to political maneuvering.

"In the end, we're going to rise above the politics of this and get something," said Senate Energy Committee member Chuck Hagel, R-Neb. "It won't be perfect, it won't be what everybody wants, it won't be what the president wants totally, but it will be reasonable." ◆

Speaker Pulls Out All the Stops For a Win on Managed Care

Moderates grow reflective over leadership bill's similarities to Ganske-Dingell

Quick Contents

A Republican win on patients' rights would give Speaker J. Dennis Hastert a chance to prove he can deliver when it comes to an issue he has worked on for much of his congressional career.

After years of trying to pass a patients' rights measure, Speaker J. Dennis Hastert may have finally found the winning strategy: produce a bill that has much in common with your opponents' measure and push Republicans to back their party and their president.

A victory would enable the Illinois Republican to heal his party after bitter fights over campaign finance legislation and President Bush's "charitable choice" bill. It also would help Bush and the GOP rechart the course of patients' rights after a bruising defeat in the Senate and claim the issue well before the 2002 elections.

Hastert must prove that, unlike during the last patients' rights debate two years ago, he can deliver, especially when it comes to an issue he has worked on for much of his congressional career. Supporters of a leadership-backed patients' rights bill (HR 2315), sponsored by Ernie Fletcher, R-Ky., say Hastert just might pull it off.

"There's just a few [members] left we're working on," Fletcher said after a July 18 GOP conference meeting. "We've narrowed

CQ Weekly July 21, 2001

it down substantially."

Charlie Norwood, R-Ga., who is backing a rival bill (HR 2563) sponsored by Greg Ganske, R-Iowa, and John D. Dingell, D-Mich., said he and the GOP leadership are also leaning on Republican moderates whose votes they need to pass a bill when the debate begins, likely late the week of July 23.

"All I can tell you is that both arms [of these members] are broken. We get one arm and they get the other," Norwood said.

Michael N. Castle, R-Del., said both parties have moved closer to agreement on how to increase regulation of health insurers, and those similarities are helping persuade Republicans who did not support the leadership bill in October 1999 to do so this time.

"The differences between the [Republican and Democratic leadership] bills are becoming almost nil," Castle said.

Unlike some previous GOP-backed bills, Fletcher's proposal would allow patients to sue health insurers in state courts, although damages would be capped at far lower levels than under Ganske-Dingell and its companion measure (S 1052) passed by the Senate. (*2001 CQ Weekly, p. 1579*)

Fletcher's liability language, and pressure from both the GOP leadership and the White House, appear to be winning converts.

Moderate Sherwood Boehlert, R-N.Y., said two visits to the White House and follow-up talks with administration officials have given him something to think about.

"I'm genuinely open to the Fletcher bill," said Boehlert, who is one of 17 House Republicans still in Congress who voted against their leadership in 1999 on patients' rights. (*1999 Almanac, p. 16-3*)

Even some Republicans who say they are committed to the Ganske bill, such as Jim Leach of Iowa and Christopher H. Smith of New Jersey, have praised the Fletcher proposal.

"Part of the reason that the leadership is in a better position this year is that they have a better alternative," Leach said. "It's made it much more difficult for me. In the end, I'm left with a judgment to make between two very reasonable bills."

Backers of the Ganske-Dingell bill, however, believe they have more than enough votes to prevail.

Dingell, left, Norwood and Ganske address a news conference July 19. The difference between their bill and a rival plan is now "almost nil," said one lawmaker.

Patients' Rights Bills Compared

The House is expected to consider competing patients' rights legislation the week of July 23. One measure (HR 2563), sponsored by Greg Ganske, R-Iowa, and John D. Dingell, D-Mich., contains liability provisions similar to those in the bill (S 1052) the Senate passed on June 29. A rival measure (HR 2315) offered by Ernie Fletcher, R-Ky., and Collin C. Peterson, D-Minn., contains more restrictive liability provisions and is supported by President Bush. The Ganske and Fletcher bills contain a number of similar protections for patients, including guaranteed coverage for specialty care and emergency care, and direct access to obstetricians and gynecologists.

ISSUE	SENATE (S 1052)	FLETCHER-PETERSON (HR 2315)	GANSKE-DINGELL (HR 2563)
Right to sue	Patients would be required to exhaust internal and external appeals before filing suit. They could sue health plans in state court under applicable state laws for disputes over medically reviewable decisions and in federal court for administrative decisions that resulted in injury or death. Patients could not pursue lawsuits in both forums at the same time.	Patients would be required exhaust internal and external appeals before filing suit and could sue in either federal or state court, but not both. Patients could sue in federal court for either medically reviewable decisions or administrative decisions that resulted in injury or death. Patients could also sue under state law where applicable if a plan disregarded decisions of an independent external reviewer.	Same as Senate bill.
Damage cap	Limits on damages in state suits would be set by state law. Punitive damages would be prohibited in federal court, but civil penalties of up to $5 million would be allowed if the plan acted in bad faith. Economic and non-economic damages would be unlimited.	Limits on damages in state suits would be set by state law. In federal court, patients could sue for up to $500,000 in non-economic damages and unlimited economic damages. Punitive damages would be prohibited.	Same as Senate bill.
Employer liability	Employers would be shielded from suits if they appointed a "designated decision-maker" to make medical decisions and the employer did not participate in such decisions. Plans that self-insure and self-administer would be exempt from suits in federal court.	Employers would be shielded from lawsuits if they appointed a "dedicated decision-maker," such as an insurer or other third party, with authority over both medical and administrative health care decisions.	Same as Senate bill.
States' rights	States laws would have to "substantially comply" with federal law.	A governor could ask the secretary of Health and Human Services to certify that state laws are "substantially equivalent" to federal law.	Same as Senate bill.
Scope	All Americans in private insurance or employer-sponsored plans, plus people covered under Medicare, Medicaid and other federal health plans, would be covered.	All Americans in private or employer-sponsored insurance plans would be covered.	All Americans in private or employer-sponsored insurance plans would be covered.

Politics and Public Policy

To help win over undecided Republicans, Bush invited several lawmakers to the White House on July 16 so he and top administration officials could make their pitch. Following the meeting, participants said a number of Republicans who are publicly undecided were persuaded to vote for the Fletcher bill.

More White House meetings are likely when Bush returns from an economic summit in Italy. "There's intense pressure," said Bob Barr, R-Ga., a conservative who said he is inclined to vote for the Ganske-Dingell bill, just as he did in 1999.

Billy Tauzin, R-La., chairman of the Energy and Commerce Committee, said Republicans have a lot more work ahead of them.

"It's a lot less than 50 but a little more than five," Tauzin said July 19 when he was asked how many more votes are needed for passage of Fletcher's bill.

"I don't think anyone has a hard count yet," Hastert said the same day.

Business and health care lobbyists who back the GOP proposal said they are concentrating their efforts on Republicans who have shown a new willingness to consider the Fletcher bill.

"There's still a lot of searching going around to see where the votes are," said Neil Trautwein, a top health care lobbyist for the National Association of Manufacturers. "The focus of the House is shifting in greater earnest to the debate. There are a lot of people scratching their heads right now."

Mark Souder, R-Ind., said the Fletcher bill may have picked up a few more Republican supporters. A firm count is hard to get because many members are "trading" — asking for earmarks in appropriations bills and for certain bills to come to the floor in exchange for supporting the leadership on patients' rights, Souder said.

One of the biggest obstacles Fletcher faces is in trying to convince Republicans who voted for Norwood-Dingell in 1999 that they can switch now without opening themselves up to criticism from political rivals in 2002.

"A flip-flop is always devastating," said Souder. When he won his seat in 1994, Souder said, he charged that his opponent, Rep. Jill L. Long (1989-95) had changed her position on President Bill Clinton's health care plan in 1993.

To give House Republicans cover from such accusations, Ways and Means Committee Chairman Bill Thomas, R-Calif., is focusing on how GOP leaders have changed the bill — beefing up its dispute resolution provisions, for example — as evidence that members would be voting for a stronger bill now.

Blue Dogs Wooed

Democrats are concentrating on keeping their own moderates in line on Ganske-Dingell. The Southern-dominated conservative "Blue Dog" Democrats have officially endorsed the bill. But some individual members have expressed interest in the Fletcher proposal and are under heavy pressure from Democratic leaders to back the Ganske measure.

Fletcher's bill is "a legitimate compromise that has merit," said Cal Dooley, D-Calif., who was criticized by the Democratic leadership about a month ago after approaching Republicans to discuss liability. "But [the Fletcher bill] is too late arriving on the scene. It's difficult for members to reposition themselves."

Supporters of the Ganske bill say they are concerned the leadership could stack the deck against them with a rule for floor debate that sets high procedural hurdles.

But a number of Republicans said they expect a fair rule. Moderates complained bitterly July 12 when GOP leaders tried to force advocates of campaign finance legislation (HR 2356) to navigate a series of votes on 14 amendments, a framework that the bill's supporters said was unfair. (*2001 CQ Weekly*, p. 1672)

Republicans do not expect their leaders to try a similar approach on patients' rights. "Oh, my Lord, I hope they learned something," said Marge Roukema, R-N.J., who said she would vote for the Ganske bill.

Norwood said he is seeking a rule that would allow a "reasonable" number of amendments from both sides.

Republican leaders say the debate will be fair. "We know there are basically two bills that have standing upon the members of Congress," House Majority Leader Dick Armey, R-Texas, said July 17. "Both of those will have, I'm sure, a place in the room."

GOP leaders and the White House did not want the campaign finance overhaul to pass, but they feel a strong political need to enact a patients' rights bill before the 2002 elections.

That is why they may bring the Fletcher bill to the floor even if a whip count shows them to be a few votes short of victory. "I'd like to get it done and get it off the table," Hastert said July 19.

Opponents also are eager for the debate to begin. "We're just asking for a fair shake to debate our bill on the floor," Ganske said.

Liability Concerns

Ganske and Dingell have made several changes to their bill to build more support among lawmakers concerned about employers' liability, and both sides are expected to continue tinkering with details in the days before the debate.

Ganske's alterations include adding provisions from the Senate bill that would allow employers to appoint a "designated decision maker" to make medical decisions and shield employers from lawsuits. Other Senate provisions added to the bill include a requirement that patients exhaust internal and external appeals processes before filing a lawsuit. Reviewers also would be prohibited from requiring a health plan to cover treatments excluded from a plan's contract.

A key insurance industry group said July 18 that "designated-decision maker" clauses in both House versions and the Senate bill would not shield employers from costly lawsuits.

According to the Health Insurance Association of America, even if a company were to appoint an outside decision maker, it could still be sued. The group said plaintiffs' attorneys could force companies that provide health insurance to their employees to prove they had nothing to do with the medical decision in question.

Complying with these legal steps — and purchasing liability insurance to cover expenses should an employer lose a case — would cost companies thousands of dollars per case, the group said, and those expenses would be passed on to workers and consumers.

One of the key arguments against the Senate-passed bill is that its liability provisions would raise employers' premiums and cause companies to drop workers' coverage.

Amy Jensen, chief House lobbyist for the National Federation of Independent Business, a trade group representing small companies, said just being deposed and named in a lawsuit "is enough to put some of our guys out of business." ◆

Student-Testing Drive Marks An Attitude Shift for Congress

As school 'accountability' plan gains acceptance, are other solutions being shortchanged?

On a sunny April day, Michele Forman stood proudly in the Rose Garden as President Bush named her the National Teacher of the Year — and then listened politely as he used the occasion to make another pitch for his plan to overhaul the nation's education laws.

Forman held her peace that afternoon as the president spoke of "accountability" and "excellence for every child" and urged the Senate to pass the legislation. It was not the time to raise doubts, she knew, not when Bush was paying her the ultimate honor for a lifetime of work. But if Bush had asked her opinion, he might have heard what was really on her mind: Like many other teachers, Forman is afraid Congress is about to put way too much faith in testing as the ticket to better schools.

"The type of test I have no use for as a teacher is one that ranks students and ranks schools," Forman, a teacher at Middlebury Union High School in Middlebury, Vt., said in a June 22 interview. A low score, she said, "might mean the students aren't learning. It might mean the teachers aren't teaching. But it might mean a lot of other things. It might mean it's a bad test."

There was a time when the idea of imposing a new battery of government-mandated tests on school children was so controversial that it brought school improvement plans to a screeching halt. In 1997, President Bill Clinton called for voluntary national tests in reading and math; the idea seemed tailor-made to fit conservatives' fears of a national curriculum, and Republicans killed it outright. (*1997 Almanac, p. 9-50*)

This year, however, there is no turning back. The ranking of schools, with rewards for the best ones and penalties for the worst, is at the heart of the landmark education overhaul (HR 1) that is close to becoming law. (*2001 CQ Weekly, p. 1431*)

By embracing the key element of Bush's education plan, lawmakers have marked a fundamental shift in the way Congress views federal aid to education, much as the 1996 welfare overhaul (PL 104-193) marked a sea change in how Congress thought about helping the needy.

Then, lawmakers at both ends of the political spectrum had to accept time limits on government assistance if they wanted to be taken seriously on the issue. Now, there is widespread agreement in Congress that annual testing is needed to find out what is happening in the nation's schools. (*1996 Almanac, p. 6-3*)

In both instances, Congress sent the unmistakable message that government assistance comes with responsibilities. Just as lawmakers were willing to cut off assistance to poor people who would not work, they are now endorsing the same kind of carrot-and-stick approach to federal aid to the schools. Rewards would be given to the best schools and penalties to the worst — and the schools and educators that teach the most disadvantaged children will no longer be allowed to argue that their students' fates are beyond their control.

"Even a couple of years ago, no president would have proposed, and no Congress would have passed, the accountability provisions that are part of this bill," said Sen. Thomas R. Carper, D-Del., a former governor who staked much of his 2000 Senate campaign on his state's education overhauls. "What was considered progressive thinking a few years ago . . . has now become accepted."

When House and Senate conferees meet to work out the final version of the education bill after the July Fourth recess, there is little doubt Bush will get the main thing he wants: annual testing in reading and math in third through eighth grades. Conferees have not been named yet, but most observers say final passage of the education bill could come before the August recess.

In part, the shift to testing has happened because Bush convinced many lawmakers there is no other way to measure how much, or how little, students are learning — and that schools will not improve unless the information is made public.

"Without yearly testing, we don't know who is falling behind and who needs help," Bush said in January when he unveiled his education plan.

But it also happened because the center of political gravity on the issue was shifting even before Bush took office. Democrats such as Sens. Joseph I. Lieberman of Connecticut and Jeff Bingaman of New Mexico were arguing in 2000 that rewards and penalties would motivate schools to change.

And just as the 1996 welfare overhaul came after a series of state experiments with time limits, this education proposal follows a wave of state laws that used testing to force changes in the schools. When Bush made "accountability" a central theme of his plan, bolstered by the success that Texas had with a similar system during his tenure as governor, congressional Republicans bought into it.

The Narrowing Debate

Because the entire debate has focused on testing, some educators and lawmakers say important debates about deeper causes of the "achievement gap" between disadvantaged students and their peers are getting short shrift.

For example, the funding inequities between rich and poor school districts, a problem often highlighted by liberal analysts, received only a brief flurry of attention before the Senate rejected an amendment by Christopher J. Dodd, D-Conn., that would have forced states to address it.

A conservative priority — allowing parents of children in underperforming schools to use federal funds for private school tuition — was also set back. Both the House and Senate rejected Bush's proposal for private school vouchers

Roxanne Walters and her fourth-grade classmates at Northeast Elementary School in Kearney, Neb., practice in February for a state test to determine their proficiency in reading and writing.

are firm believers in the testing and accountability provisions. "I think it's time for the federal government to expect results for the money it continues to spend on our schools," said Boehner.

For Edward M. Kennedy, D-Mass., who will lead Senate conferees, the task will be to fight for as much of a funding increase as possible. Otherwise, he says, there will not be enough money to help the neediest schools meet the new standards, and "I think we will have a very significant missed opportunity."

Republicans view the testing issue as political gold. With the Bush plan taking center stage in Congress, an ABC News/Washington Post poll released June 4 found the president in a virtual tie with Democrats over who would do a better job on education policy — a turnaround from the days when Democrats generally won broader support on the issue.

and declined to allow even a demonstration program.

This narrowing of the debate has frustrated some lawmakers. "The table has been set, and the idea of adding anything to the menu is out of the question," Dodd said.

For others, however, it is simply the inevitable product of a closely divided Congress. "Because of this delicate balance in the House and Senate, you're not going to be able to move any legislation that's seen as too far to the left or the right," said James C. Greenwood, R-Pa., a member of the House Education and the Workforce Committee. "By necessity, the education bill has moved toward the center."

The contours of the bill are now well defined and are unlikely to change radically when conferees sit down to work out the final version. That means Congress will have to hope that testing and "accountability" for low-performing schools — a national expansion of the overhauls already in place in 49 states — will help bring poor and minority students' test scores in line with the national average.

For Bush and Congress, the political stakes are enormous. The bill is likely to be the most significant reauthorization of the Elementary and Secondary Education Act (ESEA), the main source of federal aid to the public schools, since the law was enacted 36 years ago.

Bush has a lot riding on its success; he calls the education overhaul "my No. 1 priority." But the stakes will also be high for lawmakers from both parties who have joined forces with him, since they have already made tradeoffs that were unpopular with their party colleagues.

For House Education and the Workforce Chairman John A. Boehner, R-Ohio, who is expected to chair the conference, the trick will be to win as much state and local flexibility as possible to keep conservative Republicans happy. He will have to do that without alienating his ranking Democrat, George Miller of California, who has fought to keep his own members in line. *(2001 CQ Weekly, p. 1314)*

The good news for Bush is that both Boehner and Miller

Improving State Results

Based on the states' experience, lawmakers and the president have some reason to be optimistic. Texas, which put a similar accountability system in place in the 1990s, has seen gains in minority students' reading, writing and math scores. And nationwide math scores increased by an average of 1 percentage point a year in the 1990s, according to a July 2000 study by RAND, a public policy think tank based in Santa Monica, Calif.

Those numbers would suggest that state overhauls are working. But there remains the very real possibility of a backlash against more testing. At least four states have already revised their tests because of alarmingly high failure rates. In one well-publicized rebellion, parents in Scarsdale, N.Y., kept their children at home to boycott the state science test because they believed the standardized testing trend has gotten out of hand.

There is also the danger of inflated expectations. When President Lyndon B. Johnson declared a "war on poverty" 37 years ago, historians believe he set up the nation for disappointment because he was implying that the war could be won and poverty would disappear. Now, some analysts say, Bush may be similarly setting the expectations too high on education.

By choosing the phrase "No Child Left Behind" as the slogan for his plan, they say, Bush has chosen another lofty rhetorical goal that may be impossible to achieve. And because Congress has to work out the actual details of the plan, they say, lawmakers may have the most to lose with voters if the plan does not work.

"The president set the terms of the debate," said John F. Jennings, director of the Center on Education Policy, a liberal group that advocates greater support for the public schools. "Now, he's letting the politicians in Congress do his dirty work so he can come in and claim credit at the end. And the politicians are sweating bullets."

That means conference committee deliberations are not likely to go quickly. For Democrats and some moderate Republicans, the most obvious question is how much additional ESEA funding should accompany the overhaul beyond the $18.6 billion the programs received for fiscal 2001.

That issue is almost certain to become intertwined with the fiscal 2002 Labor, Health and Human Services and Education appropriations bill, where the money would be provided.

Bush and congressional negotiators will somehow have to bridge the difference between the $4 billion increase the administration has floated and the $14.4 billion increase authorized in the Senate bill, since the budget resolution (H Con Res 83) leaves no room for any education increase beyond inflation. (*2001 CQ Weekly, p. 1081*)

"If President Bush comes up for re-election and he hasn't funded the testing, it's all going to fall apart for him," said Patsy T. Mink of Hawaii, one of the Democrats who negotiated the House bill.

For conservative Republicans, the biggest priority will be to preserve the state and local flexibility Bush wanted as a tradeoff for the strict new standards. That means fighting for the "Straight A's" demonstration in the Senate bill, which would let seven states and 25 school districts consolidate most program funds into block grants to spend as they see fit.

House Democrats say they will not vote for a conference report if it includes "Straight A's," but Republicans in both chambers believe they have already compromised enough by agreeing to a demonstration rather than a nationwide version.

"From where we started, it's a pretty weak version that's left," said Sen. Tim Hutchinson, R-Ark.

The issue most likely to give lawmakers and administration officials migraines, however, is the formula for determining when to penalize states and schools for poor performance.

Education analysts say this fine-print issue could make all the difference between an overhaul that works and one that either has no impact or hurts too many schools.

The Senate formula has been criticized as both too complex and too easy on the states, but the House version is considered so harsh that most schools would be labeled failures.

"We think there's a third way," said Lisa Graham Keegan, chief executive officer of the Education Leaders Council, a group of state education officials that has influenced the GOP education agenda.

"We'd like to take it to the conference committee and say, 'Let's get a fresh start,' " Keegan said.

The Dividing Lines

Despite the bills' overwhelming votes in the House and Senate, Congress remains divided over the issue of how to improve schools in much the same way the nation itself is divided. Lawmakers with close ties to the education system have little use for more testing; most of the rest think the schools are unlikely to improve without it.

The lawmakers who put the education bills together — including Boehner and Kennedy — agree with education experts and business groups that it is critical to be able to measure what students are learning.

"We know that if we don't test, we don't know, and children fall behind," said Boehner.

Boehner and Kennedy were never teachers, however. Those lawmakers who have been in the classroom are more forgiving of teachers and more skeptical of how much Congress can accomplish by adding tests.

"As a neophyte here, I was kind of taken aback at how quickly [the House bill] was jammed through," said freshman Rep. Michael M. Honda, D-Calif., a former teacher and principal. "We sometimes don't listen to the professionals in the field because we think they're trying to make excuses. . . . If we had more teachers in Congress, our education policy would look much different."

So far, a large backlash has not arisen against the testing already mandated by the states. According to a September survey by Public Agenda, a public opinion research and information organization, only 11 percent of 803 parents polled said their children were having to take too many standardized tests; 55 percent said the amount was "about right." The group said opposition did not appear to be higher in cities with extensive testing programs.

But only 15 states currently test students every year between third and eighth grade. And the others are likely

to have problems early on, based on the experience of states that use "high-stakes" exams, which students must pass to graduate from high school.

Four of those states — Virginia, California, Massachusetts and Wisconsin — have had to revise their exams because of high failure rates, according to an April report by the Education Commission of the States, an education policy research organization.

In Virginia, where students had a high initial failure rate on the Standards of Learning (SOL) exams, more than half of the 1,031 parents surveyed by The Washington Post in August 2000 concluded the testing program was not working.

Five other states — Michigan, Minnesota, North Carolina, Oklahoma and Washington — are phasing in or delaying their annual tests because of logistical problems and growing public opposition.

"Clearly, if you look around the country, the implementation of these tests has been very problematic," said Joseph Olchefske, superintendent of the Seattle public schools.

Olchefske supports the idea of testing to improve schools, but notes that only 23 percent of Washington state fourth-graders passed all four parts of the Washington Assessment of Student Learning exam last year. That will have to change quickly: This is the class that will have to pass all parts of the 10th-grade exam in order to graduate in 2008.

In addition, there are signs that the public does not want test scores to be used the way Congress intends. In a CBS News-New York Times poll released June 20, 74 percent of the people polled said they supported mandatory testing to find out how well the schools are educating students. But by a 2-to-1 margin, they opposed giving extra federal funds to the best schools and withholding them from the worst.

The conference committee's biggest challenge may be damage control: making sure the bill does not have draconian consequences.

From the state level down to districts and individual schools, the key to the proposed accountability system is that schools must make "adequate yearly progress" to avoid sanctions.

For states and school districts, the penalties for failure could include a partial loss of federal administrative funds. Failing schools could be turned

Education Bills Compared

The House passed its education bill (HR 1) on May 23 and the Senate passed its version of HR 1 on June 14. Here are high- lights of the two measures, both of which would reauthorize the 1965 Elementary and Secondary Education Act (ESEA).

ISSUE	SENATE	HOUSE
Funding levels	ESEA programs would get a $14.4 billion increase in fis- cal 2002, nearly doubling the current funding level of $18.6 billion. That includes an additional $6.4 billion in Title I aid to disadvantaged schools — $132 billion over 10 years — to ensure the program reaches all eligible children.	ESEA programs would get a $4.6 billion increase in fiscal 2002. Title I funding would double over five years, reach- ing $17.2 billion by fiscal 2006.
Testing	States would have to test students in reading and math every year in grades 3 through 8 starting in the 2005-06 school year. Test scores would be broken down by sub- groups, including students' race, ethnicity, income, Eng- lish proficiency and disabilities. To gauge the tests' diffi- culty, scores would be checked against the National Assessment of Educational Progress. States could sus- pend testing if Congress does not appropriate at least $370 million in fiscal 2002, rising to $430 million in fis- cal 2008, to offset the costs.	States would have to test students in reading and math every year in grades 3 through 8, starting in the 2004-05 school year. Test scores would be broken down by sub- groups, including students' race, ethnicity, income, Eng- lish proficiency and disabilities. Scores would be checked against the National Assessment of Educational Progress or an alternative test chosen by the state.
Accountability	Penalties for states, school districts and schools would kick in if the percentage of students from each subgroup that reaches the "proficient" level did not improve by at least 1 percentage point a year, averaged out over three years, or if state improvement goals were not met. Those goals would have to be calculated to bring all students up to "proficiency" level within 10 years. Performance to- ward these objectives could be combined to develop a "grade" for overall performance.	Penalties for states, school districts and schools would kick in if all students' scores did not improve enough to bring them up to "proficiency" level within 12 years and if academic achievement gaps between the groups were not closed.
Consequences	**Schools:** If a school failed to make "adequate yearly progress" for one year, it would receive technical assis- tance and be required to develop a plan for improve- ment. After three years, districts would have to take "cor- rective action," such as changing the school's structure, replacing its staff or imposing a new curriculum. After four years, the school would either be re-opened as a charter school, have all staff replaced or be taken over by the state or a private entity. **School Districts:** If a district failed to make "adequate yearly progress" for two years, it would receive technical assistance and have to develop a plan for improvement. After four years, the state would have to take "corrective action" against the district. That might include imple- menting a new curriculum, restructuring or abolishing the district, replacing personnel, removing schools from a district's jurisdiction, appointing a trustee or receiver to run the district or withholding funds. **States:** After two years of declining test scores, states could lose 30 percent of their federal administrative funds. If scores did not show enough improvement after another year, states could lose another 45 percent of those funds.	**Schools:** If a school did not make "adequate yearly progress" for one year, it would receive technical assis- tance and be required to develop a plan for improve- ment. After two years, the district would have to take "corrective action" such as replacing the staff, imple- menting a new curriculum or appointing outside experts to advise the school. After three years, a school could be re-opened as a charter school, have all employees re- placed or be taken over by the state or another entity. **School Districts:** If a district failed to make "adequate yearly progress" for two years, it would receive technical assistance and have to develop a plan for improvement. After four years, the state would have to take "corrective action." That might include withholding funds, replacing personnel, removing schools from a district's jurisdiction, appointing a trustee or receiver to run the district, abol- ishing or restructuring the district or allowing students to transfer to another district. **States:** After two years of declining test scores, states could lose 30 percent of their federal administrative funds. If scores did not show enough improvement after another two years, states could lose another 45 percent of the funds.

ISSUE	SENATE	HOUSE
School choice	If a school failed to make "adequate yearly progress" for three years, the district would have to provide public school choice or state-approved public or private tutoring services, using up to 15 percent of its Title I funds. Private school tuition would not be covered. The bill includes $125 million in grants to develop new approaches to public school choice and $400 million to help provide facilities and start-up costs for charter schools.	If a school failed to make "adequate yearly progress" for one year, the district would have to provide public school choice. After three years of failure, up to 40 percent of the school's Title I funds could be used for state-approved public or private tutoring services. Private school tuition would not be covered. Up to 15 percent of a district's Title I funds could be used for transportation expenses.
Flexibility	Seven states and 25 school districts could participate in a "Straight A's" pilot program that would consolidate most ESEA funds into block grants. The experiment would be terminated in any state or school district that did not meet the standard of "adequate yearly progress" for two years or exceed it for three years.	States and school districts could shift up to 50 percent of funds among four ESEA programs — teacher quality, the Innovative Programs block grant, Safe and Drug Free Schools, and technology grants — or into Title I programs. The categorical programs would be maintained under current rules, and no funds could be taken out of Title I. A "super local flex" experiment would allow 100 school districts to consolidate non-Title I funds from the same four programs and be relieved of their current rules if the funds are spent for educational purposes.
Special education	States and school districts would get $181 billion over 10 years to cover 40 percent of their costs in complying with the 1975 Individuals with Disabilities Education Act (PL 94-142). *(1975 Almanac, p. 651).*	No provision.
Class-size reduction	The three-year-old program to reduce class sizes by hiring 100,000 new teachers would be consolidated into a block grant with other teacher quality programs.	Same provision.
School renovation	The $1.2 billion program of grants and loans for emergency school repairs created in the fiscal 2001 omnibus appropriations bill (PL 106-554) would not be authorized. However, some block grant funds could be used for school construction. *(2000 CQ Weekly, p. 2862)*	The $1.2 billion program of grants and loans for emergency school repairs created in the fiscal 2001 omnibus appropriations bill (PL 106-554) would not be authorized.
Title I targeting	Language in the 1994 ESEA reauthorization (PL 103-382) requiring any increase in Title I appropriations to be distributed through targeted grants would be maintained. A new trigger mechanism would prevent any Title I increase unless the bulk of the funds is distributed through the targeted grants to ensure the money reaches the poorest districts. *(1994 Almanac, p. 383)*	Language in the 1994 ESEA reauthorization requiring any increase in Title I appropriations to be distributed through targeted grants would be maintained.
Discipline	Students with disabilities could be suspended or expelled for bad behavior, such as selling drugs or bringing a weapon to school, if the incident was not related to their disability. If it was related, they would still receive educational services but could be sent to another school.	Students with disabilities could be suspended or expelled for bad behavior, such as selling drugs or bringing a weapon to school. Districts could continue to provide educational services to expelled students but would not be required to do so.
Boy Scouts	Districts could lose federal funds if they deny the Boy Scouts or other "patriotic societies" (as identified in Title 36 of the U.S. Code) access to school facilities because they refuse to accept homosexual members. An alternate proposal, also adopted, would require districts to give such groups equal access to school facilities but would not threaten violators with a loss of federal funds.	Districts could lose federal funds if they deny the Boy Scouts or "any other youth group" access to school facilities because they refuse to accept homosexual members.

into charter schools (freed from regulations but expected to show better student achievement), have all of their teachers and administrators replaced or be taken over by the state or a private entity.

The Senate has already softened its bill, dropping language that would have imposed penalties if all groups of students, including children from different racial, ethnic and economic backgrounds, were not making enough progress to reach "proficient" levels in reading and math within 10 years.

As passed by the Senate, the measure would not penalize states or schools unless the portion of each group reaching "proficiency" did not improve by at least 1 percentage point a year, averaged out over three years.

Lawmakers moved away from the tougher language after Republican aides on the Senate Health, Education, Labor and Pensions Committee ran estimates of how many states would have made "adequate yearly progress" under the original language. They found none that would have passed the test.

Even in Texas and North Carolina, two of the states that have had the most success with similar overhauls, almost every school would have failed.

"The goal . . . was both admirable and entirely unrealistic," said James M. Jeffords of Vermont, who was chairman of the Senate education committee before he left the Republican Party to become an Independent.

Democrats rejected that analysis, but they agreed to the changes to make sure no schools are penalized if a single group of students fails.

The House bill sticks closer to the Senate's original language. Its penalties would kick in if students do not make enough annual progress to ensure that all reach the "proficient" level in reading and math in 12 years. Because of the Senate aides' study, however, most education groups do not expect that language to survive.

"This is going to be a huge problem in implementation," said Frederick M.

Hess, assistant professor of education and government at the University of Virginia and author of "Spinning Wheels: The Politics of Urban School Reform."

What is likely to happen, Hess said, is a "culture clash" between urban school districts, where many teachers are not used to high expectations, and suburban districts, where some teachers may feel they have to water down their lessons to fit the tests.

Bush congratulates Forman at an April 23 ceremony. She later said tests should not be the only means of assessing progress.

What Was Left Out

Those issues may seem like a full plate for Congress, but they barely address the fixes that many lawmakers, educators and analysts believe would be needed to make a lasting difference in the nation's schools.

Among the issues they believe were left out of the mix are:

• **School financing.** During the Senate debate, Dodd proposed language that would have taken federal funds from states that did not do more to equalize funding between rich and poor school districts.

To Republicans, that would have constituted massive overreaching by Washington because it would have given the federal government leverage over the local property taxes that finance much of the nation's school systems.

Dodd's amendment was rejected, but the issue is likely to be revisited. Some lawmakers and analysts say the Bush overhaul plan stands little chance of success if state and local financing inequities are not addressed — because that is where the real money is. Only 7 percent of all education spending comes from federal funds; 48 percent comes from state expenditures and 45 percent from local spending.

The Education Trust, a group that promotes high standards for disadvantaged students and supports increased testing, released a report in March it says underscores the extent of the problem. Its study found that in 42 out of 49 states, school districts with the greatest number of poor children had less money to spend on each student than those with the fewest poor children.

In New York, the state with the worst inequities, the study found a $2,794-per-student gap in spending between the richest districts and the poorest ones.

Because so much of the nation's education spending is concentrated at the state and local level, experts say even the Title I program of aid for disadvantaged students can only do so much to close the gaps.

"The intent of Title I is to give poor kids extra, but all it does is give them a minimal, miniscule amount to close the gaps in states with these massively inequitable financing systems," said Amy Wilkins, principal partner at the Education Trust.

• **Private school choice.** For conservatives who believe greater competition is the key to better schools, there is some good news. The House and Senate bills contain funding for programs that would expand choice among public schools and allow federal funds to be spent on private tutoring services for children in schools that have performed poorly for three years.

However, Bush's original proposal, which would have given private school vouchers to the parents of students in underperforming schools, was dropped because of opposition from Democrats and moderate Republicans.

Their argument — that vouchers would drain needed funds from the public schools — carried so much weight that neither the Senate nor the House was able to muster the votes for even a demonstration program.

Still, voucher supporters are pointing to the bipartisan support for public school choice as a sign that the debate is moving in their direction.

"Increasingly, Democrats are having to move over and say, 'Yeah, yeah, we support public school choice.' Ten years ago, you never would have heard that," said Terry M. Moe, professor of political science at Stanford University and co-author of "Politics, Markets, and America's Schools," a 1990 book that influenced the growth of the school choice movement.

That is why lawmakers and other supporters of school choice believe Congress will end up approving vouchers within a few years. "The public's way ahead of Congress," said Hutchinson.

"The more comfortable people are with public school choice, the more comfortable they'll be in 10, 15, 20 years with the idea of expanded school choice, and that will include private school vouchers," said Moe.

• **Smaller class sizes.** Congress has turned class-size reduction into a running partisan battle, with Democrats arguing for targeted federal spending and Republicans insisting that states should decide whether to spend money on more teachers or better ones.

This year, Republicans won. Both the House and Senate bills would end a three-year old federal program to reduce class sizes by hiring 100,000 new teachers. Instead, block grant funds to improve teacher quality — $3 billion for fiscal 2002 in the Senate bill, $1.9 billion in the House version — could be spent to hire new teachers or train current ones.

"If you need more teachers, you can hire them. . . . If you need better teachers, you can try to improve teachers' ability," Judd Gregg, R-N.H., said during the Senate debate.

"It is a much more logical and flexible approach, which addresses the needs of school districts in a much more practical way rather than simply command and control from here in Washington," he said.

There is little question among teachers, however, that smaller class sizes do make a difference.

"If I had 15 kids in my classroom, do you know how quickly I could move them along?" said Maryann Hoffman, who teaches English as a second language at Francis C. Hammond Middle School in Alexandria, Va.

In practice, she said, "you could have 25 kids" crammed into the classes.

• **The best teachers.** One basic problem that neither party has addressed, according to many experts, is that the schools most in need of better teachers will never get them.

That is because most union contracts allow teachers with the greatest seniority to choose where they want to teach. They often pick high-performing schools, leaving the newest teachers to teach at the worst ones.

"Often, these new teachers are very bright, but they don't know what they're doing," said Wilkins of the Education Trust.

Republicans had little interest in raising the issue, however, because they did not want to interfere in local control over education, while Democrats did not want to anger the teachers' unions that are an important part of their political base, Wilkins said.

On the Front Lines

For Vermont's Michele Forman and other teachers, the real trick will be to make sure that states are not forced to use poorly written, off-the-shelf tests.

Forman says she has nothing against standardized testing as long as it is considered along with students' other work. She simply does not want to see annual tests become the sole measure of how much students are learning — or a tool for punishing schools that do poorly.

"There's no room for the punitive approach in education," Forman said.

Other teachers say that state tests such as Virginia's Standards of Learning exams have already had an unwelcome impact on what they can teach in their classrooms.

"If it's not going to be covered on the SOLs, it's not going to be covered

in my class until May," said Joanne Godwin, who teaches fifth-grade science at Tuckahoe Elementary school in Arlington, Va.

"If I didn't have an SOL to prep for, I would do a unit on flight, which I know would be fun for the kids. But because I know it's not going to be on the test, we don't cover it," said Godwin. However, she added, "there's always one question on the test about the difference between animal and plant cells, so we spend two days on it."

Teachers' opinions matter, experts say, because they will have to make the education overhaul work once Bush has signed it into law.

In urban schools, "they're going to dig in their heels," predicted Hess. "They're going to say, 'These kids come in with tremendous disadvantages. If they're not reading at grade level by third grade, how can I be expected to solve that?' "

Congress can, however, count on the support of many school superintendents.

"You should have the same requirements for all children, whether they're from poor families or wealthy families," said Roy Romer, the former Colorado governor and Democratic National Committee chairman who is now superintendent of the Los Angeles Unified School District.

Romer, who is trying to add 850 literacy and math instruction coaches to his school system, says, "The key is what do you change in the classroom. . . . My word is, 'If it isn't about improving instruction, I don't want to know about it.' "

The actual testing would not begin until the 2004-05 school year in the House bill and 2005-06 under the Senate bill — after Bush has run for re-election. With all of the work that states and teachers will have to do to prepare, however, any trouble developing the tests or holding public support would likely surface before then.

That is why the bills' supporters in Congress are urging people to give the effort sufficient time to work.

"The biggest problem with education reform is patience," said Republican Rep. Johnny Isakson of Georgia, a former chairman of that state's Board of Education. "A lot of times, politicians wait five or six years and then get impatient and change everything." ◆

Appendix

The Legislative Process in Brief

Note: Parliamentary terms used below are defined in the glossary.

Introduction of Bills

A House member (including the resident commissioner of Puerto Rico and non-voting delegates of the District of Columbia, Guam, the Virgin Islands and American Samoa) may introduce any one of several types of bills and resolutions by handing it to the clerk of the House or placing it in a box called the hopper. A senator first gains recognition of the presiding officer to announce the introduction of a bill. If objection is offered by any senator, the introduction of the bill is postponed until the following day.

As the next step in either the House or Senate, the bill is numbered, referred to the appropriate committee, labeled with the sponsor's name and sent to the Government Printing Office so that copies can be made for subsequent study and action. Senate bills may be jointly sponsored and carry several senators' names. Until 1978, the House limited the number of members who could cosponsor any one bill; the ceiling was eliminated at the beginning of the 96th Congress. A bill written in the executive branch and proposed as an administration measure usually is introduced by the chairman of the congressional committee that has jurisdiction.

Bills — Prefixed with HR in the House, S in the Senate, followed by a number. Used as the form for most legislation, whether general or special, public or private.

Joint Resolutions — Designated H J Res or S J Res. Subject to the same procedure as bills, with the exception of a joint resolution proposing an amendment to the Constitution. The latter must be approved by two-thirds of both houses and is thereupon sent directly to the administrator of general services for submission to the states for ratification instead of being presented to the president for his approval.

Concurrent Resolutions — Designated H Con Res or S Con Res. Used for matters affecting the operations of both houses. These resolutions do not become law.

Resolutions — Designated H Res or S Res. Used for a matter concerning the operation of either house alone and adopted only by the chamber in which it originates.

Committee Action

With few exceptions, bills are referred to the appropriate standing committees. The job of referral formally is the responsibility of the Speaker of the House and the presiding officer of the Senate, but this task usually is carried out on their behalf by the parliamentarians of the House and Senate. Precedent, statute and the jurisdictional mandates of the committees as set forth in the rules of the House and Senate determine which committees receive what kinds of bills. An exception is the referral of private bills, which are sent to

whatever committee is designated by their sponsors. Bills are technically considered "read for the first time" when referred to House committees.

When a bill reaches a committee it is placed on the committee's calendar. At that time the bill comes under the sharpest congressional focus. Its chances for passage are quickly determined — and the great majority of bills falls by the legislative roadside. Failure of a committee to act on a bill is equivalent to killing it; the measure can be withdrawn from the committee's purview only by a discharge petition signed by a majority of the House membership on House bills, or by adoption of a special resolution in the Senate. Discharge attempts rarely succeed.

The first committee action taken on a bill usually is a request for comment on it by interested agencies of the government. The committee chairman may assign the bill to a subcommittee for study and hearings, or it may be considered by the full committee. Hearings may be public, closed (executive session) or both. A subcommittee, after considering a bill, reports to the full committee its recommendations for action and any proposed amendments.

The full committee then votes on its recommendation to the House or Senate. This procedure is called "ordering a bill reported." Occasionally a committee may order a bill reported unfavorably; most of the time a report, submitted by the chairman of the committee to the House or Senate, calls for favorable action on the measure since the committee can effectively "kill" a bill by simply failing to take any action.

After the bill is reported, the committee chairman instructs the staff to prepare a written report. The report describes the purposes and scope of the bill, explains the committee revisions, notes proposed changes in existing law and, usually, includes the views of the executive branch agencies consulted. Often committee members opposing a measure issue dissenting minority statements that are included in the report.

Usually, the committee "marks up" or proposes amendments to the bill. If they are substantial and the measure is complicated, the committee may order a "clean bill" introduced, which will embody the proposed amendments. The original bill then is put aside and the clean bill, with a new number, is reported to the floor.

The chamber must approve, alter or reject the committee amendments before the bill itself can be put to a vote.

Floor Action

After a bill is reported back to the house where it originated, it is placed on the calendar.

There are five legislative calendars in the House, issued in one cumulative calendar titled *Calendars of the United States House of Representatives and History of Legislation*. The House

How a Bill Becomes a Law

This graphic shows the most typical way in which proposed legislation is enacted into law. There are more complicated, as well as simpler, routes, and most bills never become law. The process is illustrated with two hypothetical bills, House bill No. 1 (HR 1) and Senate bill No. 2 (S 2). Bills must be passed by both houses in identical form before they can be sent to the president. The path of HR 1 is traced by a gray line, that of S 2 by a black line. In practice, most bills begin as similar proposals in both houses.

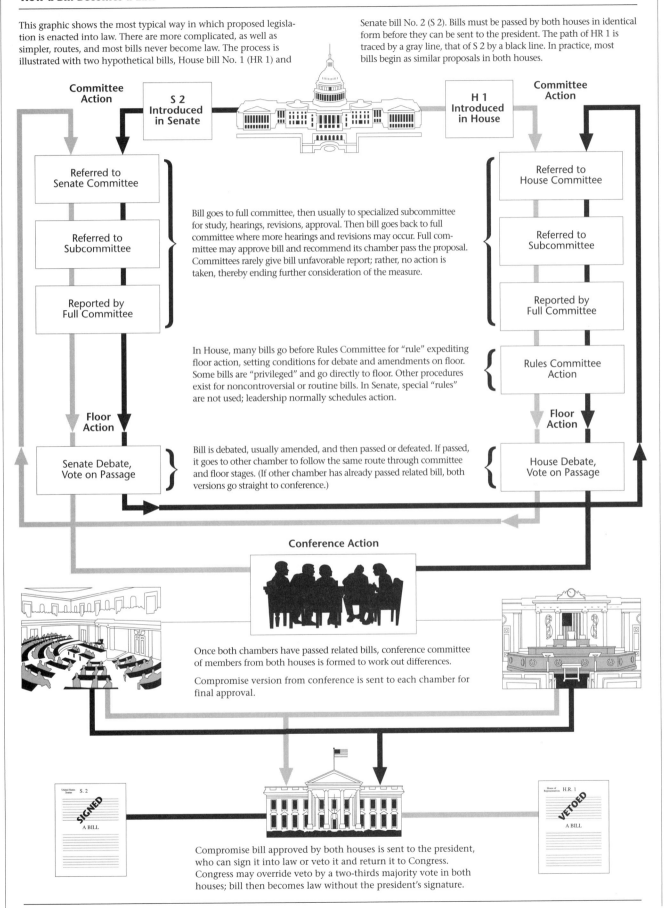

Committee Action

S 2 Introduced in Senate

H 1 Introduced in House

Committee Action

Referred to Senate Committee

Referred to Subcommittee

Reported by Full Committee

Bill goes to full committee, then usually to specialized subcommittee for study, hearings, revisions, approval. Then bill goes back to full committee where more hearings and revisions may occur. Full committee may approve bill and recommend its chamber pass the proposal. Committees rarely give bill unfavorable report; rather, no action is taken, thereby ending further consideration of the measure.

Referred to House Committee

Referred to Subcommittee

Reported by Full Committee

In House, many bills go before Rules Committee for "rule" expediting floor action, setting conditions for debate and amendments on floor. Some bills are "privileged" and go directly to floor. Other procedures exist for noncontroversial or routine bills. In Senate, special "rules" are not used; leadership normally schedules action.

Rules Committee Action

Floor Action

Senate Debate, Vote on Passage

Bill is debated, usually amended, and then passed or defeated. If passed, it goes to other chamber to follow the same route through committee and floor stages. (If other chamber has already passed related bill, both versions go straight to conference.)

Floor Action

House Debate, Vote on Passage

Conference Action

Once both chambers have passed related bills, conference committee of members from both houses is formed to work out differences.

Compromise version from conference is sent to each chamber for final approval.

United States Senate S 2
SIGNED
A BILL

House of Representatives H.R. 1
VETOED
A BILL

Compromise bill approved by both houses is sent to the president, who can sign it into law or veto it and return it to Congress. Congress may override veto by a two-thirds majority vote in both houses; bill then becomes law without the president's signature.

calendars are:

The Union Calendar to which are referred bills raising revenues, general appropriations bills and any measures directly or indirectly appropriating money or property. It is the Calendar of the Committee of the Whole House on the State of the Union.

The House Calendar to which are referred bills of public character not raising revenue or appropriating money.

The Corrections Calendar to which are referred bills to repeal rules and regulations deemed excessive or unnecessary when the Corrections Calendar is called the second and fourth Tuesday of each month. (Instituted in the 104th Congress to replace the seldom-used Consent Calendar.) A three-fifths majority is required for passage.

The Private Calendar to which are referred bills for relief in the nature of claims against the United States or private immigration bills that are passed without debate when the Private Calendar is called the first and third Tuesdays of each month.

The Discharge Calendar to which are referred motions to discharge committees when the necessary signatures are signed to a discharge petition.

There is only one legislative calendar in the Senate and one "executive calendar" for treaties and nominations submitted to the Senate. When the Senate Calendar is called, each senator is limited to five minutes' debate on each bill.

Debate. A bill is brought to debate by varying procedures. If a routine measure, it may await the call of the calendar. If it is urgent or important, it can be taken up in the Senate either by unanimous consent or by a majority vote. The majority leader, in consultation with the minority leader and others, schedules the bills that will be taken up for debate.

In the House, precedence is granted if a special rule is obtained from the Rules Committee. A request for a special rule usually is made by the chairman of the committee that favorably reported the bill, supported by the bill's sponsor and other committee members. The request, considered by the Rules Committee in the same fashion that other committees consider legislative measures, is in the form of a resolution providing for immediate consideration of the bill. The Rules Committee reports the resolution to the House where it is debated and voted on in the same fashion as regular bills. If the Rules Committee fails to report a rule requested by a committee, there are several ways to bring the bill to the House floor — under suspension of the rules, on Calendar Wednesday or by a discharge motion.

The resolutions providing special rules are important because they specify how long the bill may be debated and whether it may be amended from the floor. If floor amendments are banned, the bill is considered under a "closed rule," which permits only members of the committee that first reported the measure to the House to alter its language, subject to chamber acceptance.

When a bill is debated under an "open rule," amendments may be offered from the floor. Committee amendments always are taken up first but may be changed, as may all amendments up to the second degree; that is, an amendment to an amendment to an amendment is not in order.

Duration of debate in the House depends on whether the bill is under discussion by the House proper or before the House when it is sitting as the Committee of the Whole House on the State of the Union. In the former, the amount of time for debate either is determined by special rule or is allocated with an hour for each member if the measure is under consideration without a rule. In the Committee of the Whole the amount of time agreed on for general debate is equally divided between proponents and opponents. At the end of general discussion, the bill is read section by section for amendment. Debate on an amendment is limited to five minutes for each side; this is called the "five-minute rule." In practice, amendments regularly are debated more than ten minutes, with members gaining the floor by offering pro forma amendments or obtaining unanimous consent to speak longer than five minutes.

Senate debate usually is unlimited. It can be halted only by unanimous consent by "cloture," which requires a three-fifths majority of the entire Senate except for proposed changes in the Senate rules. The latter requires a two-thirds vote.

The House considers almost all important bills within a parliamentary framework known as the Committee of the Whole. It is not a committee as the word usually is understood; it is the full House meeting under another name for the purpose of speeding action on legislation. Technically, the House sits as the Committee of the Whole when it considers any tax measure or bill dealing with public appropriations. It also can resolve itself into the Committee of the Whole if a member moves to do so and the motion is carried. The Speaker appoints a member to serve as the chairman. The rules of the House permit the Committee of the Whole to meet when a quorum of 100 members is present on the floor and to amend and act on bills, within certain time limitations. When the Committee of the Whole has acted, it "rises," the Speaker returns as the presiding officer of the House and the member appointed chairman of the Committee of the Whole reports the action of the committee and its recommendations. The Committee of the Whole cannot pass a bill; instead it reports the measure to the full House with whatever changes it has approved. The full House then may pass or reject the bill — or, on occasion, recommit the bill to committee. Amendments adopted in the Committee of the Whole may be put to a second vote in the full House.

Votes. Voting on bills may occur repeatedly before they are finally approved or rejected. The House votes on the rule for the bill and on various amendments to the bill. Voting on amendments often is a more illuminating test of a bill's support than is the final tally. Sometimes members approve final passage of bills after vigorously supporting amendments that, if adopted, would have scuttled the legislation.

The Senate has three different methods of voting: an untabulated voice vote, a standing vote (called a division) and a recorded roll call to which members answer "yea" or "nay" when their names are called. The House also employs voice and standing votes, but since January 1973 yeas and nays have been recorded by an electronic voting device, eliminating the need for time-consuming roll calls.

Another method of voting, used in the House only, is the teller vote. Traditionally, members filed up the center aisle past counters; only vote totals were announced. Since 1971, one-fifth of a quorum can demand that the votes of individual members be recorded, thereby forcing them to take a public position on amendments to key bills. Electronic voting now is commonly used for this purpose.

After amendments to a bill have been voted upon, a vote may be taken on a motion to recommit the bill to committee. If carried, this vote removes the bill from the chamber's calendar and is usually a death blow to the bill. If the motion is unsuccessful, the bill then is "read for the third time." An actual reading usually is dispensed with. Until 1965, an opponent of a bill could delay this move by objecting and asking for a full reading of an engrossed (certified in final form) copy of the bill. After the "third reading," the vote on final passage is taken.

Examples of Legislative Documents

Appendix

The final vote may be followed by a motion to reconsider, and this motion may be followed by a move to lay the motion on the table. Usually, those voting for the bill's passage vote for the tabling motion, thus safeguarding the final passage action. With that, the bill has been formally passed by the chamber. While a motion to reconsider a Senate vote is pending on a bill, the measure cannot be sent to the House.

Action in Second House

After a bill is passed it is sent to the other chamber. This body may then take one of several steps. It may pass the bill as is — accepting the other chamber's language. It may send the bill to committee for scrutiny or alteration, or reject the entire bill, advising the other house of its actions. Or it simply may ignore the bill submitted while it continues work on its own version of the proposed legislation. Frequently, one chamber may approve a version of a bill that is greatly at variance with the version already passed by the other house, and then substitute its contents for the language of the other, retaining only the latter's bill number.

A provision of the Legislative Reorganization Act of 1970 permits a separate House vote on any non-germane amendment added by the Senate to a House-passed bill and requires a majority vote to retain the amendment. Previously the House was forced to act on the bill as a whole; the only way to defeat the non-germane amendment was to reject the entire bill.

Often the second chamber makes only minor changes. If these are readily agreed to by the other house, the bill then is routed to the president. However, if the opposite chamber significantly alters the bill submitted to it, the measure usually is "sent to conference." The chamber that has possession of the "papers" (engrossed bill, engrossed amendments, messages of transmittal) requests a conference and the other chamber must agree to it. If the second house does not agree, the bill dies.

Conference, Final Action

Conference. A conference works out conflicting House and Senate versions of a legislative bill. The conferees usually are senior members appointed by the presiding officers of the two houses, from the committees that managed the bills. Under this arrangement the conferees of one house have the duty of trying to maintain their chamber's position in the face of amending actions by the conferees (also referred to as "managers") of the other house.

The number of conferees from each chamber may vary, the range usually being from three to nine members in each group, depending upon the length or complexity of the bill involved. There may be five representatives and three senators on the conference committee, or the reverse. But a majority vote controls the action of each group so that a large representation does not give one chamber a voting advantage over the other chamber's conferees.

Theoretically, conferees are not allowed to write new legislation in reconciling the two versions before them, but this curb sometimes is bypassed. Many bills have been put into acceptable compromise form only after new language was provided by the conferees. The 1970 Reorganization Act attempted to tighten restrictions on conferees by forbidding them to introduce any language on a topic that neither chamber sent to conference or to modify any topic beyond the scope of the different House and Senate versions.

Frequently the ironing out of difficulties takes days or even weeks. Conferences on involved appropriations bills sometimes are particularly drawn out.

As a conference proceeds, conferees reconcile differences between the versions, but generally they grant concessions only insofar as they remain sure that the chamber they represent will accept the compromises. Occasionally, uncertainty over how either house will react, or the positive refusal of a chamber to back down on a disputed amendment, results in an impasse, and the bills die in conference even though each was approved by its sponsoring chamber.

Conferees sometimes go back to their respective chambers for further instructions, when they report certain portions in disagreement. Then the chamber concerned can either "recede and concur" in the amendment of the other house or "insist on its amendment."

When the conferees have reached agreement, they prepare a conference report embodying their recommendations (compromises). The report, in document form, must be submitted to each house.

The conference report must be approved by each house. Consequently, approval of the report is approval of the compromise bill. In the order of voting on conference reports, the chamber which asked for a conference yields to the other chamber the opportunity to vote first.

Final Steps. After a bill has been passed by both the House and Senate in identical form, all of the original papers are sent to the enrolling clerk of the chamber in which the bill originated. He then prepares an enrolled bill, which is printed on parchment paper. When this bill has been certified as correct by the secretary of the Senate or the clerk of the House, depending on which chamber originated the bill, it is signed first (no matter whether it originated in the Senate or House) by the Speaker of the House and then by the president of the Senate. It is next sent to the White House to await action.

If the president approves the bill, he signs it, dates it and usually writes the word "approved" on the document. If he does not sign it within 10 days (Sundays excepted) and Congress is in session, the bill becomes law without his signature.

However, should Congress adjourn before the 10 days expire, and the president has failed to sign the measure, it does not become law. This procedure is called the pocket veto.

A president vetoes a bill by refusing to sign it and, before the 10-day period expires, returning it to Congress with a message stating his reasons. The message is sent to the chamber that originated the bill. If no action is taken on the message, the bill dies. Congress, however, can attempt to override the president's veto and enact the bill, "the objections of the president to the contrary notwithstanding." Overriding a veto requires a two-thirds vote of those present, who must number a quorum and vote by roll call.

Debate can precede this vote, with motions permitted to lay the message on the table, postpone action on it or refer it to committee. If the president's veto is overridden by a two-thirds vote in both houses, the bill becomes law. Otherwise it is dead.

When bills are passed finally and signed, or passed over a veto, they are given law numbers in numerical order as they become law. There are two series of numbers, one for public and one for private laws, starting at the number "1" for each two-year term of Congress. They are then identified by law number and by Congress — for example, Private Law 21, 97th Congress; Public Law 250, 97th Congress (or PL 97–250).

124

The Budget Process in Brief

Through the budget process, the president and Congress decide how much to spend and tax during the upcoming fiscal year. More specifically, they decide how much to spend on each activity, ensure that the government spends no more and spends it only for that activity, and report on that spending at the end of each budget cycle.

The President's Budget

The law requires that, by the first Monday in February, the president submit to Congress his proposed federal budget for the next fiscal year, which begins on October 1. In order to accomplish this, the president establishes general budget and fiscal policy guidelines. Based on these guidelines, executive branch agencies make requests for funds and submit them to the White House's Office of Management and Budget (OMB) nearly a year prior to the start of a new fiscal year. The OMB, receiving direction from the president and administration official, reviews the agencies' requests and develops a detailed budget by December. From December to January the OMB prepares the budget documents, so that the president can deliver it to Congress in February.

The president's budget is the executive branch's plan for the next year — but it is just a proposal. After receiving it, Congress has its own budget process to follow from February to October. Only after Congress passes the required spending bills — and the president signs them — has the government created its actual budget.

Action in Congress

Congress first must pass a "budget resolution" — a framework within which the members of Congress will make their decisions about spending and taxes. It includes targets for total spending, total revenues, and the deficit, and allocations within the spending target for the two types of spending — discretionary and mandatory.

Discretionary spending, which currently accounts for about 33 percent of all federal spending, is what the president and Congress must decide to spend for the next year through the thirteen annual appropriations bills. It includes money for such activities as the FBI and the Coast Guard, for housing and education, for NASA and highway and bridge construction, and for defense and foreign aid.

Mandatory spending, which currently accounts for 67 percent of all spending, is authorized by laws that have already been passed. It includes entitlement spending — such as for Social Security, Medicare, veterans' benefits, and food stamps — through which individuals receive benefits because they are eligible based on their age, income, or other criteria. It also includes interest on the national debt, which the government pays to individuals and institutions that hold Treasury bonds and other government securities. The only way the president and Congress can change the spending on entitlement and other mandatory programs is if they change the laws that authorized the programs.

Currently, the law imposes a limit or "cap" through 1998 on total annual discretionary spending. Within the cap, however, the president and Congress can, and often do, change the spending levels from year to year for the thousands of individual federal programs.

In addition, the law requires that legislation that would raise mandatory spending or lower revenues — compared to existing law — be offset by spending cuts or revenue increases. This requirement, called "pay-as-you-go" is designed to prevent new legislation from increasing the deficit.

Once Congress passes the budget resolution, it turns its attention to passing the thirteen annual appropriations bills and, if it chooses, "authorizing" bills to change the laws governing mandatory spending and revenues.

Congress begins by examining the president's budget in detail. Scores of committees and subcommittees hold hearings on proposals under their jurisdiction. The House and Senate Armed Services Authorizing Committees, and the Defense and Military Construction Subcommittees of the Appropriations Committees, for instance, hold hearings on the president's defense budget. The White House budget director, cabinet officers, and other administration officials work with Congress as it accepts some of the president's proposals, rejects others, and changes still others. Congress can change funding levels, eliminate programs, or add programs not requested by the president. It can add or eliminate taxes and other sources of revenue, or make other changes that affect the amount of revenue collected. Congressional rules require that these committees and subcommittees take actions that reflect the congressional budget resolution.

The president's budget, the budget resolution, and the appropriations or authorizing bills measure spending in two ways — "budget authority" and "outlays." Budget authority is what the law authorizes the federal government to spend for certain programs, projects, or activities. What the government actually spends in a particular year, however, is an outlay. For example, when the government decides to build a space exploration system, the president and Congress may agree to appropriate $1 billion in budget authority. But the space system may take ten years to build. Thus, the government may spend $100 million in outlays in the first year to begin construction and the remaining $900 million during the next nine years as the construction continues.

Congress must provide budget authority before the federal agencies can obligate the government to make outlays. When Congress fails to complete action on one or more of the regular annual appropriations bills before the fiscal year begins on October 1, budget authority may be made on a temporary basis through continuing resolutions. Continuing resolutions make budget authority available for limited periods of time, generally at rates related through some formula to the rate provided in the previous year's appropriation.

Monitoring the Budget

Once Congress passes and the president signs the federal appropriations bills or authorizing laws for the fiscal year, the government monitors the budget through (1) agency program managers and budget officials, including the Inspectors General, who report only to the agency head; (2) the Office of Management and Budget; (3) congressional committees; and (4) the General Accounting Office, an auditing arm of Congress.

This oversight is designed to (1) ensure that agencies comply with legal limits on spending, and that they use budget authority only for the purposes intended; (2) see that programs are operating consistently with legal requirements and existing policy; and (3) ensure that programs are well managed and achieving the intended results.

The president may withhold appropriated amounts from obligation only under certain limited circumstances — to provide for contingencies, to achieve savings made possible through changes in requirements or greater efficiency of operations, or as otherwise provided by law. The Impoundment Control Act of 1974 specifies the procedures that must be followed if funds are withheld. Congress can also cancel previous authorized budget authority by passing a rescissions bill — but it also must be signed by the president.

Glossary of Congressional Terms

Absolute Majority—A vote requiring approval by a majority of all members of a house rather than a majority of members present and voting. Also referred to as constitutional majority.

Act—(1) A bill passed in identical form by both houses of Congress and signed into law by the president or enacted over his veto. A bill also becomes an act without the president's signature if he does not return it to Congress within 10 days (Sundays excepted) and if Congress has not adjourned within that period. (2) Also, the technical term for a bill passed by at least one house and engrossed.

Adjourn for More Than Three Days—Under Article I, Section 5, of the Constitution, neither house may adjourn for more than three days without the approval of the other. The necessary approval is given in a concurrent resolution and agreed to by both houses, which may permit one or both to take such an adjournment.

Adjournment Sine Die—Final adjournment of an annual or two-year session of Congress; literally, adjournment without a day. The two houses must agree to a privileged concurrent resolution for such an adjournment. A sine die adjournment precludes Congress from meeting again until the next constitutionally fixed date of a session (January 3 of the following year) unless Congress determines otherwise by law or the president calls it into special session. Article II, Section 3, of the Constitution authorizes the president to adjourn both houses until such time as he thinks proper when the two houses cannot agree to a time of adjournment, but no president has ever exercised this authority.

Adjournment to a Day (and Time) Certain—An adjournment that fixes the next date and time of meeting for one or both houses. It does not end an annual session of Congress.

Advice and Consent—The Senate's constitutional role in consenting to or rejecting the president's nominations to executive branch and judicial offices and the treaties he submits. Confirmation of nominees requires a simple majority vote of the senators present and voting. Treaties must be approved by a two-thirds majority of senators present and voting.

Amendment—A formal proposal to alter the text of a bill, resolution, amendment, motion, treaty, or some other text. Technically, it is a motion. An amendment may strike out (eliminate) part of a text, insert new text, or strike out and insert—that is, replace all or part of the text with new text. The texts of amendments considered on the floor are printed in full in the *Congressional Record*.

Amendment in the Nature of a Substitute—Usually, an amendment to replace the entire text of a measure. It strikes out everything after the enacting clause and inserts a version that may be somewhat, substantially, or entirely different. When a committee adopts extensive amendments to a measure, it often incorporates them into such an amendment. Occasionally, the term is applied to an amendment that replaces a major portion of a measure's text.

Annual Authorization—Legislation that authorizes appropriations for a single fiscal year and usually for a specific amount. Under the rules of the authorization-appropriation process, an annually authorized agency or program must be reauthorized each year if it is to receive appropriations for that year. Sometimes Congress fails to enact the reauthorization but nevertheless provides appropriations to continue the program, circumventing the rules by one means or another.

Appeal—A member's formal challenge of a ruling or decision by the presiding officer. On appeal, a house or a committee may overturn the ruling by majority vote. The right of appeal ensures the body against arbitrary control by the chair. Appeals are rarely made in the House and are even more rarely successful. Rulings are more frequently appealed in the Senate and occasionally overturned, in part because its presiding officer is not the majority party's leader, as in the House.

Apportionment—The action, after each decennial census, of allocating the number of members in the House of Representatives to each state. By law, the total number of House members (not counting delegates and a resident commissioner) is fixed at 435. The number allotted to each state is based approximately on its proportion of the nation's total population. Since the Constitution guarantees each state one representative no matter how small its population, exact proportional distribution is virtually impossible. The mathematical formula currently used to determine the apportionment is called the Method of Equal Proportions. (*See Method of Equal Proportions.*)

Appropriation—(1) Legislative language that permits a federal agency to incur obligations and make payments from the Treasury for specified purposes, usually during a specified period of time. (2) The specific amount of money made available by such language. The Constitution prohibits payments from the Treasury except "in Consequence of Appropriations made by Law." With some exceptions, the rules of both houses forbid consideration of appropriations for purposes that are unauthorized in law or of appropriation amounts larger than those authorized in law. The House of Representatives claims the exclusive right to originate appropriation bills—a claim the Senate denies in theory but accepts in practice.

Authorization—(1) A statutory provision that establishes or continues a federal agency, activity or program for a fixed or indefinite period of time. It may also establish policies and restrictions and deal with organizational and administrative matters. (2) A statutory provision that authorizes appropriations for an agency, activity, or program. The appropriations may be authorized for one year, several years, or an indefinite period of time, and the authorization may be for a specific amount of money or an indefinite amount ("such sums as may be necessary"). Authorizations of specific amounts are construed as ceilings on the amounts that subsequently may be appropriated in an appropriation bill, but not as minimums; either house may appropriate lesser amounts or nothing at all.

Backdoor Spending Authority—Authority to incur obligations that evades the normal congressional appropriations process because it is provided in legislation other than appropriation acts. The most common forms are borrowing authority, contract authority, and entitlement authority.

Baseline—A projection of the levels of federal spending, revenues, and the resulting budgetary surpluses or deficits for the upcoming and subsequent fiscal years, taking into account laws enacted to date and assuming no new policy decisions. It provides a benchmark for measuring the budgetary effects of proposed changes in federal revenues or spending, assuming certain economic conditions.

Bill—The term for the chief vehicle Congress uses for enacting laws. Bills that originate in the House of Representatives are designated as H.R., those in the Senate as S., followed by a number assigned in the order in which they are introduced during a two-year Congress. A bill becomes a law if passed in identical language by both houses and signed by the president, or passed over his veto, or if the president fails to sign it within 10 days after he has received it while Congress is in session.

Bills and Resolutions Introduced—Members formally present measures to their respective houses by delivering them to a clerk in the chamber when their house is in session. Both houses permit any number of members to join in introducing a bill or resolution. The first member listed on the measure is the sponsor; the other members listed are its cosponsors.

Bills and Resolutions Referred—After a bill or resolution is introduced, it is normally sent to one or more committees that have jurisdiction over its subject, as defined by House and Senate rules and precedents. A Senate measure is usually referred to the committee with jurisdiction over the predominant subject of its text, but it may be sent to two or more committees by unanimous consent or on a motion offered jointly by the majority and minority leaders. In the House, a rule requires the Speaker to refer a measure to the committee that has primary jurisdiction. The Speaker is also authorized to refer measures sequentially to additional committees.

Borrowing Authority—Statutory authority permitting a federal agency, such as the Export-Import Bank, to borrow money from the public or the Treasury to finance its operations. It is a form of backdoor spending. To bring such spending under the control of the congressional appropriation process, the Congressional Budget Act requires that new borrowing authori-

ty shall be effective only to the extent and in such amounts as are provided in appropriations acts.

Budget—A detailed statement of actual or anticipated revenues and expenditures during an accounting period. For the national government, the period is the federal fiscal year (October 1–September 30). The budget usually refers to the president's budget submission to Congress early each calendar year. The president's budget estimates federal government income and spending for the upcoming fiscal year and contains detailed recommendations for appropriation, revenue, and other legislation. Congress is not required to accept or even vote directly on the president's proposals, and it often revises the president's budget extensively. (*See Fiscal Year.*)

Budget Act—Common name for the Congressional Budget and Impoundment Control Act of 1974, which established the basic procedures of the current congressional budget process; created the House and Senate Budget committees; and enacted procedures for reconciliation, deferrals, and rescissions. (*See Budget Process, Deferral, Impoundment, Reconciliation, Rescission. See also Gramm-Rudman-Hollings Act of 1985.*)

Budget and Accounting Act of 1921—The law that, for the first time, authorized the president to submit to Congress an annual budget for the entire federal government. Prior to the act, most federal agencies sent their budget requests to the appropriate congressional committees without review by the president.

Budget Authority—Generally, the amount of money that may be spent or obligated by a government agency or for a government program or activity. Technically, it is statutory authority to enter into obligations that normally result in outlays. The main forms of budget authority are appropriations, borrowing authority, and contract authority. It also includes authority to obligate and expend the proceeds of offsetting receipts and collections. Congress may make budget authority available for only one year, several years, or an indefinite period, and it may specify definite or indefinite amounts.

Budget Process—(1) In Congress, the procedural system it uses (a) to approve an annual concurrent resolution on the budget that sets goals for aggregate and functional categories of federal expenditures, revenues, and the surplus or deficit for an upcoming fiscal year; and (b) to implement those goals in spending, revenue, and, if necessary, reconciliation and debt-limit legislation. (2) In the executive branch, the process of formulating the president's annual budget, submitting it to Congress, defending it before congressional committees, implementing subsequent budget-related legislation, impounding or sequestering expenditures as permitted by law, auditing and evaluating programs, and compiling final budget data. The Budget and Accounting Act of 1921 and the Congressional Budget and Impoundment Control Act of 1974 established the basic elements of the current budget process. Major revisions were enacted in the Gramm-Rudman-Hollings Act of 1985 and the Budget Enforcement Act of 1990.

Budget Resolution—A concurrent resolution in which Congress establishes or revises its version of the federal budget's broad financial features for the upcoming fiscal year and several additional fiscal years. Like other concurrent resolutions, it does not have the force of law, but it provides the framework within which Congress subsequently considers revenue, spending, and other budget-implementing legislation. The framework consists of two basic elements: (1) aggregate budget amounts (total revenues, new budget authority, outlays, loan obligations and loan guarantee commitments, deficit or surplus, and debt limit); and (2) subdivisions of the relevant aggregate amounts among the functional categories of the budget. Although it does not allocate funds to specific programs or accounts, the budget committees' reports accompanying the resolution often discuss the major program assumptions underlying its functional amounts. Unlike those amounts, however, the assumptions are not binding on Congress.

By Request—A designation indicating that a member has introduced a measure on behalf of the president, an executive agency, or a private individual or organization. Members often introduce such measures as a courtesy because neither the president nor any person other than a member of Congress can do so. The term, which appears next to the sponsor's name, implies that the member who introduced the measure does not necessarily endorse it. A House rule dealing with by-request introductions dates from 1888, but the practice goes back to the earliest history of Congress.

Calendar—A list of measures or other matters (most of them favorably reported by committees) that are eligible for floor consideration. The House has five calendars; the Senate has two. A place on a calendar does not guarantee consideration. Each house decides which measures and matters it will take up, when, and in what order, in accordance with its rules and practices.

Calendar Wednesday—A House procedure that on Wednesdays permits its committees to bring up for floor consideration nonprivileged measures they have reported. The procedure is so cumbersome and susceptible to dilatory tactics, however, that committees rarely use it.

Call of the Calendar—Senate bills that are not brought up for debate by a motion, unanimous consent, or a unanimous consent agreement are brought before the Senate for action when the calendar listing them is "called." Bills must be called in the order listed. Measures considered by this method usually are noncontroversial, and debate on the bill and any proposed amendments is limited to a total of five minutes for each senator.

Caucus—(1) A common term for the official organization of each party in each house. (2) The official title of the organization of House Democrats. House and Senate Republicans and Senate Democrats call their organizations "conferences." (3) A term for an informal group of members who share legislative interests, such as the Black Caucus, Hispanic Caucus, and Children's Caucus.

Censure—The strongest formal condemnation of a member for misconduct short of expulsion. A house usually adopts a resolution of censure to express its condemnation, after which the presiding officer reads its rebuke aloud to the member in the presence of his colleagues.

Chamber—The Capitol room in which a house of Congress normally holds its sessions. The chamber of the House of Representatives, officially called the Hall of the House, is consider-

ably larger than that of the Senate because it must accommodate 435 representatives, four delegates, and one resident commissioner. Unlike the Senate chamber, members have no desks or assigned seats. In both chambers, the floor slopes downward to the well in front of the presiding officer's raised desk. A chamber is often referred to as "the floor," as when members are said to be on or going to the floor. Those expressions usually imply that the member's house is in session.

Christmas Tree Bill—Jargon for a bill adorned with amendments, many of them unrelated to the bill's subject, that provide benefits for interest groups, specific states, congressional districts, companies, and individuals.

Classes of Senators—A class consists of the 33 or 34 senators elected to a six-year term in the same general election. Since the terms of approximately one-third of the senators expire every two years, there are three classes.

Clean Bill—After a House committee extensively amends a bill, it often assembles its amendments and what is left of the bill into a new measure that one or more of its members introduces as a "clean bill." The revised measure is assigned a new number.

Clerk of the House—An officer of the House of Representatives responsible principally for administrative support of the legislative process in the House. The clerk is invariably the candidate of the majority party.

Cloture—A Senate procedure that limits further consideration of a pending proposal to 30 hours in order to end a filibuster. Sixteen senators must first sign and submit a cloture motion to the presiding officer. One hour after the Senate meets on the second calendar day thereafter, the chair puts the motion to a yea-and-nay vote following a live quorum call. If three-fifths of all senators (60 if there are no vacancies) vote for the motion, the Senate must take final action on the cloture proposal by the end of the 30 hours of consideration and may consider no other business until it takes that action. Cloture on a proposal to amend the Senate's standing rules requires approval by two-thirds of the senators present and voting.

Code of Official Conduct—A House rule that bans certain actions by House members, officers, and employees; requires them to conduct themselves in ways that "reflect creditably" on the House; and orders them to adhere to the spirit and the letter of House rules and those of its committees. The code's provisions govern the receipt of outside compensation, gifts, and honoraria, and the use of campaign funds; prohibit members from using their clerk-hire allowance to pay anyone who does not perform duties commensurate with that pay; forbids discrimination in members' hiring or treatment of employees on the grounds of race, color, religion, sex, handicap, age, or national origin; orders members convicted of a crime who might be punished by imprisonment of two or more years not to participate in committee business or vote on the floor until exonerated or reelected; and restricts employees' contact with federal agencies on matters in which they have a significant financial interest. The Senate's rules contain some similar prohibitions.

College of Cardinals—A popular term for the subcommittee chairmen of the appropriations committees, reflecting their influence over appropriation measures. The chairmen of the full appropriations committees are sometimes referred to as popes.

Committee—A panel of members elected or appointed to perform some service or function for its parent body. Congress has four types of committees: standing, special or select, joint, and, in the House, a Committee of the Whole.

Committees conduct investigations, make studies, issue reports and recommendations, and, in the case of standing committees, review and prepare measures on their assigned subjects for action by their respective houses. Most committees divide their work among several subcommittees. With rare exceptions, the majority party in a house holds a majority of the seats on its committees, and their chairmen are also from that party.

Committee of the Whole—Common name of the Committee of the Whole House on the State of the Union, a committee consisting of all members of the House of Representatives. Measures from the union calendar must be considered in the Committee of the Whole before the House officially completes action on them; the committee often considers other major bills as well. A quorum of the committee is 100, and it meets in the House chamber under a chairman appointed by the Speaker. Procedures in the Committee of the Whole expedite consideration of legislation because of its smaller quorum requirement, its ban on certain motions, and its five-minute rule for debate on amendments. Those procedures usually permit more members to offer amendments and participate in the debate on a measure than is normally possible. The Senate no longer uses a Committee of the Whole.

Committee Veto—A procedure that requires an executive department or agency to submit certain proposed policies, programs, or action to designated committees for review before implementing them. Before 1983, when the Supreme Court declared that a legislative veto is unconstitutional, these provisions permitted committees to veto the proposals. They no longer do so, and the term is now something of a misnomer. Nevertheless, agencies usually take the pragmatic approach of trying to reach a consensus with the committees before carrying out their proposals, especially when an appropriations committee is involved.

Concurrent Resolution—A resolution that requires approval by both houses but is not sent to the president for his signature and therefore cannot have the force of law. Concurrent resolutions deal with the prerogatives or internal affairs of Congress as a whole. Designated H. Con. Res. in the House and S. Con. Res. in the Senate, they are numbered consecutively in each house in their order of introduction during a two-year Congress.

Conference—(1) A formal meeting or series of meetings between members representing each house to reconcile House and Senate differences on a measure (occasionally several measures). Since one house cannot require the other to agree to its proposals, the conference usually reaches agreement by compromise. When a conference completes action on a measure, or as much action as appears possible, it sends its recommendations to both houses in the form of a conference report, accompanied by an explanatory statement. (2) The official title of the organization of all Democrats or Republicans in the Senate and of all Republicans in the House of Representatives. (*See Party Caucus.*)

Confirmations—(*See Nomination.*)

Congress—(1) The national legislature of the United States, consisting of the House of Representatives and the Senate. (2) The national legislature in office during a two-year period. Congresses are numbered sequentially; thus, the 1st Congress of 1789–1791 and the 102d Congress of 1991–1993. Before 1935, the two-year period began on the first Monday in December of odd-numbered years. Since then it has extended from January of an odd-numbered year through noon on January 3 of the next odd-numbered year. A Congress usually holds two annual sessions, but some have had three sessions and the 67th Congress had four. When a Congress expires, measures die if they have not yet been enacted.

Congressional Record—The daily, printed, and substantially verbatim account of proceedings in both the House and Senate chambers. Extraneous materials submitted by members appear in a section titled "Extensions of Remarks." A "Daily Digest" appendix contains highlights of the day's floor and committee action plus a list of committee meetings and floor agendas for the next day's session.

Although the official reporters of each house take down every word spoken during the proceedings, members are permitted to edit and "revise and extend" their remarks before they are printed. In the Senate section, all speeches, articles, and other material submitted by senators but not actually spoken or read on the floor are set off by large black dots, called bullets. However, bullets do not appear when a senator reads part of a speech and inserts the rest. In the House section, undelivered speeches and materials are printed in a distinctive typeface. The term "permanent *Record*" refers to the bound volumes of the daily *Record*s of an entire session of Congress.

Congressional Terms of Office—A term normally begins on January 3 of the year following a general election and runs two years for representatives and six years for senators. A representative chosen in a special election to fill a vacancy is sworn in for the remainder of his predecessor's term. An individual appointed to fill a Senate vacancy usually serves until the next general election or until the end of the predecessor's term, whichever comes first. Some states, however, require their governors to call a special election to fill a Senate vacancy shortly after an appointment has been made.

Continuing Resolution (CR)—A joint resolution that provides funds to continue the operation of federal agencies and programs at the beginning of a new fiscal year if their annual appropriation bills have not yet been enacted; also called continuing appropriations.

Contract Authority—Statutory authority permitting an agency to enter into contracts or incur other obligations even though it has not received an appropriation to pay for them. Congress must eventually fund them because the government is legally liable for such payments. The Congressional Budget Act of 1974 requires that new contract authority may not be used unless provided for in advance by an appropriation act, but it permits a few exceptions.

Controllable Expenditures—Federal spending that is permitted but not mandated by existing authorization law and therefore may be adjusted by congressional action in appropriation bills. *(See Appropriation.)*

Correcting Recorded Votes—The rules of both houses prohibit members from changing their votes after a vote result has been announced. Nevertheless, the Senate permits its members to withdraw or change their votes, by unanimous consent, immediately after the announcement. In rare instances, senators have been granted unanimous consent to change their votes several days or weeks after the announcement.

Votes tallied by the electronic voting system in the House may not be changed. But when a vote actually given is not recorded during an oral call of the roll, a member may demand a correction as a matter of right. On all other alleged errors in a recorded vote, the Speaker determines whether the circumstances justify a change. Occasionally, members merely announce that they were incorrectly recorded; announcements can occur hours, days, or even months after the vote and appear in the *Congressional Record.*

Corrections Calendar—Members of the House may place on this calendar bills reported favorably from committee that repeal rules and regulations considered excessive or unnecessary. Bills on the Corrections Calendar normally are called on the second and fourth Tuesday of each month at the discretion of the Speaker in consultation with the minority leader. A bill must be on the calendar for at least three legislative days before it can be brought up for floor consideration. Once on the floor, a bill is subject to one hour of debate equally divided between the chairman and ranking member of the committee of jurisdiction. A vote may be called on whether to recommit the bill to committee with or without instructions. To pass, a three-fifths majority, or 261 votes if all House members vote, is required.

Cosponsor—A member who has joined one or more other members to sponsor a measure. *(See Bills and Resolutions Introduced.)*

Current Services Estimates—Executive branch estimates of the anticipated costs of federal programs and operations for the next and future fiscal years at existing levels of service and assuming no new initiatives or changes in existing law. The president submits these estimates to Congress with his annual budget and includes an explanation of the underlying economic and policy assumptions on which they are based, such as anticipated rates of inflation, real economic growth, and unemployment, plus program caseloads and pay increases.

Custody of the Papers—Possession of an engrossed measure and certain related basic documents that the two houses produce as they try to resolve their differences over the measure.

Dance of the Swans and the Ducks—A whimsical description of the gestures some members use in connection with a request for a recorded vote, especially in the House. When a member wants his colleagues to stand in support of the request, he moves his hands and arms in a gentle upward motion resembling the beginning flight of a graceful swan. When he wants his colleagues to remain seated in order to avoid such a vote, he moves his hands and arms in a vigorous downward motion resembling a diving duck.

Dean—Within a state's delegation in the House of Representatives, the member with the longest continuous service.

Debt Limit—The maximum amount of outstanding federal public debt permitted by law. The limit (or ceiling) covers virtually all debt incurred by the government except agency debt. Each congressional budget resolution sets forth the new debt limit that may be required under its provisions.

Deferral—An impoundment of funds for a specific period of time that may not extend beyond the fiscal year in which it is proposed. Under the Impoundment Control Act of 1974, the president must notify Congress that he is deferring the spending or obligation of funds provided by law for a project or activity. Congress can disapprove the deferral by legislation.

Deficit—The amount by which the government's outlays exceed its budget receipts for a given fiscal year. Both the president's budget and the annual congressional budget resolution provide estimates of the deficit or surplus for the upcoming and several future fiscal years.

Degrees of Amendment—Designations that indicate the relationships of amendments to the text of a measure and to each other. In general, an amendment offered directly to the text of a measure is an amendment in the first degree, and an amendment to that amendment is an amendment in the second degree. Both houses normally prohibit amendments in the third degree—that is, an amendment to an amendment to an amendment.

Dilatory Tactics—Procedural actions intended to delay or prevent action by a house or a committee. They include, among others, offering numerous motions, demanding quorum calls and recorded votes at every opportunity, making numerous points of order and parliamentary inquiries, and speaking as long as the applicable rules permit. The Senate's rules permit a battery of dilatory tactics, especially lengthy speeches, except under cloture. In the House, possible dilatory tactics are more limited. Speeches are always subject to time limits and debate-ending motions. Moreover, a House rule instructs the Speaker not to entertain dilatory motions and lets the Speaker decide whether a motion is dilatory. However, the Speaker may not override the constitutional right of a member to demand the yeas and nays, and in practice usually waits for a point of order before exercising that authority. *(See Cloture.)*

Discharge a Committee—Remove a measure from a committee to which it has been referred in order to make it available for floor consideration. Noncontroversial measures are often discharged by unanimous consent. However, because congressional committees have no obligation to report measures referred to them, each house has procedures to extract controversial measures from recalcitrant committees. Six discharge procedures are available in the House of Representatives. The Senate uses a motion to discharge, which is usually converted into a discharge resolution.

Discharge Calendar—The House calendar to which motions to discharge committees are referred when they have the required number of signatures (218) and are awaiting floor action.

Discharge Petition—(*See Discharge a Committee.*)

Discharge Resolution—In the Senate, a special motion that any senator may introduce to relieve a committee from consideration of a bill before it. The resolution can be called up for Senate approval or disapproval in the same manner as any other Senate business. (*House procedure, see Discharge a Committee.*)

Division Vote—A vote in which the chair first counts those in favor of a proposition and then those opposed to it, with no record made of how each member votes. In the Senate, the chair may count raised hands or ask senators to stand, whereas the House requires members to stand; hence, often called a standing vote. Committees in both houses ordinarily use a show of hands. A division usually occurs after a voice vote and may be demanded by any member or ordered by the chair if there is any doubt about the outcome of the voice vote. The demand for a division can also come before a voice vote. In the Senate, the demand must come before the result of a voice vote is announced. It may be made after a voice vote announcement in the House, but only if no intervening business has transpired and only if the member was standing and seeking recognition at the time of the announcement. A demand for the yeas and nays or, in the House, for a recorded vote, takes precedence over a division vote.

Enacting Clause—The opening language of each bill, beginning "Be it enacted by the Senate and House of Representatives of the United States of America in Congress assembled..." This language gives legal force to measures approved by Congress and signed by the president or enacted over his veto. A successful motion to strike it from a bill kills the entire measure.

Engrossed Bill—The official copy of a bill or joint resolution as passed by one chamber, including the text as amended by floor action, and certified by the clerk of the House or the secretary of the Senate (as appropriate). Amendments by one house to a measure or amendments of the other also are engrossed. House engrossed documents are printed on blue paper; the Senate's are printed on white paper.

Enrolled Bill—The final official copy of a bill or joint resolution passed in identical form by both houses. An enrolled bill is printed on parchment. After it is certified by the chief officer of the house in which it originated and signed by the House Speaker and the Senate president pro tempore, the measure is sent to the president for his signature.

Entitlement Program—A federal program under which individuals, businesses, or units of government that meet the requirements or qualifications established by law are entitled to receive certain payments if they seek such payments. Major examples include Social Security, Medicare, Medicaid, unemployment insurance, and military and federal civilian pensions. Congress cannot control their expenditures by refusing to appropriate the sums necessary to fund them because the government is legally obligated to pay eligible recipients the amounts to which the law entitles them.

Executive Calendar—The Senate's calendar for committee reports on its executive business, namely treaties and nominations. The calendar numbers indicate the order in which items were referred to the calendar but have no bearing on when or if the Senate will consider them. The Senate, by motion or unanimous consent, resolves itself into executive session to consider them.

Executive Document—A document, usually a treaty, sent by the president to the Senate for approval. It is referred to a committee in the same manner as other measures. Resolutions to ratify treaties have their own "treaty document" numbers. For example, the first treaty submitted in the 106th Congress would be "Treaty Doc 106-1."

Executive Order—A unilateral proclamation by the president that has a policy-making or legislative impact. Members of Congress have challenged some executive orders on the grounds that they usurped the authority of the legislative branch. Although the Supreme Court has ruled that a particular order exceeded the president's authority, it has upheld others as falling within the president's general constitutional powers.

Executive Privilege—The assertion that presidents have the right to withhold certain information from Congress. Presidents have based their claim on: (1) the constitutional separation of powers; (2) the need for secrecy in military and diplomatic affairs; (3) the need to protect individuals from unfavorable publicity; (4) the need to safeguard the confidential exchange of ideas in the executive branch; and (5) the need to protect individuals who provide confidential advice to the president.

Executive Session—A meeting of a Senate or House committee (or occasionally of either chamber) that only its members may attend. Witnesses regularly appear at committee meetings in executive session — for example, Defense Department officials during presentations of classified defense information. Other members of Congress may be invited, but the public and press are not to attend.

Expenditures—The actual spending of money as distinguished from the appropriation of funds. Expenditures are made by the disbursing officers of the administration; appropriations are made only by Congress. The two are rarely identical in any fiscal year. In addition to some current budget authority, expenditures may represent budget authority made available one, two, or more years earlier.

Expulsion—A member's removal from office by a two-thirds vote of his house; the super majority is required by the Constitution. It is the most severe and most rarely used sanction a house can invoke against a member. Although the Constitution provides no explicit grounds for expulsion, the courts have ruled that it may be applied only for misconduct during a member's term of office, not for conduct before the member's election. Generally, neither house will consider expulsion of a member convicted of a crime until the judicial processes have been exhausted. At that stage, members sometimes resign rather than face expulsion. In 1977 the House adopted a rule urging members convicted of certain crimes to voluntarily abstain from voting or participating in other legislative business.

Federal Debt—The total amount of monies borrowed and not yet repaid by the federal government. Federal debt consists of public debt and agency debt. Public debt is the portion of the federal debt borrowed by the Treasury or the Federal Financing Bank directly from the public or from another federal fund or account. For example, the Treasury regularly borrows money from the Social Security trust fund. Public debt accounts for about 99 percent of the federal debt. Agency debt refers to the debt incurred by federal agencies like the Export-Import Bank, but excluding the Treasury and the Federal Financing Bank, which are authorized by law to borrow funds from the public or from another government fund or account.

Filibuster—The use of obstructive and time-consuming parliamentary tactics by one member or a minority of members to delay, modify, or defeat proposed legislation or rules changes. Filibusters are also sometimes used to delay urgently needed measures in order to force the body to accept other legislation. The Senate's rules permitting unlimited debate and the extraordinary majority it requires to impose cloture make filibustering particularly effective in that chamber. Under the stricter rules of the House, filibusters in that body are short-lived and therefore ineffective and rarely attempted

Fiscal Year—The federal government's annual accounting period. It begins October 1 and ends on the following September 30. A fiscal year is designated by the calendar year in which it ends and is often referred to as FY. Thus, fiscal year 1999 began October 1, 1998, ended September 30, 1999, and is called FY99. In theory, Congress is supposed to complete action on all budgetary measures applying to a fiscal year before that year begins. It rarely does so.

Five-Minute Rule—In its most common usage, a House rule that limits debate on an amendment offered in Committee of the Whole to five minutes for its sponsor and five minutes for an opponent. In practice, the committee routinely permits longer debate by two devices: the offering of pro forma amendments, each debatable for five minutes, and unanimous consent for a member to speak longer than five minutes. Also a House rule that limits a committee member to five minutes when questioning a witness at a hearing until each member has had an opportunity to question that witness.

Floor Manager—A majority party member responsible for guiding a measure through its floor consideration in a house and for devising the political and procedural strategies that might be required to get the measure passed. The presiding officer gives the floor manager priority recognition to debate, offer amendments, oppose amendments, and make crucial procedural motions.

Frank—Informally, a member's legal right to send official mail postage free under his or her signature; often called the franking privilege. Technically, it is the autographic or facsimile signature used on envelopes instead of stamps that permits members and certain congressional officers to send their official mail free of charge. The franking privilege has been authorized by law since the first Congress, except for a few months in 1873. Congress reimburses the U.S. Postal Service for the franked mail it handles.

Function or Functional Category—A broad category of national need and spending of budgetary significance. A category provides an accounting method for allocating and keeping track of budgetary resources and expenditures for that function because it includes all budget accounts related to the functions subject or purpose such as agriculture, administration of justice,

commerce and housing and energy. Functions do not necessarily correspond with appropriations acts or with the budgets of individual agencies.

Germane—Basically, on the same subject as the matter under consideration. A House rule requires that all amendments be germane. In the Senate, only amendments proposed to general appropriation bills and budget resolutions or under cloture must be germane. Germaneness rules can be evaded by suspension of the rules in both houses, by unanimous consent agreements in the Senate, and by special rules from the Rules Committee in the House.

Gerrymandering—The manipulation of legislative district boundaries to benefit a particular party, politician, or minority group. The term originated in 1812 when the Massachusetts legislature redrew the lines of state legislative districts to favor the party of Gov. Elbridge Gerry, and some critics said one district looked like a salamander.

Gramm-Rudman-Hollings Act of 1985—Common name for the Balanced Budget and Emergency Deficit Control Act of 1985, which established new budget procedures intended to balance the federal budget by fiscal year 1991. The timetable subsequently was extended and then deleted. The act's chief sponsors were senators Phil Gramm (R-Texas), Warren Rudman (R-N.H.), and Ernest Hollings (D-S.C.).

Grandfather Clause—A provision in a measure, law, or rule that exempts an individual, entity, or a defined category of individuals or entities from complying with a new policy or restriction. For example, a bill that would raise taxes on persons who reach the age of 65 after a certain date inherently grandfathers out those who are 65 before that date. Similarly, a Senate rule limiting senators to two major committee assignments also grandfathers some senators who were sitting on a third major committee prior to a specified date.

Grants-in-Aid—Payments by the federal government to state and local governments to help provide for assistance programs or public services.

Hearing—Committee or subcommittee meetings to receive testimony from witnesses on proposed legislation during investigations or for oversight purposes. Relatively few bills are important enough to justify formal hearings. Witnesses often include experts, government officials, spokespersons for interested groups, officials of the General Accounting Office, and members of Congress. Also, the printed transcripts of hearings.

Hold—A senator's request that his or her party leaders delay floor consideration of certain legislation or presidential nominations. The majority leader usually honors a hold for a reasonable period of time, especially if its purpose is to assure the senator that the matter will not be called up during his or her absence or to give the senator time to gather necessary information.

Hold-Harmless Clause—In legislation providing a new formula for allocating federal funds, a clause to ensure that recipients of those funds do not receive less in a future year than they did in the current year if the new formula would result in a reduction for them. Similar to a grandfather clause, it has been used most frequently to soften the impact of sudden reductions in federal grants. (*See Grandfather Clause.*)

Hopper—A box on the clerk's desk in the House chamber into which members deposit bills and resolutions to introduce them. In House jargon, to drop a bill in the hopper is to introduce it.

Hour Rule—(1) A House rule that permits members, when recognized, to hold the floor in debate for no more than one hour each. The majority party member customarily yields one-half the time to a minority member. Although the hour rule applies to general debate in Committee of the Whole as well as in the House, special rules routinely vary the length of time for such debate and its control to fit the circumstances of particular measures.

House—The House of Representatives, as distinct from the Senate, although each body is a "house" of Congress.

House as in Committee of the Whole—A hybrid combination of procedures from the general rules of the House and from the rules of the Committee of the Whole, sometimes used to expedite consideration of a measure on the floor.

House Calendar—The calendar reserved for all public bills and resolutions that do not raise revenue or directly or indirectly appropriate money or property when they are favorably reported by House committees.

House Manual—A commonly used title for the handbook of the rules of the House of Representatives, published in each Congress. Its official title is *Constitution, Jefferson's Manual, and Rules of the House of Representatives*.

House of Representatives—The house of Congress in which states are represented roughly in proportion to their populations, but every state is guaranteed at least one representative. By law, the number of voting representatives is fixed at 435. Four delegates and one resident commissioner also serve in the House; they may vote in their committees but not on the House floor. Although the House and Senate have equal legislative power, the Constitution gives the House sole authority to originate revenue measures. The House also claims the right to originate appropriation measures, a claim the Senate disputes in theory but concedes in practice. The House has the sole power to impeach, and it elects the president when no candidate has received a majority of the electoral votes. It is sometimes referred to as the lower body.

Immunity—(1) Members' constitutional protection from lawsuits and arrest in connection with their legislative duties. They may not be tried for libel or slander for anything they say on the floor of a house or in committee. Nor may they be arrested while attending sessions of their houses or when traveling to or from sessions of Congress, except when charged with treason, a felony, or a breach of the peace. (2) In the case of a witness before a committee, a grant of protection from prosecution based on that person's testimony to the committee. It is used to compel witnesses to testify who would otherwise refuse to do so on the constitutional ground of possible self-incrimination. Under such a grant, none of a witness testimony may be used against him or her in a court proceeding except in a prosecution for perjury or for giving a false statement to Congress.

Impeachment—The first step to remove the president, vice president, or other federal civil officers from office and to disqualify them from any future federal office "of honor, Trust or Profit." An impeachment is a formal charge of treason, bribery, or "other high Crimes and Misdemeanors." The House has the sole power of impeachment and the Senate the sole power of trying the charges and convicting. The House impeaches by a simple majority vote; conviction requires a two-thirds vote of all senators present.

Impoundment—An executive branch action or inaction that delays or withholds the expenditure or obligation of budget authority provided by law. The Impoundment Control Act of 1974 classifies impoundments as either deferrals or rescissions, requires the president to notify Congress about all such actions, and gives Congress authority to approve or reject them. The Constitution is unclear on whether a president may refuse to spend appropriated money, but Congress usually expects the president to spend at least enough to achieve the purposes for which the money was provided whether or not he agrees with those purposes.

Joint Committee—A committee composed of members selected from each house. The functions of most joint committees involve investigation, research, or oversight of agencies closely related to Congress. Permanent joint committees, created by statute, are sometimes called standing joint committees. Once quite numerous, only four joint committees remained as of 1997: Joint Economic, Joint Taxation, Joint Library, and Joint Printing. No joint committee has authority to report legislation.

Joint Resolution—A legislative measure that Congress uses for purposes other than general legislation. Like a bill, it has the force of law when passed by both houses and either approved by the president or passed over the president's veto. Unlike a bill, a joint resolution enacted into law is not called an act; it retains its original title.

Most often, joint resolutions deal with such relatively limited matters as the correction of errors in existing law, continuing appropriations, a single appropriation, or the establishment of permanent joint committees. Unlike bills, however, joint resolutions also are used to propose constitutional amendments; these do not require the president's signature and become effective only when ratified by three-fourths of the states. The House designates joint resolutions as H.J. Res., the Senate as S.J. Res. Each house numbers its joint resolutions consecutively in the order of introduction during a two-year Congress.

Journal—The official record of House or Senate actions, including every motion offered, every vote cast, amendments agreed to, quorum calls, and so forth. Unlike the *Congressional Record*, it does not provide reports of speeches, debates, statements, and the like. The Constitution requires each house to maintain a *Journal* and to publish it periodically.

King of the Mountain (or Hill) Rule—(*See Queen of the Hill Rule.*)

Lame Duck—Jargon for a member who has not been reelected, or did not seek reelection, and is serving the balance of his or her term.

Lame Duck Session—A session of a Congress held after the election for the succeeding Congress, so-called after the lame duck members still serving.

Law—An act of Congress that has been signed by the president, passed over the president's veto, or allowed to become law without the president's signature.

Legislative Day—The day that begins when a house meets after an adjournment and ends when it next adjourns. Because the House of Representatives normally adjourns at the end of a daily session, its legislative and calendar days usually coincide. The Senate, however, frequently recesses at the end of a daily session, and its legislative day may extend over several calendar days, weeks, or months. Among other uses, this technicality permits the Senate to save time by circumventing its morning hour, a procedure required at the beginning of every legislative day

Legislative Veto—A procedure, declared unconstitutional in 1983, that allowed Congress or one of its houses to nullify certain actions of the president, executive branch agencies, or independent agencies. Sometimes called congressional vetoes or congressional disapprovals. Following the Supreme Court's 1983 decision, Congress amended several legislative veto statutes to require enactment of joint resolutions, which are subject to presidential veto, for nullifying executive branch actions.

Live Pair—A voluntary and informal agreement between two members on opposite sides of an issue under which the member who is present for a recorded vote withholds or withdraws his or her vote because the other member is absent.

Loan Guarantee—A statutory commitment by the federal government to pay part or all of a loans principal and interest to a lender or the holder of a security in case the borrower defaults.

Lobby—To try to persuade members of Congress to propose, pass, modify, or defeat proposed legislation or to change or repeal existing laws. A lobbyist attempts to promote his or her own preferences or those of a group, organization, or industry. Originally the term referred to persons frequenting the lobbies or corridors of legislative chambers in order to speak to lawmakers. In a general sense, lobbying includes not only direct contact with members but also indirect attempts to influence them, such as writing to them or persuading others to write or visit them, attempting to mold public opinion toward a desired legislative goal by various means, and contributing or arranging for contributions to members election campaigns. The right to lobby stems from the First Amendment to the Constitution, which bans laws that abridge the right of the people to petition the government for a redress of grievances.

Logrolling—Jargon for a legislative tactic or bargaining strategy in which members try to build support for their legislation by promising to support legislation desired by other members or by accepting amendments they hope will induce their colleagues to vote for their bill.

Mace—The symbol of the office of the House sergeant at arms. Under the direction of the Speaker, the sergeant at arms is responsible for preserving order on the House floor by holding up the mace in front of an unruly member, or by carrying the mace up and down the aisles to quell boisterous behavior. When the House is in session, the mace sits on a pedestal at the Speaker's right; when the House is in Committee of the Whole, it is moved to a lower pedestal. The mace is 46 inches high and consists of 13 ebony rods bound in silver and topped by a silver globe with a silver eagle, wings outstretched, perched on it.

Majority Leader—The majority party's chief floor spokesman, elected by that party's caucus—sometimes called floor leader. In the Senate, the majority leader also develops the party's political and procedural strategy, usually in collaboration with other party officials and committee chairmen. He negotiates the Senates agenda and committee ratios with the minority leader and usually calls up measures for floor action. The chamber traditionally concedes to the majority leader the right to determine the days on which it will meet and the hours at which it will convene and adjourn. In the House, the majority leader is the Speaker's deputy and heir apparent. He helps plan the floor agenda and the party's legislative strategy and often speaks for the party leadership in debate.

Majority Whip—In effect, the assistant majority leader, in either the House or Senate. His job is to help marshal majority forces in support of party strategy and legislation.

Manual—The official handbook in each house prescribing in detail its organization, procedures, and operations.

Marking Up a Bill—Going through the contents of a piece of legislation in committee or subcommittee to, for example, consider its provisions in large and small portions, act on amendments to provisions and proposed revisions to the language, and insert new sections and phraseology. If the bill is extensively amended, the committee's version may be introduced as a separate bill, with a new number, before being considered by the full House or Senate. (*See Clean Bill.*)

Method of Equal Proportions—The mathematical formula used since 1950 to determine how the 435 seats in the House of Representatives should be distributed among the 50 states in the apportionment following each decennial census. It minimizes as much as possible the proportional difference between the average district population in any two states. Because the Constitution guarantees each state at least one representative, 50 seats are automatically apportioned. The formula calculates priority numbers for each state, assigns the first of the 385 remaining seats to the state with the highest priority number, the second to the state with the next highest number, and so on until all seats are distributed. (*See Apportionment.*)

Midterm Election—The general election for members of Congress that occurs in November of the second year in a presidential term.

Minority Leader—The minority party's leader and chief floor spokesman, elected by the party caucus; sometimes called minority floor leader. With the assistance of other party officials and the ranking minority members of committees, the minority leader devises the party's political and procedural strategy.

Minority Whip—Performs duties of whip for the minority party. (*See also Majority Whip.*)

Minority Staff—Employees who assist the minority party members of a committee. Most committees hire separate majority and minority party staffs, but they also may hire nonpartisan staff.

Motion—A formal proposal for a procedural action, such as to consider, to amend, to lay on the table, to reconsider, to recess, or to adjourn. It has been estimated that at least 85 motions are possible under various circumstances in the House of Representatives, somewhat fewer in the Senate. Not all motions are created equal; some are privileged or preferential and enjoy priority over others. And some motions are debatable, amendable or divisible, while others are not.

Nomination—A proposed presidential appointment to a federal office submitted to the Senate for confirmation. Approval is by majority vote. The Constitution explicitly requires confirmation for ambassadors, consuls, public Ministers (department heads), and Supreme Court justices. By law, other federal judges, all military promotions of officers, and many high-level civilian officials must be confirmed.

Oath of Office—Upon taking office, members of Congress must swear or affirm that they will "support and defend the Constitution . . . against all enemies, foreign and domestic," that they will "bear true faith and allegiance" to the Constitution, that they take the obligation "freely, without any mental reservation or purpose of evasion," and that they will "well and faithfully discharge the duties" of their office. The oath is required by the Constitution; the wording is prescribed by a statute. All House members must take the oath at the beginning of each new Congress.

Obligations—Orders placed, contracts awarded, services received, and similar transactions during a given period that will require payments during the same or future period. Such amounts include outlays for which obligations had not been previously recorded and reflect adjustments for differences between obligations previously recorded and actual outlays to liquidate those obligations.

Omnibus Bill—A measure that combines the provisions of several disparate subjects into a single and often lengthy bill.

One-Minute Speeches—Addresses by House members at the beginning of a legislative day. The speeches may cover any subject but are limited to one minute's duration.

Order of Business (House)—The sequence of events during the meeting of the House on a new legislative day prescribed by a House rule; also called the general order of business. The sequence consists of (1) the chaplain's prayer; (2) approval of the *Journal*; (3) pledge of allegiance (4) correction of the reference of public bills; (5) disposal of business on the Speaker's table; (6) unfinished business; (7) the morning hour call of committees and consideration of their bills (largely obsolete); (8) motions to go into Committee of the Whole; and (9) orders of the day (also obsolete). In practice, on days specified in the rules, the items of business that follow approval of the *Journal* are supplanted in part by the special order of business (for example, the corrections, discharge, or private calendars or motions to suspend the rules) and on any day by other privileged business (for example, general appropriation bills and special rules)

or measures made in order by special rules. By this combination of an order of business with privileged interruptions, the House gives precedence to certain categories of important legislation, brings to the floor other major legislation from its calendars in any order it chooses, and provides expeditious processing for minor and noncontroversial measures.

Order of Business (Senate)—The sequence of events at the beginning of a new legislative day prescribed by Senate rules. The sequence consists of (1) the chaplain's prayer; (2) *Journal* reading and correction; (3) morning business in the morning hour; (4) call of the calendar during the morning hour; and (5) unfinished business.

Outlays—Amounts of government spending. They consist of payments, usually by check or in cash, to liquidate obligations incurred in prior fiscal years as well as in the current year, including the net lending of funds under budget authority. In federal budget accounting, net outlays are calculated by subtracting the amounts of refunds and various kinds of reimbursements to the government from actual spending.

Override a Veto—Congressional enactment of a measure over the president's veto. A veto override requires a recorded two-thirds vote of those voting in each house, a quorum being present. Because the president must return the vetoed measure to its house of origin, that house votes first, but neither house is required to attempt an override, whether immediately or at all. If an override attempt fails in the house of origin, the veto stands and the measure dies.

Oversight—Congressional review of the way in which federal agencies implement laws to ensure that they are carrying out the intent of Congress and to inquire into the efficiency of the implementation and the effectiveness of the law. The Legislative Reorganization Act of 1946 defined oversight as the function of exercising continuous watchfulness over the execution of the laws by the executive branch.

Pairing—A procedure that permits two or three members to enter into voluntary arrangements that offset their votes so that one or more of the members can be absent without changing the result. The names of paired members and their positions on the vote (except on general pairs) appear in the *Congressional Record*. Members can be paired on one vote or on a series of votes.

Parliamentarian—The official advisor to the presiding officer in each house on questions of procedure. The parliamentarian and his assistants also answer procedural questions from members and congressional staff, refer measures to committees on behalf of the presiding officer, and maintain compilations of the precedents. The House parliamentarian revises the House Manual at the beginning of every Congress and usually reviews special rules before the Rules Committee reports them to the House. Either a parliamentarian or an assistant is always present and near the podium during sessions of each house.

Party Caucus—Generic term for each party's official organization in each house. Only House Democrats officially call their organization a caucus. House and Senate Republicans and Senate Democrats call their organizations conferences. The party caucuses elect their leaders, approve committee assignments and chairmanships (or ranking minority members, if the party is in the minority), establish party committees and study groups, and discuss party and legislative policies. On rare occasions, they have stripped members of committee seniority or expelled them from the caucus for party disloyalty.

Petition—A request or plea sent to one or both chambers from an organization or private citizens' group asking support of particular legislation or favorable consideration of a matter not yet receiving congressional attention. Petitions are referred to appropriate committees.

Pocket Veto—The indirect veto of a bill as a result of the president withholding approval of it until after Congress has adjourned sine die. A bill the president does not sign, but does not formally veto while Congress is in session, automatically becomes a law 10 days (excluding Sundays) after it is received. But if Congress adjourns its annual session during that 10-day period, the measure dies even if the president does not formally veto it.

Point of Order—A parliamentary term used in committee and on the floor to object to an alleged violation of a rule and to demand that the chair enforce the rule. The point of order immediately halts the proceedings until the chair decides whether the contention is valid.

Pork or Pork Barrel Legislation—Pejorative terms for federal appropriations, bills, or policies that provide funds to benefit a legislator's district or state, with the implication that the legislator presses for enactment of such benefits to ingratiate himself or herself with constituents rather than on the basis of an impartial, objective assessment of need or merit.

The terms are often applied to such benefits as new parks, post offices, dams, canals, bridges, roads, water projects, sewage treatment plants, and public works of any kind, as well as demonstration projects, research grants, and relocation of government facilities. Funds released by the president for various kinds of benefits or government contracts approved by him allegedly for political purposes are also sometimes referred to as pork.

Postcloture Filibuster—A filibuster conducted after the Senate invokes cloture. It employs an array of procedural tactics rather than lengthy speeches to delay final action. The Senate curtailed the postcloture filibusters effectiveness by closing a variety of loopholes in the cloture rule in 1979 and 1986.

President of the Senate—The vice president of the United States in his constitutional role as presiding officer of the Senate. The Constitution permits the vice president to cast a vote in the Senate only to break a tie, but he is not required to do so.

President Pro Tempore—Under the Constitution, an officer elected by the Senate to preside over it during the absence of the vice president of the United States. Often referred to as the "pro tem," he is usually the majority party senator with the longest continuous service in the chamber and also, by virtue of his seniority, a committee chairman. When attending to committee and other duties, the president pro tempore appoints other senators to preside.

Previous Question—A nondebatable motion which, when agreed to by majority vote, usually cuts off further debate, prevents the offering of additional amendments, and brings the pending matter to an immediate vote. It is a major debate-limiting device in the House; it is not permitted in Committee of the Whole or in the Senate.

Printed Amendment—A House rule guarantees five minutes of floor debate in support and five minutes in opposition, and no other debate time, on amendments printed in the Congressional Record at least one day prior to the amendment's consideration in the Committee of the Whole. In the Senate, although amendments may be submitted for printing, they have no parliamentary standing or status. An amendment submitted for printing in the Senate, however, may be called up by any senator.

Private Bill—A bill that applies to one or more specified persons, corporations, institutions, or other entities, usually to grant relief when no other legal remedy is available to them. Many private bills deal with claims against the federal government, immigration and naturalization cases, and land titles.

Private Calendar—Commonly used title for a calendar in the House reserved for private bills and resolutions favorably reported by committees. The private calendar is officially called the Calendar of the Committee of the Whole House.

Privilege—An attribute of a motion, measure, report, question, or proposition that gives it priority status for consideration. Privileged motions and motions to bring up privileged questions are not debatable.

Privileged Questions—The order in which bills, motions, and other legislative measures are considered by Congress is governed by strict priorities. A motion to table, for instance, is more privileged than a motion to recommit. Thus, a motion to recommit can be superseded by a motion to table, and a vote would be forced on the latter motion only. A motion to adjourn, however, takes precedence over a tabling motion and thus is considered of the "highest privilege." (*See also Questions of Privilege.*)

Pro Forma Amendment—In the House, an amendment that ostensibly proposes to change a measure or another amendment by moving "to strike the last word" or "to strike the requisite number of words." A member offers it not to make any actual change in the measure or amendment but only to obtain time for debate.

Proxy Voting—The practice of permitting a member to cast the vote of an absent colleague in addition to his own vote. Proxy voting is prohibited on the floors of the House and Senate, but the Senate permits its committees to authorize proxy voting, and most do. In 1995, House rules were changed to prohibit proxy voting in committee.

Public Law—A public bill or joint resolution enacted into law. It is cited by the letters P.L. followed by a hyphenated number. The digits before the hyphen indicate the number of the Congress in which it was enacted; the digits after the hyphen indicate its position in the numerical sequence of public measures that became law during that Congress. For example, the

Budget Enforcement Act of 1990 became P.L. 101-508 because it was the 508th measure in that sequence for the 101st Congress. (*See also Private Bill.*)

Queen of the Hill Rule—A special rule from the House Rules Committee that permits votes on a series of amendments, especially complete substitutes for a measure, in a specified order, but directs that the amendment receiving the greatest number of votes shall be the winning one. This kind of rule permits the House to vote directly on a variety of alternatives to a measure. In doing so, it sets aside the precedent that once an amendment has been adopted, no further amendments may be offered to the text it has amended. Under an earlier practice, the Rules Committee reported "king of the hill" rules under which there also could be votes on a series of amendments, again in a specified order. If more than one of the amendments was adopted under this kind of rule, it was the last amendment to receive a majority vote that was considered as having been finally adopted, whether or not it had received the greatest number of votes.

Questions of Privilege—These are matters affecting members of Congress individually or collectively. Matters affecting the rights, safety, dignity, and integrity of proceedings of the House or Senate as a whole are questions of privilege in both chambers.

Questions involving individual members are called questions of "personal privilege." A member rising to ask a question of personal privilege is given precedence over almost all other proceedings. An annotation in the House rules points out that the privilege rests primarily on the Constitution, which gives a member a conditional immunity from arrest and an unconditional freedom to speak in the House. (*See also Privileged Questions.*)

Quorum—The minimum number of members required to be present for the transaction of business. Under the Constitution, a quorum in each house is a majority of its members: 218 in the House and 51 in the Senate when there are no vacancies. By House rule, a quorum in Committee of the Whole is 100. In practice, both houses usually assume a quorum is present even if it is not, unless a member makes a point of no quorum in the House or suggests the absence of a quorum in the Senate. Consequently, each house transacts much of its business, and even passes bills, when only a few members are present.

For House and Senate committees, chamber rules allow a minimum quorum of one-third of a committee's members to conduct most types of business.

Ramseyer Rule—A House rule that requires a committee's report on a bill or joint resolution to show the changes the measure, and any committee amendments to it, would make in existing law.

Readings of Bills—Traditional parliamentary procedure required bills to be read three times before they were passed. This custom is of little modern significance. Normally a bill is considered to have its first reading when it is introduced and printed, by title, in the *Congressional Record*. In the House, its second reading comes when floor consideration begins. (This is the most likely point at which there is an actual reading of the bill, if there is any.) The second reading in the Senate is supposed to occur on the legislative day after the measure is introduced, but

before it is referred to committee. The third reading (again, usually by title) takes place when floor action has been completed on amendments.

Reapportionment—(*See Apportionment.*)

Recess—(1) A temporary interruption or suspension of a meeting of a chamber or committee. Unlike an adjournment, a recess does not end a legislative day. Because the Senate often recesses from one calendar day to another, its legislative day may extend over several calendar days, weeks, or even months. (2) A period of adjournment for more than three days to a day certain, especially over a holiday or in August during odd-numbered years.

Recognition—The power of recognition of a member is lodged in the Speaker of the House and the presiding officer of the Senate. The presiding officer names the member who will speak first when two or more members simultaneously request recognition.

Recommit—To send a measure back to the committee that reported it; sometimes called a straight motion to recommit to distinguish it from a motion to recommit with instructions. A successful motion to recommit kills the measure unless it is accompanied by instructions.

Reconciliation—A procedure for changing existing revenue and spending laws to bring total federal revenues and spending within the limits established in a budget resolution. Congress has applied reconciliation chiefly to revenues and mandatory spending programs, especially entitlements. Discretionary spending is controlled through annual appropriation bills.

Reconsider a Vote—A motion to reconsider the vote by which an action was taken has, until it is disposed of, the effect of putting the action in abeyance. In the Senate, the motion can be made only by a member who voted on the prevailing side of the original question or by a member who did not vote at all. In the House, it can be made only by a member on the prevailing side.

A common practice in the Senate after close votes on an issue is a motion to reconsider, followed by a motion to table the motion to reconsider. On this motion to table, senators vote as they voted on the original question, which allows the motion to table to prevail, assuming there are no switches. The matter then is finally closed and further motions to reconsider are not entertained. In the House, as a routine precaution, a motion to reconsider usually is made every time a measure is passed. Such a motion almost always is tabled immediately, thus shutting off the possibility of future reconsideration, except by unanimous consent.

Motions to reconsider must be entered in the Senate within the next two days of actual session after the original vote has been taken. In the House they must be entered either on the same day or on the next succeeding day the House is in session.

Recorded Vote—(1) Generally, any vote in which members are recorded by name for or against a measure; also called a record vote or roll-call vote. The only recorded vote in the Senate is a vote by the yeas and nays and is commonly called a roll-call vote. (2) Technically, a recorded vote is one demanded in the House of Representatives and supported by at least one-fifth of a quorum (44 members) in the House sitting as the House or at least 25 members in Committee of the Whole.

Report—(1) As a verb, a committee is said to report when it submits a measure or other document to its parent chamber. (2) A clerk is said to report when he or she reads a measure's title, text, or the text of an amendment to the body at the direction of the chair. (3) As a noun, a committee document that accompanies a reported measure. It describes the measure, the committee's views on it, its costs, and the changes it proposes to make in existing law; it also includes certain impact statements. (4) A committee document submitted to its parent chamber that describes the results of an investigation or other study or provides information the committee is required to provide by rule or law.

Reprimand—A formal condemnation of a member for misbehavior, considered a milder reproof than censure. The House of Representatives first used it in 1976. The Senate first used it in 1991. *(See also Censure, Code of Official Conduct, Expulsion.)*

Rescission—A provision of law that repeals previously enacted budget authority in whole or in part. Under the Impoundment Control Act of 1974, the president can impound such funds by sending a message to Congress requesting one or more rescissions and the reasons for doing so. If Congress does not pass a rescission bill for the programs requested by the president within 45 days of continuous session after receiving the message, the president must make the funds available for obligation and expenditure. If the president does not, the comptroller general of the United States is authorized to bring suit to compel the release of those funds. A rescission bill may rescind all, part, or none of an amount proposed by the president, and may rescind funds the president has not impounded.

Resolution—(1) A simple resolution; that is, a nonlegislative measure effective only in the house in which it is proposed and not requiring concurrence by the other chamber or approval by the president. Simple resolutions are designated H. Res. in the House and S. Res. in the Senate. Simple resolutions express nonbinding opinions on policies or issues or deal with the internal affairs or prerogatives of a house. (2) Any type of resolution: simple, concurrent, or joint. *(See Concurrent Resolution, Joint Resolution.)*

Revise and Extend One's Remarks—A unanimous consent request to publish in the *Congressional Record* a statement a member did not deliver on the floor, a longer statement than the one made on the floor, or miscellaneous extraneous material.

Rider—Congressional slang for an amendment unrelated or extraneous to the subject matter of the measure to which it is attached. Riders often contain proposals that are less likely to become law on their own merits as separate bills, either because of opposition in the committee of jurisdiction, resistance in the other house, or the probability of a presidential veto. Riders are more common in the Senate.

Rule—(1) A permanent regulation that a house adopts to govern its conduct of business, its procedures, its internal organization, behavior of its members, regulation of its facilities, duties of an officer, or some other subject it chooses to govern in that form. (2) In the House, a privileged simple resolution reported by the Rules Committee that provides methods and conditions for floor consideration of a measure or, rarely, several measures.

Secretary of the Senate—The chief administrative and budgetary officer of the Senate. The secretary manages a wide range of functions that support the operation of the Senate as an organization as well as those functions necessary to its legislative process, including recordkeeping, document management, certifications, housekeeping services, administration of oaths, and lobbyist registrations.

Select or Special Committee—A committee established by a resolution in either house for a special purpose and, usually, for a limited time. Most select and special committees are assigned specific investigations or studies, but are not authorized to report measures to their chambers.

Senate—The house of Congress in which each state is represented by two senators; each senator has one vote. Article V of the Constitution declares that "No State, without its Consent, shall be deprived of its equal Suffrage in the Senate." The Constitution also gives the Senate equal legislative power with the House of Representatives. Although the Senate is prohibited from originating revenue measures, and as a matter of practice it does not originate appropriation measures, it can amend both. Only the Senate can give or withhold consent to treaties and nominations from the president. It also acts as a court to try impeachments by the House and elects the vice president when no candidate receives a majority of the electoral votes. It is often referred to as "the upper body," but not by members of the House.

Senate Manual—The handbook of the Senate's standing rules and orders and the laws and other regulations that apply to the Senate, usually published once each Congress.

Senatorial Courtesy—The Senate's practice of declining to confirm a presidential nominee for an office in the state of a senator of the president's party unless that senator approves.

Sequestration—A procedure for canceling budgetary resources that is, money available for obligation or spending to enforce budget limitations established in law. Sequestered funds are no longer available for obligation or expenditure.

Sine Die—*(See Adjournment Sine Die.)*

Slip Law—The first official publication of a measure that has become law. It is published separately in unbound, single-sheet form or pamphlet form. A slip law usually is available two or three days after the date of the law's enactment.

Speaker—The presiding officer of the House of Representatives and the leader of its majority party. The Speaker is selected by the majority party and formally elected by the House at the beginning of each Congress. Although the Constitution does not require the Speaker to be a member of the House, in fact, all Speakers have been members.

Special Session—A session of Congress convened by the president, under his constitutional authority, after Congress has adjourned sine die at the end of a regular session. *(See Adjournment Sine Die.)*

Spending Authority—The technical term for backdoor spending. The Congressional Budget Act of 1974 defines it as borrowing authority, contract authority, and entitlement authority for which appropriation acts do not provide budget authority in advance. Under the Budget Act, legislation that provides new spending authority may not be considered unless it provides that the authority shall be effective only to the extent or in such amounts as provided in an appropriation act.

Sponsor—The principal proponent and introducer of a measure or an amendment.

Standing Committee—A permanent committee established by a House or Senate standing rule or standing order. The rule also describes the subject areas on which the committee may report bills and resolutions and conduct oversight. Most introduced measures must be referred to one or more standing committees according to their jurisdictions.

Standing Vote—An alternative and informal term for a division vote, during which members in favor of a proposal and then members opposed stand and are counted by the chair. (*See Division Vote.*)

Star Print—A reprint of a bill, resolution, amendment, or committee report correcting technical or substantive errors in a previous printing; so called because of the small black star that appears on the front page or cover.

Statutes at Large—A chronological arrangement of the laws enacted in each session of Congress. Though indexed, the laws are not arranged by subject matter nor is there an indication of how they affect or change previously enacted laws. The volumes are numbered by Congress, and the laws are cited by their volume and page number. The Gramm-Rudman-Hollings Act, for example, appears as 99 Stat. 1037.

Strike from the Record—Expunge objectionable remarks from the *Congressional Record*, after a member's words have been taken down on a point of order.

Strike Out the Last Word—A motion whereby a House member is entitled to speak for five minutes on an amendment then being debated by the chamber. A member gains recognition from the chair by moving to "strike out the last word" of the amendment or section of the bill under consideration. The motion is proforma, requires no vote, and does not change the amendment being debated.

Substitute—A motion, amendment, or entire bill introduced in place of the pending legislative business. Passage of a substitute measure kills the original measure by supplanting it. The substitute also may be amended. (*See also Amendment in the Nature of a Substitute.*)

Sunshine Rules—Rules requiring open committee hearings and business meetings, including markup sessions, in both houses, and also open conference committee meetings. However, all may be closed under certain circumstances and using certain procedures required by the rules.

Super Majority—A term sometimes used for a vote on a matter that requires approval by more than a simple majority of those members present and voting; also referred to as extraordinary majority.

Supplemental Appropriation Bill—A measure providing appropriations for use in the current fiscal year, in addition to those already provided in annual general appropriation bills. Supplemental appropriations are often for unforeseen emergencies.

Suspension of the Rules (House)—An expeditious procedure for passing relatively noncontroversial or emergency measures by a two-thirds vote of those members voting, a quorum being present.

Suspension of the Rules (Senate)—A procedure to set aside one or more of the Senate's rules; it is used infrequently, and then most often to suspend the rule banning legislative amendments to appropriation bills.

Table a Bill—Motions to table, or to "lay on the table," are used to block or kill amendments or other parliamentary questions. When approved, a tabling motion is considered the final disposition of that issue. One of the most widely used parliamentary procedures, the motion to table is not debatable, and adoption requires a simple majority vote.

In the Senate, however, different language sometimes is used. The motion may be worded to let a bill "lie on the table," perhaps for subsequent "picking up." This motion is more flexible, keeping the bill pending for later action, if desired. Tabling motions on amendments are effective debate-ending devices in the Senate.

Teller Vote—A voting procedure, formerly used in the House, in which members cast their votes by passing through the center aisle to be counted, but not recorded by name, by a member from each party appointed by the chair. The House deleted the procedure from its rules in 1993, but during floor discussion of the deletion a leading member stated that a teller vote would still be available in the event of a breakdown of the electronic voting system.

Treaty—A formal document containing an agreement between two or more sovereign nations. The Constitution authorizes the president to make treaties, but he must submit them to the Senate for its approval by a two-thirds vote of the senators present. Under the Senate's rules, that vote actually occurs on a resolution of ratification. Although the Constitution does not give the House a direct role in approving treaties, that body has sometimes insisted that a revenue treaty is an invasion of its prerogatives. In any case, the House may significantly affect the application of a treaty by its equal role in enacting legislation to implement the treaty.

Trust Funds—Special accounts in the Treasury that receive earmarked taxes or other kinds of revenue collections, such as user fees, and from which payments are made for special purposes or to recipients who meet the requirements of the trust funds as established by law. Of the more than 150 federal government trust funds, several finance major entitlement programs, such as Social Security, Medicare, and retired federal employees' pensions. Others fund infrastructure construction and improvements, such as highways and airports.

Unanimous Consent—Without an objection by any member. A unanimous consent request asks permission, explicitly or implicitly, to set aside one or more rules. Both houses and their committees frequently use such requests to expedite their proceedings.

Unanimous Consent Agreement—A device used in the Senate to expedite legislation. Much of the Senate's legislative business, dealing with both minor and controversial issues, is conducted through unanimous consent or unanimous consent agreements. On major legislation, such agreements usually are printed and transmitted to all senators in advance of floor debate. Once agreed to, they are binding on all members unless the Senate, by unanimous consent, agrees to modify them. An agreement may list the order in which various bills are to be considered, specify the length of time bills and contested amendments are to be debated and when they are to be voted upon, and, frequently, require that all amendments introduced be germane to the bill under consideration. In this regard, unanimous consent agreements are similar to the "rules" issued by the House Rules Committee for bills pending in the House.

Unfunded Mandate—Generally, any provision in federal law or regulation that imposes a duty or obligation on a state or local government or private sector entity without providing the necessary funds to comply. The Unfunded Mandates Reform Act of 1995 amended the Congressional Budget Act of 1974 to provide a mechanism for the control of new unfunded mandates.

Union Calendar—A calendar of the House of Representatives for bills and resolutions favorably reported by committees that raise revenue or directly or indirectly appropriate money or property. In addition to appropriation bills, measures that authorize expenditures are also placed on this calendar. The calendar's full title is the Calendar of the Committee of the Whole House on the State of the Union.

U.S. Code—Popular title for the *United States Code: Containing the General and Permanent Laws of the United States in Force on. . . .* It is a consolidation and partial codification of the general and permanent laws of the United States arranged by subject under 50 titles. The first six titles deal with general or political subjects, the other 44 with subjects ranging from agriculture to war, alphabetically arranged. A supplement is published after each session of Congress, and the entire Code is revised every six years.

Veto—The president's disapproval of a legislative measure passed by Congress. He returns the measure to the house in which it originated without his signature but with a veto message stating his objections to it. When Congress is in session, the president must veto a bill within 10 days, excluding Sundays, after he has received it; otherwise it becomes law without his signature. The 10-day clock begins to run at midnight following his receipt of the bill. (*See also Committee Veto, Item Veto, Override a Veto, Pocket Veto.*)

Voice Vote—A method of voting in which members who favor a question answer aye in chorus, after which those opposed answer no in chorus, and the chair decides which position prevails.

War Powers Resolution of 1973—An act that requires the president "in every possible instance" to consult Congress before he commits U.S. forces to ongoing or imminent hostilities. If he commits them to a combat situation without congressional consultation, he must notify Congress within 48 hours. Unless Congress declares war or otherwise authorizes the operation to continue, the forces must be withdrawn within 60 or 90 days, depending on certain conditions. No president has ever acknowleged the constitutionality of the resolution.

Whip—The majority or minority party member in each house who acts as assistant leader, helps plan and marshal support for party strategies, encourages party discipline, and advises his leader on how his colleagues intend to vote on the floor. In the Senate, the Republican whip's official title is assistant leader.

Without Objection—Used in lieu of a vote on noncontroversial motions, amendments, or bills that may be passed in either the House or Senate if no member voices an objection.

Yeas and Nays—A vote in which members usually respond "aye" or "no" (despite the official title of the vote) on a question when their names are called in alphabetical order. The Constitution requires the yeas and nays when a demand for it is supported by one-fifth of the members present, and it also requires an automatic yea-and-nay vote on overriding a veto. Senate precedents require the support of at least one-fifth of a quorum, a minimum of 11 members with the present membership of 100.

Yielding—When a member has been recognized to speak, no other member may speak unless he or she obtains permission from the member recognized. This permission is called yielding and usually is requested in the form, "Will the gentleman yield to me?" While this activity occasionally is seen in the Senate, the Senate has no rule or practice to parcel out time.

Congressional Information on the Internet

A huge array of congressional information is available for free at Internet sites operated by the federal government, colleges and universities, and commercial firms. The sites offer the full text of bills introduced in the House and Senate, voting records, campaign finance information, transcripts of selected congressional hearings, investigative reports, and much more.

THOMAS

The most important site for congressional information is THOMAS (*http://thomas.loc.gov*), which is named for Thomas Jefferson and operated by the Library of Congress. THOMAS's highlight is its databases containing the full text of all bills introduced in Congress since 1989, the full text of the *Congressional Record* since 1989, and the status and summary information for all bills introduced since 1973.

THOMAS also offers special links to bills that have received or are expected to receive floor action during the current week and newsworthy bills that are pending or that have recently been approved. Finally, THOMAS has selected committee reports, answers to frequently asked questions about accessing congressional information, publications titled *How Our Laws Are Made* and *Enactment of a Law*, and links to lots of other congressional Web sites.

House of Representatives

The U.S. House of Representatives site (*http://www.house. gov*) offers the schedule of bills, resolutions, and other legislative issues the House will consider in the current week. It also has updates about current proceedings on the House floor and a list of the next day's meeting of House committees. Other highlights include a database that helps users identify their representative, a directory of House members and committees, the House ethics manual, links to Web pages maintained by House members and committees, a calendar of congressional primary dates and candidate-filing deadlines for ballot access, the full text of all amendments to the Constitution that have been ratified and those that have been proposed but not ratified, and lots of information about Washington, D.C., for visitors.

Another key House site is The Office of the Clerk On-line Information Center (*http://clerkweb.house.gov*), which has records of all roll-call votes taken since 1990. The votes are recorded by bill, so it is a lengthy process to compile a particular representative's voting record. The site also has lists of committee assignments, a telephone directory for members and committees, mailing label templates for members and committees, rules of the current Congress, election statistics from 1920 to the present, biographies of Speakers of the House, biographies of women who have served since 1917, and a virtual tour of the House Chamber.

One of the more interesting House sites is operated by the Subcommittee on Rules and Organization of the House

Committee on Rules (*http://www.house.gov/rules/crs_reports. htm*). Its highlight is dozens of Congressional Research Service reports about the legislative process. Some of the available titles include *Legislative Research in Congressional Offices: A Primer, How to Follow Current Federal Legislation and Regulations, Investigative Oversight: An Introduction to the Law, Practice, and Procedure of Congressional Inquiry,* and *Presidential Vetoes 1789– Present: A Summary Overview.*

A final House site is the Internet Law Library (*http://uscode. house.gov*). This site has a searchable version of the U.S. Code, which contains the text of public laws enacted by Congress, and a tutorial for searching the Code. There also is a huge collection of links to other Internet sites that provide state and territorial laws, laws of other nations, and treaties and international laws.

Senate

At least in the Internet world, the Senate is not as active as the House. Its main Web site (*http://www.senate.gov*) has records of all roll-call votes taken since 1989 (arranged by bill), brief descriptions of all bills and joint resolutions introduced in the Senate during the past week, and a calendar of upcoming committee hearings. The site also provides the standing rules of the Senate, a directory of senators and their committee assignments, lists of nominations that the president has submitted to the Senate for approval, links to Web pages operated by senators and committees, and a virtual tour of the Senate.

Information about the membership, jurisdiction, and rules of each congressional committee is available at the U.S. Government Printing Office site (*http://www.access.gpo.gov/congress/ index.html*). It also has transcripts of selected congressional hearings, the full text of selected House and Senate reports, and the House and Senate rules manuals.

General Reference

The U.S. General Accounting Office, the investigative arm of Congress, operates a site (*http://www.gao.gov*) that provides the full text of its reports from 1996 to the present. The reports cover a wide range of topics: aviation safety, combating terrorism, counternarcotics efforts in Mexico, defense contracting, electronic warfare, food assistance programs, Gulf War illness, health insurance, illegal aliens, information technology, long-term care, mass transit, Medicare, military readiness, money laundering, national parks, nuclear waste, organ donation, student loan defaults, and the year 2000 computing crisis, among others.

The GAO Daybook is an excellent current awareness tool. This electronic mailing list distributes a daily list of reports and testimony released by the GAO. Subscriptions are available by sending an E-mail message to *majordomo@www.gao.gov,* and in the message area typing "subscribe daybook" (without the quotation marks).

Current budget and economic projections are provided at the Congressional Budget Office Web site (*http://www.cbo.gov*). The site also has reports about the economic and budget outlook for the next decade, the president's budget proposals, federal civilian employment, Social Security privatization, tax reform, water use conflicts in the West, marriage and the federal income tax, and the role of foreign aid in development, among other topics. Other highlights include monthly budget updates, historical budget data, cost estimates for bills reported by congressional committees, and transcripts of congressional testimony by CBO officials.

Campaign Finance

Several Internet sites provide detailed campaign finance data for congressional elections. The official site is operated by the Federal Election Commission (*http://www.fec.gov*), which regulates political spending. The site's highlight is its database of campaign reports filed from May 1996 to the present by House and presidential candidates, political action committees, and political party committees. Senate reports are not included because they are filed with the Secretary of the Senate. The reports in the FEC's database are scanned images of paper reports filed with the commission.

The FEC site also has summary financial data for House and Senate candidates in the current election cycle, abstracts of court decisions pertaining to federal election law from 1976 to 1997, a graph showing the number of political action committees in existence each year from 1974 to the present, and a directory of national and state agencies that are responsible for releasing information about campaign financing, candidates on the ballot, election results, lobbying, and other issues. Another useful feature is a collection of brochures about federal election law, public funding of presidential elections, the ban on contributions by foreign nationals, independent expenditures supporting or opposing a candidate for federal office, contribution limits, filing a complaint, researching public records at the FEC, and other topics. Finally, the site provides the FEC's legislative

recommendations, its annual report, a report about its first twenty years in existence, the FEC's monthly newsletter, several reports about voter registration, election results for the most recent presidential and congressional elections, and campaign guides for corporations and labor organizations, congressional candidates and committees, political party committees, and nonconnected committees.

The best online source for campaign finance data is FECInfo (*http://www.tray.com/fecinfo*), which is operated by former Federal Election Commission employee Tony Raymond. FECInfo's searchable databases provide extensive itemized information about receipts and expenditures by federal candidates and political action committees from 1980 to the present. The data, which are obtained from the FEC, are quite detailed. For example, for candidates contributions can be searched by Zip Code. The site also has data on soft money contributions, lists of the top political action committees in various categories, lists of the top contributors from each state, and much more.

Another interesting site is Campaign Finance Data on the Internet (*http://www1.soc.american.edu/campfin*), which is operated by the American University School of Communication. It provides electronic files from the FEC that have been reformatted in .dbf format so they can be used in database programs such as Paradox, Access, and FoxPro. The files contain data on PAC, committee, and individual contributions to individual congressional candidates.

More campaign finance data is available from the Center for Responsive Politics (*http://www.opensecrets.org*), a public interest organization. The center provides a list of all "soft money" donations to political parties of $100,000 or more in the current election cycle and data about "leadership" political action committees associated with individual politicians. Other databases at the site provide information about travel expenses that House members received from private sources for attending meetings and other events, activities of registered federal lobbyists, and activities of foreign agents who are registered in the United States.

Index